A DEVELOPMENTAL–
FUNCTIONALIST
APPROACH TO
CHILD LANGUAGE

A DEVELOPMENTAL– FUNCTIONALIST APPROACH TO CHILD LANGUAGE

Nancy Budwig
Clark University

 LAWRENCE ERLBAUM ASSOCIATES, PUBLISHERS
1995 Mahwah, New Jersey

Lawrence Erlbaum Associates, Inc., Publishers
10 Industrial Avenue
Mahwah, New Jersey 07430

Library of Congress Cataloging-in-Publication Data

Budwig, Nancy.
    A developmental-functionalist approach to child language / Nancy
Budwig.
        p.   cm.
    Includes bibliographical references and indexes.
    ISBN 0-8058-0520-6 (alk. paper)
    1. Language acquisition. 2. Child development. 3. Functionalism
(Linguistics). I. Title.
    P118.B76 1995
    401'.93–dc20   95-680
                                                                  CIP

Books published by Lawrence Erlbaum Associates are printed on acid-free paper,
and their bindings are chosen for strength and durability.

Printed in the United States of America
10 9 8 7 6 5 4 3 2 1

For Michael

Contents

PART III: MECHANISMS OF DEVELOPMENT

Preface

The work reported in this volume began during my final years as a doctoral student at University of California, Berkeley. At the time the work began, it seemed clear to me what a functionalist position was and what it wasn't, and I felt convinced that as an approach, it provided an excellent account of children's development of language. As I moved away from Berkeley, and as I traveled around to talk about my research, what had once seemed so clear was becoming more fuzzy. It was at that point that I decided to write this book, not so much as an explication of a coherent approach, but more as a way to clarify for myself, what others had meant by functionalism, the relative strengths of such an approach as an account for children's language development, and where further work needed to be done.

In reviewing what others had said about functionalist accounts of language in general, and functionalist accounts of child language in particular, it seemed to me that much of the explicit discussion centered around the issue of what one takes the *domain of language* to be. That is, most of the work seemed focused on describing a view of language as a nonautonomous system. The first chapter of this book summarizes such research, reviewing the extent to which child language researchers have picked up on trends found in functional linguistic theorizing.

A common theme among the functionalist child language literature is that children's earliest use of grammatical forms is linked to the ways they interact with the world. In chapter 2, I suggest that if we are to take this claim seriously, we must not only focus on the ways languages link forms with particular semantic and pragmatic meanings, but also weigh such knowledge in light of what research in the area of social and cognitive development has shown. I illustrate this with an examination of the linguistic as well as developmental psychological literature on notions of agency and control. This review provides evidence for the claim that languages across the world draw linguistic distinctions based on degree of agentivity and control; and at the same time, highlights evidence from the developmental literature which suggests that children, around the age of beginning to first combine words, most likely make use of more restricted notions of agency and intentionality having to do primarily with self. I argue that a review such as that offered in chapter 2, which attempts to link what we know from the crosslinguistic study of languages, with what is known about children's budding conceptual and social development, is another central aspect of many (but not all) functional approaches to child language that distinguishes them from other approaches toward child language.

One problem noted with focusing much of the functionalist work in the area of child language around the issue of domain is that other aspects of functionalist approaches—such as a particular view of development—remain implicit and unnoticed. This has led some to wonder, if a functionalist approach is defined in terms of an approach that relates syntax or grammar to other levels of language functioning, such as semantics or pragmatics, then couldn't everyone who has recently worked in the area of child language theorizing be considered a functionalist (P. Bloom, p.c.)? Part II of this book is an attempt to make *explicit* that functionalist approaches take a radically different position on the notion of development. Part II presents an analysis of six children's language development. Here it is argued that at a time before the young children refer to others, they temporarily borrow first person pronominal forms as markers of various degrees of agentivity and control. The central theme of these chapters, which is said to distinguish functionalist approaches from, say, maturational approaches to child language, is the claim that development is protracted. It is argued that children go through a series of phases en route to adult-like systems. Thus, the point is made that although much of the discussion of what constitutes a functionalist position has explicitly centered around the issue of *domain*, another way in which functionalist positions can be distinguished from other approaches is in terms of the way they view *course of development* (see Budwig, 1993a).

Finally, in Part III of this book we turn to a discussion of *mechanisms* of development from the standpoint of a functionalist perspective. Given that we are only beginning to understand the nature of the *course of development* for certain areas of linguistic development, I suggest that functionalist approaches are only in the very early phases of understanding what leads children to originally organize systems as they do, and what pushes them to give up their original form–function pairings in order to replace them with alternative systematizations. In chapter 9, I review various proposals that have been offered regarding both organizational and reorganizational processes, drawing on both conceptual and environmental accounts. Chapter 10 suggests that in order to tease apart the various contributions much further research is needed. A specific program of research is discussed that I believe will help us unravel what remains to be one of the central questions for researchers interested in the development of children's language.

In recent years there has been much confusion surrounding the issue of what constitutes a functionalist position. It has been argued that much of what has been criticized about functionalist approaches to child language falls under what can be referred to as "Straw Man Functionalism" (see Bates & MacWhinney, 1988). The aim of this book is two-fold. First, it is an attempt to begin to untangle some of the confusion about functionalist approaches to child language. Second, this book aims to identify issues, such as the notion of development and mechanisms of development, which those adopting a functionalist approach to child language have only begun to consider in any explicit detail and for which much future inquiry is required.

ACKNOWLEDGMENTS

The material covered in this volume goes well beyond the original plan of simply reworking my 1986 dissertation into book format. The decision to go this route came in part due to the support and interest of numerous colleagues who have attempted to influence and challenge my thinking along the way. It is really quite gratifying to reconsider the number of individuals who have directly impacted on the nature of my thinking over the last years. I was fortunate to have a supportive group of professors and fellow students at U. C. Berkeley to discuss the original ideas with and lucky to find a similar engaging environment at Clark University over the last years. In the time spanning between these two locations I have had the opportunity to test out a variety of ideas with colleagues at the Stanford Child Language Research Forum, The Boston University Conference on Language Development, Society for Research in Child Development, the International Congress for the Study of Child Language, and the Max-Planck Institute for Psycholinguistics. While there are too many individuals to mention, many will see the ways in which our discussions have led to revisions in the manuscript.

There has been a group of individuals who have had a more constant role in assisting me with this project. My original dissertation committee consisting of Susan Ervin-Tripp, John Gumperz, and Dan Slobin all went beyond the role of mentors in shaping the original thesis. Since that time Dan and Sue have also continued to play a major role in helping me articulate the ideas put forward in this book and both have been a wonderful source of inspiration. Members of the Department of Psychology at Clark University have also provided a most supportive working environment and great technical assistance. In particular, I would like to thank my colleagues in the developmental psychology program Bernie Kaplan, Ina Uzgiris, and Jim Wertsch who have all impacted on my thinking about the notions of development and semiotic systems in our joint teachings and discussions. Former students, Jessica Everett, Pate Mahoney, Heather Quick, Andrew Rosner, and Angela Wiley made suggestions from a student's perspective. Colleagues from farther away regularly have engaged in dialogues with me both in their review of portions of manuscript and in ongoing discussions. Ruth Berman, Melissa Bowerman, Eve Clark, Werner Deutsch, Julie Gerhardt, Elena Lieven, Ann Peters, and Bambi Schieffelin have all been influential, often by raising exactly the issues that I would have preferred to leave unnoticed. I am also thankful for the help provided by the staff at Lawrence Erlbaum Associates. Judi Amsel provided constant encouragement and friendly reminders that the book was getting behind schedule. In the final phases of production Sondra Guideman made sure that I attended to all the slippery and tedious corrections.

This project could not have been carried out without the support of various institutions. I gratefully acknowledge assistance from The National Academy of Education Spencer Fellowship Program, The Max Planck Institute for Psycholinguistics, and The Frances L. Hiatt Endowment for Faculty Research, Clark University.

Closer to home there has been a group of family members who provided a most delicate balance between interest and disinterest in this project. My parents, RoJene and Sam Budwig, have shown great enthusiasm and have been equally accepting of each aspect of the manuscript regardless of its theoretical flaws. They have always reminded me to create a space for the best thinking possible, even if it meant leaning on them financially, and for this support I am most grateful. My children, Zachary and Jeremy, have also been willing to engage in passionate discussions concerning language development, but also persuaded me of the joy to be found in pursuing other activities. Finally, this book would never have been completed without the loving support of my husband, Michael Bamberg, who has provided ongoing encouragement as a family member and at the same time acted as my best critic. He has found a most delicate balance between accepting and challenging just about every idea presented in this book.

Nancy Budwig

PART ONE

FOUNDATIONS

Functional Approaches to Child Language

The approach adopted in this book is a *developmental-functionalist* approach to child language. From the start it is important to explain what is meant by the term *developmental* and what is meant by the term *functionalist*. Often it is assumed that any approach to child language is necessarily a developmental approach—what is one studying if not language development? I argue throughout this book that we need to be far more concerned with the notion of development than much child language research has been in recent years (see also Bamberg, Budwig, & Kaplan, 1991; Bloom, 1991; Tomasello, 1992). The goal of this chapter is to familiarize the reader with various kinds of *functional* approaches and to lay out, in particular, some of the assumptions guiding the use of the term *developmental-functionalist* in this book. I begin with a general discussion of the notion of function. I then describe how this term has been used in linguistic theorizing and in child language research. I conclude this chapter with a discussion of some of the problems inherent in current child language research that has been considered functional in nature.

THE NOTION OF FUNCTION
IN LINGUISTIC THEORIZING

From the outset I should clarify that the use of the term *functional* in functional approaches to language should not be confused with uses of the term *functionalism* in psychology and philosophy. Functional approaches to language share little with programs of behaviorists such as Skinner (1957) that have been referred to as a kind of functionalism. The use of the term *functional* within linguistics and psycholinguistics can also be distinguished from uses within computer science and artificial intelligence that refer to mathematical functions (see Bates & MacWhinney, 1989, for further discussion). To assist in severing the connection between these other uses and the use of the term *function* in linguistic and child language theorizing, I avoid the term *functionalism* and use the term *functional.*

It is important to note that within linguistic theorizing there has been no single functional theory of language. Rather, we find a variety of functional theories, models, and approaches, which differ from one another to various degrees. Although, as we see here, there are many important differences between the various uses of *functional* in linguistic theorizing, it is possible to find some assumptions that are agreed upon by all (see also Budwig, 1993). I briefly discuss these similarities before focusing on the differences between the various uses.

The first and most important assumption shared by the various approaches that could be considered functional is the belief that language has evolved and is acquired in relation to the communicative functions it serves. Language thus is not an arbitrary and autonomous system but, rather, is organized in relation to the needs of those who use it. As a consequence, all theorists taking a functional approach share the belief that language must be studied in relation to context, regardless of what they take context to mean.

A second and related similarity between the various uses of *functional* is the belief that language is a system of forms and meanings. Forms are a vehicle through which the meanings can be realized. Thus, in functionally oriented research, forms are viewed as a means to an end rather than as an end.

It has often been suggested that there are basically two broad orientations within linguistic theorizing: a formal orientation and a functional orientation (see for instance, Bates & MacWhinney, 1989; Foley & Van Valin, 1984). We might suggest that what unites various functional theories is a shared disbelief in formal orientations. Functionalists join in rejecting the formalist assumption that language consists of a set of structural descriptions of sentences, as well as formalist beliefs about how language ought to be studied and how language is acquired by the child (see, for instance, Chomsky, 1957, 1975, for a more complete discussion of these points). Although on the one hand, one can draw a division between formal and functional orientations, it seems important to keep in mind that at another level of analysis one could construe formalist accounts of language as reflecting a kind of functionalist orientation (see Silverstein, 1987, for a discussion of this possibility). In addition, as Silverstein (1991) more recently pointed out, some functionalist orientations share many features of formal orientations. The point is that the distinction between the two orientations may not be as clear as it might seem.

More relevant to child language theorizing and the various uses of the notion of function in the child language literature is an understanding of some of the differences between various kinds of functional approaches. I begin now to distinguish some of these approaches (see also Silverstein, 1987). It should be made clear that the numerous orientations falling under the general heading of functional do not divide into neat groups. Nevertheless, for the sake of presentation here, I have opted to divide the various kinds of functional perspectives to language into four groups. First, I discuss a group with a *cognitive functional* orientation. I then discuss a group that can be characterized as bearing a *textual functional* orientation. A third group is referred to as adopting a *social functional* orientation. Members of the final group share an interest in a combination of these orientations; this group will be referred to as adopting a *multifunctional* orientation. Other groupings are possible, but for the general goal of understanding the role of functional linguistic theorizing in child language research, this grouping seems most appropriate.

Cognitive Orientation

The group labeled cognitive in orientation holds together in a belief that languages are organized around event schemes. Members of this group include Comrie (1981), DeLancey (1984, 1987), Fillmore (1968), and Lakoff (1977), among others. A central assumption for this group is that particular linguistic devices are organized around various perspectives speakers take on events. The events are thought to be organized around prototypes, and deviations from the prototype are thought to be marked by deviations in morphosyntactic patterns. The idea, then, is not simply that particular linguistic devices can be correlated with particular event perspectives but, rather, that the relations between various form-event pairings can be linked at a higher level of organization into a larger system of form-meaning correspondences. The central claim is that alternations between particular grammatical devices (i.e., case markers) indicate a related change in the view the speaker adopts on a given action frame (i.e., degree of participant involvement). These action frames consist of a bundle of both semantic and pragmatic features that are organized around a prototype (see Holisky, 1987, for an illustration of the semantic and pragmatic clusters thought to motivate the use of ergative case with subjects of some intransitive verbs in Tsova-Tush [Batsi]).

Textual Orientation

Approaches in the second group to be discussed can be considered similar (despite important differences) in that they are concerned with the ordering and organization of units of discourse both within and between sentences. Members of this group include proponents of what has been referred to as

Prague School functionalism (Firbas, 1964; Firth, 1951, among others), British functionalism (Halliday, 1973), Role and Reference Grammar (Foley & Van Valin, 1984; Van Valin, 1993), as well as Chafe (1980), Tomlin (1987), and others. In contrast to the cognitive functional group, this group is interested in the relation between various aspects of formal structure and the way texts are organized. Focus on narrative discourse has been central to this group.

With regard to the organization of information units within sentences, many of those working within this orientation have focused on two kinds of sentential elements: first, the speaker's point of departure (referred to as either the *theme*, the *topic*, or *given information*), and second, what is said about this (referred to as the *theme*, the *comment*, or *new information*). Research falling under this heading has illustrated the extent to which various linguistic means (i.e., lexical, intonational, or word order phenomena) mark such a contrast.

With regard to the overall organization of texts, other research has examined how certain linguistic devices (i.e., tense-aspect markers, pronominal-nominal shifts) segment given texts into smaller textual units informing the listener/reader about various aspects of the global structuring of information (see, for instance, Chafe, 1980; Tomlin, 1987).

In a separate but related line of theorizing, Foley and Van Valin (1984) and Van Valin (1993) outlined Role and Reference Grammar (RRG), which focuses on the relations between clause-internal morphosyntax, clause linkage, and cross-clause reference tracking mechanisms. This leads to a consideration of such aspects of language as the semantic structure of the clause, case marking, intraclausal syntax, and systems of discourse cohesion. The general point here, shared with many others in the textual functional group, is that the analysis of various aspects of morphosyntax must start from a discourse perspective.

Social Orientation

The first two groups were said to be interested in the connections between grammar and event schemata, and grammar and text organization. The third group is unified by a joint interest in social aspects of language use. We can include under this heading at least three kinds of social functional approaches: first, that of a group of philosophers of language who developed a theory of speech acts; second, that of a group of theorists who examined the relation between language and broader sociological issues; and third, that of a group who focused on sociocultural issues and language functioning. I briefly consider each of these groups.

One subgroup bearing a social orientation can be characterized by an interest in a theory of speech acts. This group (i.e., Austin, 1962; Grice,

1975; Searle, 1969, 1979) worked within the logico-semantic tradition, where the central question concerns the principles by which utterances are assigned meaning in particular settings. This group set out to show that utterances function not only to express propositions about the world (which then can be tested against truth conditions), but also to perform certain actions. Its members were not particularly interested in working with real conversational data occurring in real event time but, rather, tended to work with made-up examples with very little emphasis on aspects of the situations in which such utterances were supposed to take place. The general point of such work was to challenge prevailing views concerning the centrality of truth-conditional analyses of sentence meaning, and to develop a theory of politeness and interaction (see Levinson, 1983, for an excellent summary of this tradition).

Although theorists like Austin and Searle were intrigued by the fact that one and the same utterance could function differently in different language contexts, they never really were interested in broader sociological issues. The second subgroup falling under the social functional orientation focused on these issues. One group of theorists, working within the tradition of conversation analysis, focused on real utterances sequenced in time and was concerned with the internal structure of conversation (see Sacks, Schegloff, & Jefferson, 1974). Another group was more interested in the issue of conversational inference as well as the notion of *contextualization cues*—surface devices that play an important role in negotiated meaning in social contexts (Gumperz, 1982).

A final subgroup includes sociocultural approaches to language functioning. This group, though closely related to the sociological one just reviewed, can be distinguished in terms of its emphasis on the relation between language and the cultural setting within which language occurs. What is different here is that focus is not placed so much on the goal-directed nature of an individual's functioning within a given context as on the role of societal issues. The general approach adopted within this framework is ethnographic in nature (see Duranti, 1985; Hymes, 1974, for further elaboration).

Pulling together these separate traditions, what unites such approaches is the belief that language is an instrument of social action. Furthermore, there is a shared belief among these theorists that the use of particular linguistic devices can be related to speakers' attempts to achieve particular social goals. This emphasis on the relation between grammar and the social world is what distinguishes the various kinds of functionalist perspectives grouped under this heading from the approaches described under the previous two headings. Those interested in the relationship between grammar and event schemata or between grammar and text have not been primarily concerned with social issues.

Multifunctional Orientation

Several approaches that can be labeled functional in nature do not fit neatly into one division but, rather, are best characterized as integrating aspects of more than one of the orientations discussed here. I refer to these as multifunctional. Although there are large differences among the various approaches discussed here, for the present purposes it can be noted that a major similarity among most of the approaches labeled as multifunctional is that they attempt to integrate two of the levels of analysis. The most common kind of linkage drawn in multifunctional approaches is between the event schemata orientation and the textual orientation. This kind of integration is illustrated in several different lines of work (see Comrie, 1981; Givón, 1979, 1984a, 1990; Hopper & Thompson, 1980, among others).

One way to illustrate the multifunctional orientation of this group is to consider how such an orientation would approach a given issue. One common issue is that of the relation between grammar, agency, and topicality. Some working within what has been labeled the multifunctional orientation not only draw a connection between the use of particular grammatical forms and reference to agents versus patients—thereby appealing to the event schema orientation—but also examine the relationship between such connections and broader textual issues such as topicality. For instance, Bates and MacWhinney (1989) argued that often particular forms link up with overlaps of semantic and discourse meanings. They argued that many languages show a tendency to recruit one grammatical device to mark both agents and topics because these semantic and discourse functions represent a natural coalition because agents typically are topics in natural discourse.

Others have argued that certain form-meaning correspondences can be accounted for only by considering discursive phenomena. For instance, rather than arguing for form-meaning-function bundles, Hopper and Thompson (1980) suggested that certain regularities in the relation between particular grammatical devices and semantic meanings can be accounted for only by considering discourse functions such as foregrounding and backgrounding. Thus, although there has been a tendency within the multifunctional orientation to link form, meaning, and discourse function, differences exist in the degree to which a particular group is suggesting an overlap or a causal connection between the different levels of analysis.

What is important to note is the general reluctance in this area to draw a connection between what we have referred to as the social functional orientation and the other orientations (however, see Holisky, 1987; and van Oosten, 1986, for exceptions).[1]

---

[1] It should be noted that with regard to the study of children's use of passives, Budwig noted that it well may be that the early passive use also links up with textual and social functional characteristics and that the focus on the cognitive functional orientation was guided by the nature of the data (see Budwig, 1990). It can also be noted that Slobin (1988) suggested the importance of integrating a pragmatic dimension of analysis.

THE NOTION OF FUNCTION
IN CHILD LANGUAGE THEORIZING

Just as was noted to be the case for linguistic theorizing, the notion of function has been used in many different ways in the area of child language acquisition. Although there are many different uses of the term *functional* in the literature, the various uses share the assumption that language develops in relation to the communicative functions it serves. Various child language researchers differ with regard to the degree to which they believe the telos of language development to be functional in nature. The relevant point is that it is possible to believe that children begin with functionally oriented language systems, and yet over development these systems become more abstract (see, for instance, Werner & Kaplan, 1984, for such a discussion). A second commonality across the various uses of the term *functional* in the child language literature is the reliance on a notion of system. This similarity was noted also in the linguistic literature. With regard to children, the notion of system comes in when accounting for the relation between one language function and others, as well as that between various language devices and various functions.

With these similarities in mind we can turn to a brief discussion of some of the differences in the way the term *function* is used in the study of language development. The various kinds of functional orientations noted earlier also can be found in the child language literature, though they have played a different role. It should be noted that most of the work in child language that can be considered functional in nature has fallen under what was labeled earlier the *social functional orientation*. Before turning to a more systematic review of some of the different uses of function in the child language literature, it should also be noted that my review is not exhaustive. The discussion here is limited to child language research that has been concerned with the relationship between language structure and language function, because this is most central to the research outlined in subsequent chapters of this book. This restriction has meant that much of the research that would have fallen under the *social functional* heading, consisting of detailed typologies of the functions of children's language, is not reviewed here (see, though, Atkinson, 1982; Budwig & Bamberg, in press; Cook-Gumperz, Corsaro, & Streeck, 1986; Ervin-Tripp & Mitchell-Kernan, 1977; Ochs & Schieffelin, 1979). With these comments in mind, we can now consider child language research that falls under the headings of *cognitive orientation, textual orientation, social orientation,* and *multifunctional orientation*.

Cognitive Orientation

The best example of the cognitive functional orientation can be found in the work of Slobin (1981, 1985). In summarizing the relationship between various linguistic forms and their developmental routes Slobin suggested that many forms are first used to take particular perspectives on events. This is best illustrated in Slobin's discussion of the grammatical encoding of the manipulative activity scene. From cross-linguistic comparisons of very different kinds of languages, Slobin concluded that one of the opening wedges for grammar is the linguistic encoding of a scene in which an agent brings about a change of state in an object. Although the kind of linguistic treatment may vary from language to language, this event is said to receive linguistic treatment in the very early phases of grammatical development by children across the world. What is particularly interesting about the examples that Slobin discussed concerns the relationship between the children's system and the target languages the children are acquiring. Slobin's claim highlights the creative nature of the children's use of grammatical forms. In my discussion of the cognitive orientation within linguistic theorizing I pointed out that languages across the world have been noted to give special linguistic treatment to a cluster of related notions having to do with agency and transitivity; the interesting aspect of Slobin's finding is that the children are not merely copying the adult system but, in fact, are creating their own form-function pairings. Slobin suggested that children across the world begin with what he called Basic Child Grammar—a grammar marking specific notions that are not necessarily marked in the target language but that nevertheless are important conceptual distinctions within the world of the child.

A second illustration of the cognitive orientation stems from the study of early use of passives by young children. Examining the use of passive sentences in children between the ages of 2 and 10 as well as in adults, in both longitudinal and cross-sectional data, I argued that the children contrastively employ the auxiliary forms *get* and *be* in order to mark a different perspective on events. The use of *be* links up with talk about an event involving a generic or unknown agent, or one who is irrelevant to the discourse. The use of *get* is found in utterances that refer to an event in which an action brings about negative consequences. What is central to the children's use of passive constructions, regardless of auxiliary choice, is that talk focuses on a scene involving an agent who is not in focus (see Budwig, 1990).

Abstracting across these two studies, we find the principle features of the cognitive functional orientation. Note that the examination of specific linguistic forms in context has been crucial. The cognitive functional orientation involves the examination of how particular grammatical devices mark shifts in perspective on events. The central claim is that children exploit particular devices to mark various kinds of perspectives that can be taken on a given scene. Furthermore, it is claimed that these devices function to provide a wedge into the formal adult system. Note that this functional orientation differs from the textual orientation in that there is no focus on the use of particular devices across stretches of discourse. Also there is little concern for how the devices function socially. Within the cognitive functional approach the assumption is that language is representing the child's view of the world and not that it is used as a tool of social action, as is characteristic of the social orientation.

Textual Orientation

In general there has been little focus on the textual orientation within the study of child language. Much of the research, as we see here, has focused on aspects of later language development. One of the most complete studies of particular linguistic devices and how they function to structure the flow of the ongoing discourse is that of Paprotté and Sinha (1987). Paprotté and Sinha explored the relevance of central notions of the Prague functional sentence perspective to the study of language acquisition. With regard to the early phases of language development, Paprotté and Sinha argued against communicative pressure guiding the functional motivation for syntax. Instead, they argued that principles governing the organization of sentential information can be related to the "evidentiality of the information" (Paprotté & Sinha, 1987, p. 219). At later points of development, children are said to become concerned with linking discourse over consecutive sentences.

The study of subsequent phases of language development (i.e., beyond the two-word stage) has focused primarily on children's narrative abilities and how various linguistic devices indicate textual cohesion and coherence (see Bamberg, 1987; Berman & Slobin, 1984; Hickmann, 1987; Karmiloff-Smith, 1986). These studies revealed that children acquiring a variety of languages make use of several different linguistic devices (i.e., pronominal-nominal shifts, tense-aspect markers) to segment a text into cohesive chunks that ultimately establish larger conceptual units making up a narrative. As I noted with regard to the cognitive orientation, the children's early use of specific devices does not necessarily match up with adult usage. That is, there seems to be little evidence that the children are simply listening to adult uses of similar forms and then making use of such forms for similar functions. What we find reported in the studies cited here is an extended developmental sequence in which the children reinterpret such devices for various textual functions that, though consistently used, are sometimes at odds with the input they receive.

With regard to the textual orientation, the issue of central importance is the extent to which particular linguistic devices are employed to help organize stretches of discourse both intrasententially and across broader stretches of text. In general, the relationship between the use of particular devices and the perspective taken on a given event is not important, nor is the social function of the language examined.[2]

---

[2]Note, though, that Bamberg (1991) argued that cohesive divices also play a role in indicating what perspective the speaker takes on an event. That is, he claimed that textual devices simultaneously indicate how the speaker views the event being described.

Social Orientation

As has been noted, most of the work within a functional perspective with regard to child language development can be characterized as falling under the heading of *social functional orientation*. However, as I have noted, much of it has focused on social functional aspects of children's talk without specific focus on the relationship between particular linguistic devices and such functions. In this section I limit myself to a discussion of only some of the work bearing a social functional orientation, with special reference to the nature of the relationship posited between forms and social functions.

Much of the work in this area has focused on various aspects of the development of grammar and their relation to levels of analysis above the level of the sentence, such as the activity level, speech events, conversational exchanges, and speech acts (see Ervin-Tripp, 1989, for an excellent review of these studies). One area that has received more focus than others concerns the relationship between specific linguistic forms and the pragmatic force of the utterance within which such a form appears. For instance, Carter (1975, 1978a, 1978b) noted in detailed case studies that children will contrastively use particular forms, depending on whether the child desires an action to be carried out by a partner or whether the child wants to draw the communicative partner's attention to a particular object.

This sort of contrast based on the pragmatic force of the utterance was also noted by Deutsch and Budwig (1983). They suggested that children's early contrastive use of multiple first person possessive pronouns is due to the communicative force of the utterance. In a reanalysis of Brown's (1973) longitudinal data, Deutsch and Budwig claimed that the children went through an extended phase of contrastively employing *My + Possessum* (i.e., *My pencil*) versus *Own Name + Possessum*, depending on whether the utterance was indicative or volitional. Researchers examining other languages have also indicated that this sort of contrastive use of pronominal and nominal possessive forms marks a pragmatic distinction concerning utterance force (see Kolodziej, Deutsch, & Bittner, 1991; Vila, 1987; see also Halliday, 1975; Painter, 1984, for further examples of English).

Thus far my discussion of the social functional orientation has emphasized what could be viewed as fairly local aspects of the social context. Some work also has attempted to relate broader sociocultural features to various aspects of grammar. The idea that broader social and cultural systems play a role in the child's development of various grammatical systems was wonderfully illustrated by Ochs (1988) and Schieffelin (1990). Their cross-linguistic comparisons of children's acquisition of Samoan and Kaluli, for instance, pointed out that one reason children in the two cultures might acquire similar inflectional morphology at very different points in development is that in one language, usage is sociologically constrained, whereas this is not the case in the other. Given that much of the research in the area of child language has attempted to minimize cultural (and subcultural) differences, this is an area open for future research.

Multifunctional Orientation

There has been surprisingly little work in the area of child language that can be considered multifunctional in orientation. In part, this relates to the previously mentioned point that few researchers have examined child language from the perspective of the textual orientation (see earlier discussion). The most common sort of linkage noted earlier was that between the cognitive and textual orientations (see, though, Bamberg, 1987; Bates & MacWhinney, 1987; Berman & Slobin, 1994, for important exceptions). One excellent example of the multifunctional orientation is found in Gerhardt's work (Gee & Savasir, 1985; Gerhardt, 1990). Gerhardt examined various aspects of children's linguistic systems with an eye toward semantic, pragmatic, and discursive factors associated with their use. For instance, Gerhardt argued that 3-year-old children contrastively employ the forms *will* and *gonna*; a discursive analysis reveals important contextual distinctions in the use of these forms. *Gonna* appears in discourse in which the children were planning and organizing; it implies a more distant intention to act in a particular way. In contrast, *will* appears in the context of ongoing cooperative peer play and refers to an immediate intentional stance. Gerhardt's research highlights the fact that children as young as 3 years are capable of linking multiple levels of information into clusters of form-function pairings. Although we are beginning to know more about the interrelationship between semantic, pragmatic, and textual information from studies of this sort, much further research is needed to unravel the pathway between original multifunctional usage and patterns found in the input.

DEVELOPMENTAL ISSUES AND FUNCTIONAL APPROACHES TO CHILD LANGUAGE

Thus far, I have suggested that there is no single unified functional approach within the study of linguistics and child language. Several different kinds of approaches have been discussed, and I have noted some parallels between functional approaches used in linguistics and those used in child language research. In grouping various kinds of functional approaches, the divisions have focused on important distinctions in content areas. For instance, I have considered such differences as the extent to which a given functional approach emphasizes cognitive notions, textual notions, social notions, or some combination of these. There are, though, other differences that are central to various functional approaches. Three other issues are particularly relevant to our discussion of functional approaches to language development. These relate to distinctions between various approaches concerning the following developmental issues:

1. In positing a relationship between particular forms and functions, what are the specific claims, if any, about causal connections? Are there, for instance, claims that functions trigger forms or vice versa?
2. What is the endpoint of development thought to be? In particular, within the various approaches, is it suggested that the endpoint of development is the acquisition of a formal grammatical system or is the endpoint also viewed as functional in nature?
3. Where do the functional categories used in a given approach come from? Does a given approach make use of a specific functional linguistic theory or are other categories used?

Answers to these questions help clarify developmental issues related to functionalist theorizing in child language research.

Form-Function Connections in Language Development

There seem to be three different kinds of positions taken with regard to claims about form-function connections. The question here involves the directionality of influence. In suggesting that children make use of form-function pairings in acquiring a linguistic system, functionalists have differed with regard to (a) the degree of specificity regarding the nature of this connection, and (b) the status they give to both forms and functions.

One of the dominant views is that functions guide form. Here the claim is that the child has a set of functions and searches or finds forms to map onto these functions. It is important to note that various researchers differ, of course, on the nature of the functions but agree that functions are primary. This can be better illustrated by an examination of two different kinds of functional approaches that nevertheless share this view of function dominating form. One example of this position is that in Slobin (1985). Slobin argued that conceptual development plays a central role in the development of various grammatical forms. First of all, Slobin's cross-linguistic approach revealed that conceptual development provides a starting point for grammatical development. Certain salient conceptual notions (such as transitivity) are more likely than other notions to receive early grammatical treatment. As a result of this, certain preferred event perspectives are more likely to receive grammatical treatment, which in turn helps to determine which forms develop.

Slobin also suggested that the universal conceptual schemes can lead children to make grammatical distinctions that are not necessarily provided in the input the child receives. In addition, conceptual development has been noted to determine the order in which particular grammatical forms emerge. Although Slobin postulated that conceptual development is the guiding force in grammatical acquisition, and that children across the world begin with universal preferences to mark particular conceptual categories, this should not be taken to indicate that Slobin did not believe that formal pattern preferences exist in early child language development. Children do use form patterns, but often these form patterns are tied to underlying meaning patterns. Slobin believed that when languages require that the speaker combine two or more meanings in using a particular grammatical form, the child will acquire those in which there exists a kind of semantic affinity between the two semantic meanings. In addition, with regard to the placement of grammatical markers, children show a preference for placing such markers according to semantic relevance. Morphemes that go together semantically are more likely to be placed together syntactically by the child. Thus even when children work with form patterns, elements of meaning have been noted to play a role in acquisition. Although Slobin suggested that many aspects of grammatical development can be accounted for by appealing to semantic underpinnings, he also agreed that children are capable of working at the level of form independent of semantic criteria. The general claim put forth by Slobin, though, was that semantic meanings play a central role in the child's construction of grammar.

Ervin-Tripp (1989) built a similar argument suggesting that function guides form in grammatical development:

> The hypothesis of a form/function relationship suggests that in acquisition the trigger for development of certain forms may be their density and importance in the achievement of conversational goals. The social and activity context makes their meanings clear, simplifying the acquisitional process. (p. 1)

Though Ervin-Tripp had a somewhat different notion of function, the general point is the same, namely, that the development of formal devices is guided by the functions such devices serve.

All functionalists do not, though, necessarily argue that function guides form development. For instance, some researchers seem to take a somewhat neutral position with regard to causation. Gerhardt (1988, 1990) and Gerhardt and Savasir (1986), in her careful contextually based analyses of various functional aspects of children's acquisition of different grammatical systems, made no claim that it is function that guides form or vice versa. Such work is best described as highlighting the interactive nature of syntax and discourse and the importance of studying both in tandem. The important point here is that adopting a functionalist position need not imply that one believes that function guides form. Gerhardt's work is an excellent illustration of this.

In another type of position, functionalists have proposed a very complex interaction between form and function in development. Bates and MacWhinney (1989) argued, within the framework of the Competition Model, that mappings between forms and functions are best viewed in terms of both horizontal and vertical correlations (Bates & MacWhinney, 1987). Although most functional approaches focus on the vertical correlations of form-function pairings, Bates and MacWhinney suggested two kinds of horizontal correlations—one at the level of forms themselves, and one between various language functions. According to their perspective, the child is not simply acquiring form-function pairings but is also making use of formal correlations or correlations between various functions. Bates and MacWhinney suggested, though, that the vertical mappings are the most central: ". . . although the system is capable of acquiring a complex set of horizontal correlations, the mappings that drive the system are the vertical correlations" (p. 166). The model provided by Bates and MacWhinney suggests a far more complex relationship between the acquisition of form and that of function. According to their perspective the child is not simply relating forms to already acquired functions. Rather, the child often acquires functions and then seeks to express them, or the child acquires forms without being bound to a particular function.

In this section, we have seen that there are many alternative characterizations of the relationship between form and function in various functionalist approaches. At present, various approaches differ not only with regard to what they take function to mean, but also with regard to whether function is said to play an organizing role in the development of grammar or whether one believes that the developmental relationship between linguistic forms and functions is more complex in nature.

Continuity and Functional Approaches

One of the chief critiques against functional approaches has centered around the issue of continuity. The argument goes as follows: If the child uses function as a wedge into grammar, how does a researcher account for the transition into a formal abstract system? Although most of the discussions (cf. Gleitman & Wanner, 1982) of this issue have centered around a clear distinction between continuous and noncontinuous theories, the issue is really better viewed in terms of a continuum. The general assumption is that functionalist approaches must grapple with the continuity problem, that is, how the child transcends the functionally oriented early grammar and arrives at a formal abstract system. In contrast, formalist approaches are thought of as continuous in nature to the extent that the origin and end point are formal in nature. The importance of appealing to a continuum is best understood by looking more closely at some of the different ways various functional approaches deal with the continuity issue.

At one end of the continuum we find functional approaches like those that have been discussed by critics; namely, they appear to be discontinuous in nature. Under such proposals, it is held that the functionalist nature of early grammatical categories is specific to child language and that ultimately such systems give way to more formal abstract adult systems (cf. Schlesinger, 1988; Werner & Kaplan, 1984). Specific proposals are made about how the child might transcend a functionally based system.

It is important to recognize that not all functionalist approaches can be described as discontinuous in nature. At the other end of the continuum are functionalist approaches that take a continuity position. At this end of the continuum, there is no problem of discontinuity, because the telos of linguistic development is believed to be based on categories that are functional in nature. This position is best illustrated by Van Valin (1991).

There are many functionalist approaches that fall somewhere in between these two positions. On the one hand, they fit with the continuity position to the extent that they posit starting and ending points that are functional in nature. Yet they share with the discontinuity side of the continuum the belief that the functional categories and even the form-function linkages that the child creates early on are not necessarily the ones that are functioning in the adult system. As Bates and MacWhinney (1989) pointed out, many of the functions that are part of the adult system are not necessarily those to which a young child will be sensitive. To this extent, there are some functionalist approaches that deal with a less extreme version of the continuity problem.

The point here is that the continuity problem need not be a problem for functional approaches. There are functional approaches that have been construed such that they are as continuous as formal approaches. It is also important to recognize that there are nativist approaches that have had to deal with the continuity problem, as illustrated, for instance, in Pinker's discussion of semantic bootstrapping (Pinker, 1984, 1989). It is important to keep in mind that there are major differences in how particular kinds of functional approaches deal with the issue of continuity. It is equally important that any approach to child language that proposes that children's early linguistic categories differ from those thought to be functioning in the adult linguistic system also account for the mechanisms that lead the child from one point to the next.

The Source of Linguistic Categories

A third distinction between various functional approaches, and one that relates to my previous discussion of the continuity issue, concerns the source of the various linguistic categories posited in a given functionalist approach. One central distinction in various functional approaches to child language involves the extent to which a given approach either starts with a set of well-defined categories springing from a specific linguistic theory or works with categories that are not part of an accepted functionally based linguistic theory but instead develop out of an analysis of what children do with particular forms. Not surprisingly, those approaches that start with well-defined categories stemming from functional linguistic theorizing are exactly those approaches that were labeled as continuous in our previous discussion of continuity.

Perhaps the best example of child language work that draws upon functional linguistic theory can be found in Van Valin's attempts to relate RRG to children's language (see Van Valin, 1991). The approach adopted by Van Valin is quite different than the approach adopted by a number of others working within a functionalist perspective who have been less concerned with starting with built-in assumptions about how particular forms function in adult grammars and instead have sought to find out how children make use of particular linguistic devices and how such usage changes over time (cf. Bamberg, 1987; Bamberg, Budwig, & Kaplan, 1991; Berman & Slobin, 1994; Bloom, 1991; Deutsch & Budwig, 1983; Ervin-Tripp, 1989; Gerhardt, 1988, 1990; Slobin, 1988). Researchers in this second group started with few presuppositions about how forms may function for the child. Their task was to figure out what meaning the child gives to a form by examining usages in context (context meaning different things to different researchers).

As just one illustration of this difference, we can look more closely at Deutsch and Budwig's analysis of the use of *Own Name* and *My* in possessive constructions like *Adam car* and *My car*. An analysis beginning with established categories might categorize both these utterances, produced by the same child in close proximity, as possessive constructions (see Braine, 1976, for similar categorizations). Deutsch and Budwig (1983) examined functional aspects of such utterances and came to the conclusion that *Own Name + Possessum* and *My + Possessum* were two different categories for the children studied. For a period of several months the children constructed a distinction between reference to possessions in which control was not at issue (marked with *Own Name*) and reference to possessions the child would like to gain or maintain control of (marked with *My*). This example illustrates the attempt on the part of the researchers working within this perspective to find out what function children attribute to various forms. Thus, rather than referring to examples such as *Adam car* and *My car* as possessive constructions, the researchers argued that the child uses distinct forms to mark a contrast in function.

Thus far we have looked at two very different ways in which functional approaches categorize child language data. There are other possibilities that fall somewhere in between these two extremes. For instance, Karmiloff-Smith's (1979) work on the acquisition of determiners was similar to approaches that began with preestablished categories, in that Karmiloff-Smith began with some predetermined ideas about how determiners function. At the same time, her research can be viewed as similar to the research of those who examine how forms might function for children at various points in development, to the extent that she examined whether children in their initial uses of determiners employed them multifunctionally, as adults do. The work of Bates and MacWhinney (1987, 1989) also falls somewhere between these two extremes. Like Karmiloff-Smith, Bates and MacWhinney began with specific assumptions about form-function coalitions in various languages and examined which aspects of such coalitions children acquire in what order. Thus Bates and MacWhinney recognized that there are potential differences between children's form-function pairings and those of adult speakers, but at the same time they worked with predetermined ideas about how forms might function in a given language. To this extent, their work was comparable to Van Valin's. Bates and MacWhinney noted, though, that the categories they employed could be considered pretheoretical or general (i.e., agent, topic) and contrasted with the more specific categories that Van Valin used.

It is important to recognize that although functionalist approaches have often been criticized for lacking a theoretical conception of an adult grammar (cf. Atkinson, 1982; Pinker, 1989), this claim may be true only of some functionalist approaches. As Van Valin's work illustrates, functionalist approaches, like formalist approaches, at times are guided by a specific linguistic theory. It seems one of the most important challenges for functionalist approaches in years to come is the integration of the two extreme kinds of approaches described here. What we need are functional approaches that begin with clearly delineated notions of the telos or end state of grammatical development but that at the same time are sensitive to the functions children assign to forms early on (see Bamberg, Budwig, & Kaplan, 1991, for further discussion of this point).

A DEVELOPMENTAL-FUNCTIONALIST APPROACH
TO CHILD LANGUAGE

At the start of this chapter I described the approach adopted in this book as a developmental-functionalist approach to child language. Thus far, I have discussed various uses of the notion of function in both linguistic and developmental psycholinguistic studies, but until now I have had very little to say about the notion of development and, in particular, about why the approach to be adopted here is labeled as developmental in nature. One could raise the question—are not all functional approaches to child language inherently developmental in nature? The answer to this question, it seems, depends on what one takes the notion of development to mean. In this section I discuss the notion of development in various functional approaches, and I outline how this term is used in the approach adopted in this book.

There is general consensus in the field of child language that language acquisition is not instantaneous. The assumption is that the earliest phases of child language are different from the target language the child is acquiring. Various functionalist approaches have dealt with the issue of development in different ways. One major criticism of functionalist approaches has been that they have not really addressed the issue of development at all. As Pinker (1988) pointed out in a general critique of all of developmental psycholinguistics:

> . . . if language acquisition is the study of ACQUISITION (i.e., creation of new knowledge contingent on environmental inputs of LANGUAGE (i.e., adult linguistic abilities in all their complexity), then very few psychologists were studying the question. There were studies of the speech of children at one or more stages, and of their comprehension abilities, but virtually no one paid attention to the *learning* process itself (i.e., the process by which the child forms new *rules*), nor to the end state of acquisition. . . . (p. 100)

Although Pinker's claim was not particularly directed toward functional approaches to child language, one might argue that his statement holds true of certain functional approaches to child language that have examined the various functions of children's language at one or more stages en route to the adult system. Atkinson (1982) also highlighted some problems for functionally based approaches with regard to their stance toward development. Although some functional approaches to child language have not been concerned with developmental issues, there nevertheless are other functional approaches where development has played a central role. I now examine the issue of development within such approaches.

**Two Notions of Development
in the Child Language Literature**

One of the main questions we need to raise is what a particular approach takes development to be the development of. There are two main ways in which development has been perceived in functional approaches to child language. First, some researchers have examined development by questioning the *order* of acquisition. Here the central issue is: In what order do the various forms come in and how can one account for that order by appealing to functional notions? A second view of development has focused less on the order of acquisition of various forms and more on the development of particular forms or particular functions, watching for developmental changes in particular form-function pairings.

An example of a functionalist approach that looks at development in terms of order of acquisition is that of Bates and MacWhinney (1989). In their view, "learning is viewed as a process of acquiring form-function mappings" (p. 59). Their view of development was reflected in the following statement: "We have offered some strong predictions about language acqui-sition across natural languages, claiming that cue validity will determine the order in which grammatical devices are acquired" (p. 59). In talking about development, Bates and MacWhinney were primarily interested in account-ing for particular sequences in the course of development of linguistic forms—that is, why a given form is acquired at a particular time relative to another form.

Bates and MacWhinney also made use of the principle of functional readiness in accounting for developmental sequences. According to this principle, certain functions must be available before a mapping between form and function can take place. For instance, certain grammatical devices used to achieve discourse cohesion have been noted to develop later than cue validity might predict, simply because the child does not understand the function of these devices.

There seem to be two major problems with all developmental work of this sort that is based on acquisition order. First, how does one assess whether something is acquired? There are no clear-cut methods or stable criteria used by researchers in deciding whether or not a child has acquired a particular linguistic structure with regard to either production or compre-hension (see Clark, 1985, for an excellent discussion of the problem of assessing acquisition). Without a firm way of assessing whether something has been acquired, it becomes problematic to draw generalizations about ordering relations. A second problem for researchers who have approached development from the standpoint of order of acquisition concerns the issue of process. This approach forces one to view development in a static way—something either is or is not acquired. Such a vantage point ignores the process of development. This issue is taken up by a second view of the notion of development in functional approaches to child language.

The second approach, that focusing on developmental histories of given form-function pairings, begins with very different notions about acquisition. One central assumption of this approach is that the child might be using forms in a very different way than adult speakers. The developmental issue is one of examining how a given form functions at a particular point in child language and how a given set of form-function pairings undergoes developmental changes over time.

Those taking this view of development are particularly interested in the mechanisms involved in the transition from one form-function pairing to another. The work of Karmiloff-Smith is an excellent example of this kind of approach. Karmiloff-Smith (1979) outlined three phases of language ac-quisition procedures. She started with the assumption that children first approach language as if morphemes were unifunctional and that develop-ment consists in conferring on a series of unifunctional homonyms the status of a plurifunctional morpheme. In the first of three phases, roughly between the ages of 3 and 5 years, children attribute one meaning to each form. They act as if they do not understand that one form may serve multiple functions. During the second phase, roughly between 5 and 8 years, children seem to recognize two functions, as evidenced in two developments. First, the children make use of redundant markers; and second, they create somewhat ungrammatical strings to mark functional contrasts. Karmiloff-Smith suggested that these developments indicate that the child is becoming conscious of the plurifunctionality of forms. In the third phase of development, neither the redundant marking nor ungrammatical forms are used, and the child uses forms plurifunctionally. Although these phases were proposed with reference to the development of determiners, Karmiloff-Smith suggested that the form of development is very general. In particular, she suggested that development consists of two related processes: "the child's endeavour to disambiguate by overmarking, use of emphasizers, use of paralinguistic markers, etc., counterbalanced by his progressive endeavour to be economical" (Karmiloff-Smith, 1979, p. 236).

Karmiloff-Smith's view of development is quite different from one that focuses on what was discussed under the heading of order of acquisition. Karmiloff-Smith was concerned with the development from unifunctional to plurifunctional status of a given form. The general processes of disambiguation and economy motivate the changes in the system. What differs in this approach is the focus on developments that take place prior to adultlike usage. Thus we see that even within various functional approaches, several different positions can be found with regard to development. Theorists differ with regard to how much of their focus is on proposing form-function patterns in child language and how much they attempt to account for developmental sequences that take place.

Although previous functional approaches to child language have at times been concerned with the notion of development, these discussions have been largely implicit. There has been very little in the way of explicit discussion of what one means by the notion of development. One major difference between the developmental-functional approach to child language proposed here and previous functional approaches is the level of explicitness about what the notion of development is taken to mean. I now consider how development is viewed within the framework adopted here.

The Notion of Development
Within a Developmental-Functionalist Approach

In contrast to most scholars who treat the notion of development in the field of child language (and developmental psychology as well), I do not equate the notions of ontogenesis and development. I reserve the use of the term ontogenesis to refer to the actual life span of a given individual.

The notion of development will be viewed in terms of "the ways in which agents utilized or constructed 'means' for the attainment of 'ends' " (Kaplan, 1983a, p. 56). Following Werner (1957), Werner and Kaplan (1984), and Kaplan (1983a, 1983b), the notion of development as used here is taken as a heuristic, or an ideal. To this extent one can distinguish ontogenesis (the actual) from development (rarely attained ideal). The use of the notion of development here requires having a telos of development in mind prior to empirical study. As Kaplan (1983b) suggested: "Development does not lurk directly in the population(s) studied but resides fundamentally in the perspective used" (p. 196).

In order to clarify what is meant by the notion of development it is helpful to discuss the *orthogenetic principle* formulated by Werner and Kaplan (1984): "We assume that organisms are naturally directed towards a series of transformations-reflecting a tendency to move from a state of relative globality and undifferentiatedness towards states of increasing differentiation and hierarchical integration" (p. 7). According to this principle, development is defined in terms of both hierarchical integration and increasing differentiation. To this extent, the principle is something one brings to the analysis of data, rather than development being something one finds through empirical examination.

Relating this view of development to the field of child language we can see some themes from the previous discussion of functionalist approaches to child language. For instance, we saw that a clear stipulation of a telos is something that was discussed in the work of Van Valin (1991). Furthermore, having an eye for developmental differences in form-function (means-ends) relations has been discussed here as only one way in which researchers have examined development. The difference between the present approach and most previous functional approaches to child language regards the way the notion of development is viewed. As noted earlier, development is not equated with change but, rather, is viewed as a perspective adopted toward data.

The approach put forth here shares much with that of Karmiloff-Smith, and it is important from the outset to clarify the relationship between these two approaches. With regard to their similarities, we can note that Karmiloff-Smith began with a clear notion of the ideal or end point of study, and at the same time she was interested in accounting for how a child makes use of given forms across the course of development. This interest is shared in the developmental-functionalist approach adopted here. Furthermore, Karmiloff-Smith was less interested in when a form is acquired in its full adultlike sense. Instead, she wished to account for the course of development along the way, another point of similarity between her approach and the approach taken here. The major difference between the two kinds of functional approaches concerns the account of developmental change. Karmiloff-Smith argued that children go through three phases in language acquisition, moving from a level of unifunctional interpretation of grammatical devices toward plurifunctional usage. This differs from the approach adopted here in that I suggest that language development can best be accounted for in terms of hierarchical integration and increasing differentiation. Old forms do not simply add on new functions; rather, the whole system undergoes linguistic transformations such that old forms are given new functions and old functions are related to new forms (see Slobin, 1973). According to the functional-developmental approach adopted here, form-function pairs are not only viewed as developing in and of themselves but are also perceived as part of a broader linguistic system.

CHAPTER TWO

Agentivity and Control: Linguistic, Developmental Psycholinguistic, and Developmental Psychological Perspectives

In the previous chapter, I outlined the beginnings of a developmental-functionalist approach that has guided the research reported in Part II of this book. In Part II I focus on one particular area of study, namely, the linguistic marking of agentivity and control in early child language. The issue is not simply whether children refer to notions of agency but, rather, whether they contrastively employ linguistic devices to mark different perspectives on the way participants are related in ongoing discourse frames.

A number of considerations have led to the selection of the issue of the linguistic marking of agentivity and control. I show why such a selection is appropriate as I consider findings from previous studies concerning the grammatical marking of agentivity and control in various languages, cross-linguistic studies concerning the notions of agentivity and control in early child language development, and studies within the area of social cognitive development. I now discuss these three separate areas of study that have shaped the questions guiding the research outlined in Part II. In the final section of this chapter, I discuss the framework adopted here for studying agentivity and control in early child language, and I outline a set of research questions that guided the research reported in Part II.

LINGUISTIC PERSPECTIVES

In this section I review several separate strands of theorizing that have dealt with the semantic notion of agency. One broad distinction in the various studies is between those in which a theorist has viewed agency as a discrete

25

semantic category and those in which agency is viewed as a semantic category with prototypical structure. I now review research in light of this basic distinction. It should be noted that the review of the linguistic literature is not meant to be exhaustive; instead, the studies included in this discussion have been selected because they have had significant impact on the way the concept of agentivity has been discussed within child language research.

Agentivity as a Discrete Semantic Category

The separate strands of theorizing placed together in this section, although different in many important ways, can be brought together to the extent that in all cases, agentivity is seen as a discrete category. These three views include: Fillmore's (1968) case grammar, Jackendoff's (1990) discussion of the action tier dealing with actor-patient relations, and Van Valin's (1993) discussion of semantic roles.

According to Fillmore (1968),[1] agent was viewed as one among several case notions in "a set of universal, presumably innate, concepts which identify certain types of judgments human beings are capable of making about the events that are going on around them" (p. 24). The idea behind Fillmore's case grammar was to provide a bridge between descriptions of events and underlying syntactic representations. It offered "a level of linguistic organization at which universal properties of lexical structure and clause organization were to be found" (Fillmore, 1977, p. 62).

Because my discussion of the child language literature draws upon the sorts of categories that are central to Fillmore's proposal, I present Fillmore's (1968) summary of his six main case categories (pp. 24–25):

Agentive (A), the case of the typically animate perceived instigator of the action identified by the verb.

Instrumental (I), the case of the inanimate force or object causally involved in the action or state identified by the verb.

Dative (D), the case of the animate being affected by the state or action identified by the verb.

Factive (F), the case of the object or being resulting from the action or state identified by the verb, or understood as a part of the meaning of the verb.

Locative (L), the case which identifies the location or spatial orientation of the state or action identified by the verb.

Objective (O), the semantically most neutral case. . . . The term is not to be confused with the notion of direct object.

---

[1]Although Fillmore later revised his original position (see, for instance, Fillmore, 1977) I refer exclusively to the 1968 version, because related research in child language has primarily drawn on Fillmore's 1968 paper.

Central to the discussion of case grammar is the idea that there is no one-to-one match between particular case categories and specific surface relations such as subject or object. With regard to English, we find contrasts like *Charles opened the door with the key* and *The key opened the door.* In these examples, we find that both the agentive case and the instrumental case can occur in subject position.

A second approach to the notion of agent as a more or less discrete category can be found in two theoretical perspectives that differ along other dimensions. These perspectives are those of Role and Reference Grammar (RRG) (see Foley & Van Valin, 1984; Van Valin, 1993) and Conceptual Semantics (CS) (Jackendoff, 1990). What is similar about the treatment of agent in these two seemingly different theoretical perspectives is the idea that conceptual roles are best viewed in terms of tiers. In contrast to Fillmore's single tier approach, both RRG and CS propose two tiers of conceptual structure. According to RRG, there are two layers of semantic structure: microroles and macroroles. Microroles consist of case roles or thematic relations (Fillmore, 1968; Gruber, 1965), of which agent is one. Within the framework of RRG, agent is defined as a willful instigator of an action. Contrasting with the specific microroles are two macroroles. Macroroles are "generalized semantic relations between a predicate and its arguments" (Foley & Van Valin, 1984, p. 29). The *actor*, according to RRG, can be characterized as "the argument of the predicate which expresses the participant which performs, effects, instigates, or controls the situation denoted by the predicate" (p. 29). The second macrorole is referred to as the *undergoer* and is aligned with the argument "which expresses the participant which does not perform, initiate, or control any situation but rather is affected by it in some way" (p. 29).[2]

Jackendoff (1990) proposed a similar multilevel analysis within the analysis of causation. According to Jackendoff, conceptual roles are distributed in two tiers: "a *thematic tier* dealing with motion and location, and an *action tier* dealing with Actor-Patient relations" (Jackendoff, 1990, p. 126). Adding this action tier allowed Jackendoff to break down the notion of agent into three distinct components, which included instigation of action, volitionality, and the more general notion of doer.

Agentivity as a Nondiscrete Semantic Category

In the preceding discussion of agentivity as a discrete category, I have noted that some of the more recent analyses of agentivity have assumed a multilevel

---

[2]The macroroles of actor and undergoer as well as the case roles/thematic relations can be viewed in terms of the hierarchy depicted in (i) (see Van Valin, 1993):

(i) ACTOR   UNDERGOER

    →   ←

  Agent . . . Effector . . . Locative . . . Theme . . . Patient

view of agent. This is central to the view of agentivity as a nondiscrete linguistic category. Drawing upon prototype theory (Rosch, 1978), the claim is that linguistic categories such as agent are best defined in terms of a cluster of related notions in which some exemplars of a given category will be better members than others. With regard to the notion of agentivity, Lakoff (1977, p. 244) suggested the following cluster of properties for prototypical agent-patient sentences, based on his analysis of English data:

1. There is a(n) agent, who does something.
2. There is a patient, who undergoes a change to a new state.
3. The change in the patient results from the action by the agent.
4. The agent's action is volitional.
5. The agent is in control of what he does.
6. The agent is primarily responsible for what happens (his action and the resulting change).
7. The agent is the energy source in the action.
8. There is a single event.
9. There is a single definite agent.
10. There is a single definite patient.
11. The agent uses his hands, body, or some instrument.
12. The change in the patient is perceptible.
13. The agent perceives the change.
14. The agent is looking at the patient.

According to Lakoff's proposal, agent-patient sentences will vary in terms of the number of properties exhibited. The more properties a particular sentence displays, the more prototypical the sentence is said to be.

Lakoff and others have since argued that the notion of agent cannot be defined in terms of a set of necessary features, suggesting instead that agency involves a number of semantic categories including volition, animacy, and control. Hopper and Thompson (1980) claimed that agency is part of a broader cluster involving transitivity. They suggested a set of 10 parameters listed in Table 2.1, all of which have to do with the effectiveness of transferring action. Each parameter was viewed along a continuum ranging from high to low transitivity; the more an action is transferred, the higher the transitivity rating. Based on extensive examination of several languages, Hopper and Thompson concluded that morphosyntactic markings are sensitive to "transitivity as a whole, rather than the actual presence or absence of a second participant" (Hopper and Thompson, 1980, p. 254). These regularities were said to be motivated by broader discursive functions.

TABLE 2.1
Transitivity Parameters
(from Hopper and Thompson, 1980, p. 252)

Parameter	High	Low
Participants	2 or more	1 participant
Kinesis	action	nonaction
Aspect	telic	atelic
Punctuality	punctuality	nonpunctuality
Volitionality	volitional	nonvolitional
Affirmation	affirmative	negative
Mode	realis	irrealis
Agency	A high in potency	A low in potency
Affectedness of 0	0 totally affected	A not affected
Individuation	0 highly affected	0 nonindividuated

A = Agent, 0 = Object.

DeLancey (1984) claimed that agentivity is a major subcomponent of the transitivity scene:

> The general claim is that there is a cross-linguistically valid prototype for true transitivity which involves (among other things) a direct causation schema with proximate and ultimate cause both residing in the same volitionally acting causer. The prototype definition of agent is part of this schema, i.e., the prototypical agent is just such a volitional causer. Deviations from the semantic prototype are coded by deviations from prototypical transitive morphosyntax. (p.185)

Cross-linguistic research has revealed that languages tend to mark prototypical agents with different linguistic devices from those marking nonprototypical agents. Nevertheless, a review of this literature reveals that languages differ in what counts as a prototypical agent. For instance, languages differ on whether natural forces are given agentive marking or not (see DeLancey, 1984). In addition, languages differ in the range of devices used to mark prototypical agentivity and various deviations. Two of the major kinds of resources employed to mark such distinctions are case markers and voice (see Barber, 1975; Berman, 1979; Comrie, 1981; Croft, 1987, 1990; DeLancey, 1984, 1987, 1990; Eilfort, Kroeber, & Peterson, 1985; Givón, 1984a). Furthermore, such research has revealed that speaker perspective often determines what gets prototypical marking and what does not (cf. Barber, 1975; Berman, 1979, for illustration).

Comparing the two views of agents as either discrete or nondiscrete categories, two major distinctions can be found. First, with regard to the nondiscrete position, agentivity is viewed in terms of prototypicality rather than as a unitary category. A second major distinction concerns whether one posits that the semantic categorization of agentivity is reflected in particular morphosyntactic patterns. Central to the prototype approach is the claim that languages of the world mark prototypical agents differently from deviations from the prototype. Researchers who have viewed agents as a discrete semantic category have made the opposite claim; that is, case grammarians have highlighted the lack of correspondence between semantic and morphosyntactic levels of analysis. In the section that follows we see that these differences result in quite different views about the role of the category of agent in language acquisition.

DEVELOPMENTAL PSYCHOLINGUISTIC PERSPECTIVES

In this section I consider the notions of agency and control within the child language literature. Specifically, I first review literature that has dealt with semantic approaches to agentivity. Here one can draw a distinction similar to that discussed earlier between the treatment of agentivity as a discrete semantic category and the treatment of agentivity in terms of prototypicality. Next, I consider how agency has figured in recent discussions of pragmatic and activity-type approaches to child language. In these later sections, focus will shift from viewing agentivity in terms of purely physical causation toward a consideration of agentivity in terms of social control.

Semantic Approaches to Agency

Agentivity as a Discrete Semantic Category. There seem to be two very broad kinds of treatments of agentivity as a discrete semantic category in the developmental psycholinguistic literature. One group of researchers has followed up on the case grammar approach, and agent has been viewed as one among many case categories in children's early speech. This group has been interested primarily in the semantic content of children's early word combinations. A second group has followed up on the work of Jackendoff (1990) and Van Valin (1993) reviewed earlier and has examined the notion of agent at the level of thematic relations. I now review the work of the first group, because this group has generated the most empirical work relevant to the analyses reported in Part II of this book.

There have been dozens of proposals in the literature concerning the semantic content of children's early speech. Although the specifics of the various proposals differ, what is similar is the belief that children's early word combinations are best viewed in terms of semantic caselike categories rather than syntactic categories (i.e., subject, object). I briefly examine three such categorization schemes. Though others could have been selected, these have been included because they highlight some relevant distinctions in the way the notion of agent has figured in these proposals.

Brown (1973) applied Fillmore's case categories to the longitudinal data of Adam and found that all six of Fillmore's basic categories could be applied to Adam's earliest multiword utterances. In considering a wider corpus of data, Brown suggested that three of the four most common kinds of semantic relations in children's early speech relate to the notion of agentivity. These three categories include: (a) agent-action (*Adam write, Daddy go*), (b) action-object (*Change diaper*), and (c) possessor-possessed (*Adam chair, My pencil*). Brown used a notion of agent that was not restricted to animate instigators, though he noted that most agents in the various samples were in fact animate. One can also note that Brown's category of possessor-possessed would be classified under Fillmore's more general category of Dative-Objective, though Brown suggested that the frequent appearance and productivity of possessor-possessed word combinations led him to create this special category. Brown suggested that children are very interested in talking about who carries out actions, the kinds of changes undergone by objects by virtue of actions carried out on them, and the distinction between rights to control and association with particular objects. It should be emphasized that in working with these case categories, Brown, like Fillmore, was not making any specific claims about the relationship between particular surface forms and the underlying semantic case relation.

Bloom, Lightbown, and Hood (1975) also considered semantic aspects of children's early word combinations. The categories they posited did not follow Fillmore's so closely but, rather, were said to "emerge from the data" (p. 9). For the present purposes, we can note that Bloom et al. differed from Brown in that they distinguished between an action category, which might refer to "action that affected an object with movement by an agent" (p. 10), and a locative category, referring to actions "where the goal of the movement was a change in the location of a person or object" or "where the agent and affected object or person were the same" (p. 10). Examples of this contrast include *My open that, Gia ride bike,* and *I made,* as opposed to *Up Kathryn* (=child's own name) and *I get down.* Bloom et al. claimed that the action category, which involves the relation between agent, actions, and objects, is central early in development.

Although Bloom et al., like Brown, claimed that the various children studied all made use of similar semantic categories, Bloom et al. differed to the extent that they claimed that at a very early phase (before the children's MLU [mean length of utterance] was 2.0), the children could be distinguished in terms of the range of forms used—some children relied on pronominal and others on nominal forms. The variation in nominal-pronominal usage has been taken to indicate that the children are in the earliest phase of learning different kinds of syntactic-semantic systems. It can be noted, though, that Bloom et al. did not attempt to link the use of specific forms with specific meaning categories.

One final proposal highlights yet another way the notion of agentivity has figured in proposals concerning children's early word combinations. Braine (1976), in examining data from children acquiring several languages, came to the conclusion that the relational categories of young children are far narrower than previous child language research led one to believe. Of particular relevance here is his discussion of the actor-action category. Braine noted that Fillmore's agent category was more sophisticated than the actor category he posited. Braine argued that the sort of relations that children talk about early on do not involve the kinds of causal changes Fillmore referred to. Instead, Braine claimed that children talk about "simple actions like sitting, running, eating" (Braine, 1976, p. 84). For this reason, Braine referred to an actor— namely, one who carries out an action-rather than an agent.[3]

Although there is some agreement among the various semantic proposals that agentivity is a notion expressed in children's early word combinations, what remains unclear from a comparative analysis of the various proposals is the nature of the notion of agency that is expressed. Some researchers have attributed to children fairly sophisticated notions of agency similar to those referred to in Fillmore's case grammar, whereas others have been more cautious in suggesting children may simply be referring to a notion of animate doer. With regard to these various proposals, one of the major questions that has been raised concerns the issue of continuity: If children begin combining words based on semantic patterns such as agent-action, how is it that they ultimately arrive at syntactic categories such as subject-verb? I do not pursue this issue here but, rather, turn to another way agent has been viewed in the child language literature, namely, as a nondiscrete semantic category.

Agentivity as a Nondiscrete Semantic Category. Although I have noted very fundamental differences in the ways agentivity has been viewed in my discussion of child language theorizing thus far, what has held these various views together is the idea that agent is a discrete category. As I noted in the discussion of linguistic perspectives on agency, much attention in the linguistic literature has worked with an alternative conception of agentivity, namely, that it is best viewed in terms of a cluster of related semantic parameters. I now consider one semantic approach to child language that has drawn upon this claim.

Over the past decade, Slobin (1981, 1982, 1985) has suggested that particular prototypical events provide a framework for children's early organization of linguistic forms. As was noted in chapter 1, certain notions were

---

[3]It is of interest that Braine commented on the role of pragmatic purpose in children's early word combinations—a point I return to later on in this chapter. Note that Braine was not interested in the relation between utterance function and the semantic meaning categories he proposed.

said to be the first to receive linguistic treatment by children across the world. One such notion was that of linguistic transitivity. Based on a review of typologically distinct languages, Slobin provided intriguing evidence that children acquiring structurally different languages begin to use grammatical forms to mark a scene he referred to as the Manipulative Activity Scene. This scene involves "the experiential gestalt of a basic causal event in which an agent carries out a physical and perceptible change of state in a patient by means of direct body contact or with an instrument under the agent's control" (Slobin, 1985, p. 1175). Children were said to extract specific surface markers from the input language; and though the specific marker selected will vary from language to language, Slobin suggested that in all languages children will attempt to grammaticize something like the Manipulative Activity Scene. In particular, based on acquisitional data of a child acquiring Russian (Gvozdev, 1949) and children acquiring Kaluli (Schieffelin, 1985), Slobin noted that the children studied similarly restricted the use of accusative and ergative inflections. At an early phase of development the children restricted the use of the language-relevant inflections to the Manipulative Activity Scene, rather than using the accusative marker in Russian to mark all direct objects and the ergative inflection in Kaluli to mark subjects of transitive verbs.

Slobin's analysis of agentivity differs considerably from that in the developmental psycholinguistic literature discussed previously, in which agency was viewed as a discrete category. In addition to viewing agentivity in terms of a prototypical scene, Slobin also attempted to relate the use of specific linguistic devices to this scene. In fact, it was Slobin's claim that this prototypical scene plays an organizing role for the child as an entry into grammar. Although Slobin's analysis of children's special linguistic treatment of the Manipulative Activity Scene is quite similar to the analysis discussed here of transitivity and agentivity as a nondiscrete semantic category in the linguistic literature, it is important to note the following differences. First, in Slobin's discussion of the Manipulative Activity Scene, the notion of volition was not mentioned. In addition, the marking of various kinds of deviations from the agentive prototype did not receive focus. What also remains unclear is the relation between Slobin's proposed prototype and the language-specific differences noted by DeLancey (1984, 1990) and others in what counts as a prototypical agent and what counts as relevant deviations. This is a topic I return to.

Pragmatic Approaches to Agency

Thus far I have been considering the notions of agentivity and control primarily from the standpoint of physical causation. It seems, though, that by limiting the discussion of agentivity to physical causation, one misses out on a related set of issues concerning social causality. As I have noted in the first chapter of this book, language does not merely reflect reality; speakers use language to achieve social goals. In this section, I consider some of the literature on language development that focuses on children's growing use of language for social purposes. Our focus will be on the potential relationship between language structure and the particular goals of the type of action the children talk about.

There is much evidence that before children begin combining words in multiword utterances, they draw a linguistic distinction between utterances that function to bring about action and utterances that match or describe the world (cf. Halliday, 1975; Painter, 1984). In addition to using contrasting intonation patterns, children have been noted to use particular gestural and phonetic forms systematically with specific communicative sensorimotor schemata. As was noted in chapter 1, Carter (1975, 1978a, 1978b), for instance, suggested that children will contrastively use particular forms depending on whether they wanted an action to be carried out by a partner or whether they wanted to bring attention to a particular object. In chapter 1 I noted findings from Deutsch and Budwig (1983) that also suggested that children organize the use of specific linguistic forms around the notion of social control. Studies of older children's use of form contrasts have also indicated their continued interest in dimensions of social control as a way to organize linguistic forms. Shepherd (1980) claimed that preschool-aged Antiguan Creole-speaking children made an innovative contrast when using the modal forms *gon* and *go*. Although adult speakers of this English-based creole appear to use the forms nondistinctively, Shepherd claimed that the children distinguish between the two forms based on locus of control.

Gordon and Ervin-Tripp (1984) also noted that the preschool English-speaking boy they studied linked the use of three different request forms (*I want* vs. *supposed to* and *have to* vs. imperatives) with particular instrumental goals (i.e., requests oriented to rules and norms vs. requests in the context of joint activities). This sort of form-function contrast highlights the extent to which children's use of linguistic forms is organized around various kinds of social motivations for action.

Gordon, Budwig, Strage, and Carrell (1980) revealed that with continued development, children draw even further formal contrasts based on their growing ability to attend to the viewpoint of the listener. To this extent, both social motivation and social relationships are indexed in the use of particular linguistic devices. It is exactly these broad sorts of social distinctions that have not been considered in previous semantic discussions of agentivity. At the conclusion of this chapter, I return to a consideration of more specific suggestions concerning how such social aspects of causation schemes might be integrated into the notion of agentivity. First, I consider one more area of research in which agentivity has been said to play a role in acquisition.

Activity-Type Approaches to Agency

The activity-type approach is quite similar to the prototype and pragmatic approaches reviewed here. Central to the activity-type approach is the claim that children's use of particular grammatical constructions can be understood only by a consideration of the broader discursive contexts in which they are embedded (see Gee, 1985; Gee & Savasir, 1985; Gerhardt, 1990). The notion of activity-type is similar to related notions used by Ervin-Tripp (1972), Gumperz (1982), and Levinson (1979).[4] It also can be related to the notion of Scene as employed by Fillmore (1977) and Slobin (1985), which can be viewed as involving landscapes within which people act, although activity-types are more dynamic units that also take into account the ongoing inter-active frame. The activity-level construct views under one heading a variety of verbal and nonverbal properties that pattern together in ongoing action. I now consider some findings from research that suggests that activity-types relate to children's growing notions of agentivity and control.

In a study of various kinds of future markers in children's acquisition of Turkish, Savasir (1984) argued that children contrastively employ future markers in ways that deviate from adult Turkish. Although at one level the children's usage is deviant, particular forms are said to be consistently and meaningfully employed by the children. As one example of the kinds of contrasts Savasir noted, consider the activity-types associated with the use of the aorist and optative markers. Savasir claimed that the aorist form oc-curred in first and third person reference in situations where he found the child to be taking an eventive perspective on an action frame. Although the child or some other participant might have been acting as agent, focus was placed on the role of experimentation. The shift was away from agency. Similarly, the optative was viewed as a marker of nonprototypical agency. The optative was found in two related contexts—either in accounts for which the motivation for action was due to knowledge of rules of the game or in contexts in which the child's actions were adult motivated. These findings highlighted the fact that the children were distinguishing different ways to contextualize their own and others' actions that produced changes of state in objects. Although all examples could be viewed at the semantic level as agentive, a more refined analysis revealed differences in the kinds of motives for the action; the two forms appeared in different discourse contexts.

The sorts of parameters included in the activity-types suggested by Savasir are similar to those reviewed in chapter 1 with regard to Gerhardt's work on modal forms. Such research indicates the importance of including a variety of parameters that run orthogonal to the parameters of agentivity and control,

---

[4]Although Levinson (1979) used the same term, Levinson considered activity-types as macro-level categories having to do with institutionally agreed upon activities (see Gee & Savasir, 1985, for further discussion).

discussed with regard to the semantic approach to agentivity. Issues such as volition and responsibility, as well as the communicative function of the utterances under consideration, are only parts of the constellations children seem to link with linguistic forms. Gee and Savasir pointed toward the importance of also considering a variety of social factors, such as whether agents are acting in order to carry out their own goals or interpersonal goals. I return to some specific implications of the activity-type approach for the study of agentivity and control in English-speaking children's first word combinations. First, though, I briefly consider one last kind of relevant literature, namely, that concerning psychological studies of the development of children's conceptions of agentivity and control.

DEVELOPMENTAL PSYCHOLOGICAL PERSPECTIVES

Much of the developmental psycholinguistic literature starts from the assumption that children who are just beginning to combine words have relatively stable conceptual notions about agency. The question I raise here is whether such a claim can be supported when one examines research findings concerning children's understanding of the concept of agency. I have noted that agency can be viewed as a multidimensional concept that involves an understanding of causality, animacy, and intentionality. In what follows, I briefly consider some literature from developmental psychological research. This work suggests that previous psycholinguistic research may have presupposed categories that are still developing in the child who is just beginning to acquire language. After reviewing this literature, I consider the implications of such findings for theorizing about the relation between children's conceptual notions of agency and their development of language.

Piaget (1930, 1954) wrote extensively on the emergence of children's notions of causality. His central argument was that children's notions of causality are gradually constructed over the course of several years. Piaget's (1930) early claims that preschool-aged children lack causal knowledge, as evidenced in their inability to reason about causal mechanisms, has led to a multitude of studies that have attempted to show that preschoolers function similarly to adults with regard to both mechanical (see Bullock, 1979) and social (Shultz, 1980) causality. A more specific understanding of children's developing notions of causality emerges from a review of children's growing conceptions of animacy and intentionality. Much research has been directed toward children's ability to distinguish between animate and inanimate causation and toward children's growing understanding that some actions are carried out intentionally, whereas others are not.

One aspect of understanding agency is the ability to distinguish animate and inanimate causation. Several different lines of research have indicated that before children begin combining words, they understand what animate and inanimate objects can do (see Golinkoff, Harding, Carlson, & Sexton, 1984, for a review). These studies show that children as young as 2 years show surprise when they are presented with inanimate objects that move on their own (i.e., a chair suddenly moving without an external agent assisting).

With regard to understanding animate causation, much discussion has focused on the distinction between self and other. Piaget (1954) claimed that infants attribute causality to self actions before attributing independent causality to others. A similar self–other distinction has been upheld in numerous experimental studies (see Huttenlocher, Smiley, & Charney, 1983; Poulin-DuBois & Shultz, 1988; Wolf, 1982; Wolf, Rygh, & Altshuler, 1984). Most relevant to our present concern with language development is a series of studies conducted by Huttenlocher et al. In three separate studies of children's verb meanings, these researchers found that the verbs children first used encoded self actions. Only later did the children use verbs to encode the actions of others. Huttenlocher et al. claimed that at the time the children in their study were beginning to combine words into multiword utterances, the children rarely produced verbs spontaneously to refer to others' actions; and the same finding was said to hold for comprehension. Based on these findings, Huttenlocher et al. concluded that children pass through distinct developmental stages in understanding self and other as actors. This finding is particularly intriguing in light of the developmental psycholinguistic research reviewed earlier that presupposed that children's semantic category of actor encompasses both self and other.

A related question is whether children's understanding of animate beings acting with intentions need be considered in terms of a distinction between self and other as agent. Several different lines of developmental research suggest that such a distinction is necessary (see Huttenlocher et al., 1983; Poulin-DuBois & Shultz, 1988; Wolf, 1982; Wolf et al., 1984). What these studies revealed is that children first have an understanding of personal agency and only later come to understand others as acting with intentions. Although the studies differed somewhat in the specific age at which they suggested that children have a notion of independent agency, there was much agreement that at around the age of 2, the child is primarily working with a notion of personal agency. The main conclusion of such studies was that the very notion of agency undergoes development between the ages of 1 and 5. Around the age of 2, children are working primarily with a notion of personal agency rather than a more global notion of independent agency.

The findings reviewed here suggest the need for caution with regard to assumptions concerning young children's semantic notions of agentivity. As I noted earlier, agentivity is a multidimensional notion consisting of several interrelated categories. One particular finding stemming from the developmental psychological literature that is relevant to a consideration of children's use of agency as a wedge into grammar is that children seem to develop notions of agency first with respect only to the self and later for others. The question this raises is whether some of the previous studies of children's early word combinations have overestimated the breadth of children's early semantic categories (see also Braine, 1976; Huttenlocher et al., 1983, for a similar discussion). In the section that follows I explore the implications of such a claim.

A FRAMEWORK FOR STUDYING AGENTIVITY AND CONTROL IN EARLY CHILD LANGUAGE

In this chapter I have examined several different studies concerning agentivity and control. Based on a review of this work stemming from related disciplines, the choice to focus on agentivity and control seems relevant for numerous reasons. First, there is a good amount of evidence that such notions are consistently marked in the languages of the world and play a central role in the organization of grammar. Second, there is much evidence from studies of children's first word combinations that children spend a great deal of time talking about agentivity and control. If children are going to employ linguistic devices to mark salient conceptual notions, the choice of agentivity and control seems relevant. Finally, our review of cross-linguistic evidence suggests that children acquiring strikingly different languages attempt to mark linguistically the various perspectives they take on human action.

Having reviewed a number of separate lines of research that consider the notions of agentivity and control, we are now in a better position to raise questions pertaining to the linguistic marking of agentivity and control in children acquiring English. Although I have noted that the majority of developmental psycholinguistic studies have yet to examine the extent to which particular linguistic devices may reflect children's attempts to mark a cluster of notions concerning agentivity, Slobin's cross-linguistic research illustrated that children acquiring inflectional languages seek to link particular devices with a prototypical manipulative scene. This leads to the question whether children acquiring English also mark such notions in the early phases of language development. In the present investigation, I elaborate on the issue of the linguistic marking of prototypical agentivity by assessing whether children mark various deviations from the prototypical agentive scene as well. Thus my concern is with the development of systems for marking various aspects of causation schemes.

The research concerning transitivity, agentivity, and prototype semantics reviewed here suggests that the categories children are working with may not be discrete in nature. I start from the assumption that young children are working with categories with prototypical structure not only because these have been suggested for adult linguistic systems, but also because my examination of the social-cognitive developmental literature suggested that the very notions said to cluster with the notion of agentivity are themselves developing at the time grammar is emerging. It therefore seems likely that children are attempting to link specific forms with various aspects of causal vectors, and that they are working with form-meaning pairs that are built around a prototype, rather than with unitary categories such as agent-action relations.[5] In particular, I am interested in whether specific linguistic forms link up with prototypical agentivity and various deviations. For instance, Brown (1973) placed instances like *Adam write* and *I no fall* in the same Verb + Agent category. Likewise, Bloom et al. (1975) categorized utterances like *My get magazine, My open this,* and *I turn the light on* as falling within the Action category. The question of interest here is whether the forms are used contrastively to refer to prototypical agentivity and various deviations. In examining the children's use of forms in terms of whether they mark various notions of agentivity and control, I depart from a purely semantic analysis and examine whether children might also integrate a set of related notions about social causation into the agentive prototype.

Although these questions guide the present study, no specific predictions can be made about where English-speaking children might decide to mark such notions. Some subsystems of grammar, however, seem more likely candidates than others. A review of the linguistic literature concerning the linguistic marking of agentivity, as well as Slobin's cross-linguistic findings regarding young children's marking of prototypical agentivity, suggests that case markers often are employed to mark shifts in perspective on agency. English, though, does not mark nouns with case inflections and only has limited case marking in pronominal forms. Deutsch and Budwig's (1983) study indicated that children contrastively employ first person possessive pronominal forms and nominal forms to mark a contrast in degree of pragmatic control; yet other pronominal forms were not examined. The research on Turkish- and English-speaking children conducted by Savasir (1984) and Gerhardt (1990) suggested that tense, aspect, and modality markers are also employed to contrast between different perspectives on participants' involvements in fields of action. What all these subsystems share is the extent to which they relate the speaker's perspective. Although we cannot firmly predict where in the linguistic system children acquiring English might mark notions of agentivity in their early word combinations, it seems that they would be likely to draw upon linguistic structures that have been noted to

---

[5]One might suggest that the sort of tiered approach offered by Jackendoff (1990) and Van Valin (1993) could also handle developmental aspects of the broader category, though in this view one would need to explain why such information would be ignored at one phase and included at another—thus the tiered approach is not an ideal solution.

link up with speakers' expression of an inner attitude (see Benveniste, 1971; Kuroda, 1973; Lyons, 1982).

Although it is expected that 2-year-old children mark the notions of agentivity and control in the earliest phases of grammatical development, examination focuses on the breadth of the children's categories. My review of the developmental psychological literature suggests the need, before assuming that children are marking a broad notion of agent, to attend to whether the children first work with a more refined notion of personal agency. The following set of research questions summarizes the focus of the present study:

1. What distinctions concerning agentivity and control are relevant to children's organization of linguistic forms in the early phases of acquiring English?

2. Do English-speaking children make use of particular linguistic forms to mark something like a prototypical agentivity scene?

3. If so, what counts as prototypical agentivity?

4. How, if at all, do children mark deviations from a prototypical agentivity scene, and what distinctions are marked? What broader systems of agentivity marking are children organizing?

5. What role does pragmatic function play in the linguistic marking of agentivity and control? Are children attempting to relate forms to broader constellations of meaning that cut across semantic and pragmatic parameters?

6. Do young children begin with a broad notion of agentivity or do they first organize forms around notions of personal agency?

7. What happens across development? If, for instance, children's early systems do not completely match those of adult speakers of English, what developmental paths are traveled en route to an adultlike system?

8. What commonalities and differences are found among various children acquiring English?

In the chapters that follow, I deal with these questions. In chapter 3, I discuss methodological issues related to the study. In chapter 4, I review some preliminary analyses; and in chapters 5 through 8, I discuss the major findings regarding the eight questions raised here.

CHAPTER THREE

Methodology

In this chapter I consider various aspects of the overall design of the research reported in subsequent chapters of this book. In addition to covering issues such as the selection of subjects and the kinds of tasks involved, I also briefly consider two preliminary phases in arriving at the present research paradigm. A central theme in this chapter is that the research environment can be structured so that the data are ecologically valid, as well as directed at the particular question to be examined.

The findings to be reported in subsequent chapters are based on an investigation making use of a naturalistic design. Focus is on children's spontaneous linguistic productions, looking in particular at ways in which the children being studied marked the notions of agentivity and control. In gathering the data, any naturalistic study is confronted with the issue of sampling. What activities should be sampled? What partners should interact with the child? Where should the study take place? With regard to the present study, a decision was made to collect data in settings and with partners that would provide a maximum amount of language productions involving talk about agentivity and control.

In order to carry out the kind of distributional analyses and in order to sort out the interrelationships that exist between form and semantic and pragmatic function across a span of development in the detailed manner documented in Part II of this book, one must have a sufficient corpus that can provide a rich basis for such analyses. In making choices about setting, partners, and activities, the aim was to design a study that utilized a subset of activities that 2-year-old children participate in and at the same time tapped a range of talk about the issues of agentivity and control. The design was intended not merely to permit the observation of children doing what they naturally do but to create a natural environment within which talk about agentivity and control could unfold. I now consider two preliminary phases that contributed greatly to the formulation of the design that is later discussed further.

PRELIMINARY PHASES
OF DESIGNING THE INVESTIGATION

Analysis of Other Data Sources

The first step in designing the present study involved working through transcripts stemming from other research projects concerning the natural speech productions of 2-year-old children. In so doing, I made use of three different sources of information: (a) transcripts from children in Brown's (1973) longitudinal sample, (b) transcripts from naturalistic interactions of three children in Ervin and Miller's longitudinal corpus (Ervin & Miller, 1964), and (c) transcripts and video taped recordings stemming from a longitudinal investigation of mother-child and peer interaction of children between 2 and 3 years of age (Budwig, Strage, & Bamberg, 1986). The point of working through these sources was to isolate the sorts of activities that led children to talk about various kinds of agentivity and control. When did the children talk about personal agency? When did they refer to others' involvements in action frames? Did particular kinds of settings, partners, or activities lead to talk about social control?

An extensive analysis of these data sources proved helpful in the following ways. First, it became clear that talk about agentivity was not limited to particular kinds of tasks. Children talked about their own ability to carry out actions both when engaged in play activities and when no particular activity was taking place. Nevertheless, the amount of extended discourse found in different kinds of activities varied tremendously. It also became clear that there were differences in the kinds of talk about physical and social causation that took place when the children were interacting with a peer versus a caregiver. Within the context of play with peers, verbal interactions involved numerous claims to gain or maintain control of objects. In contrast, in the context of caregiver-child interactions, disputes over control of objects occurred rather infrequently and were primarily over control of objects that were in limited quantity and of high value to the adults. Finally, although the Brown and the Ervin and Miller studies took place in a single setting, namely, the child's home, the data sources involving peer and adult interactions revealed differences in the nature of the children's (and caregivers') talk when they interacted in their own home versus that of the peer (see Budwig, 1981, for further discussion).

On the basis of this examination of other transcripts, a series of preliminary decisions could be made concerning the design of the study. First, the limitation in working only with transcripts made clear the need to use video for the present study. Although at times contextual notes were sufficient, at other times it was unclear whether children were claiming objects or referring to an object they possessed. Consider the example where the child says *My purse* as the researcher and parent converse. The contextual notes suggest that the child is approaching the purse. In such an instance, it is unclear whether the purse belongs to the researcher and the child wishes to claim it, or whether the purse is the child's own and the child is pointing it out to the adults. Although at times the surrounding discourse adds clarification, often the lack of video meant that potentially useful material had to be ignored.

A second decision that came out of the analyses of other longitudinal data sources involved the importance of including peer data when studying the early phases of grammatical development. Though most previous studies of the early phases of grammatical development of English-speaking children have almost exclusively focused on adult-child interactions, it seemed important to include interactions with peers as well. This point was stressed by Demuth (1984), whose ethnographic study of Basotho children's spontaneous speech revealed that relative clause usage was highly affected by the kind of discourse partner with which one interacted. Demuth reported that relative clauses were first produced by the children in peer interactions and were not used in the context of adult-child interactions where the caregiver tended to supply much contextual information. Ervin-Tripp (1977) also pointed out that bursts of syntax are more likely to occur in contexts where pressure to communicate is strong. In the present study, the decision was to include interactions both between caregiver and child and between peer and child.

A third issue that was affected by examination of other longitudinal research involved the selection of the setting. The decision was made to pick an environment that was equally familiar to both children. Especially with regard to the issue of rights and claiming possession, this seemed important in order to make developmental comparisons. Although there are no neutral settings, the best option seemed to be to conduct the study at the day-care center that the children attended regularly and where their caregivers volunteered on a regular basis. Having narrowed down the focus to a particular setting and range of interactive partners, the second round of preliminary decision making concerning design could begin.

Entering the Day-Care Center

In selecting a day-care center where the study could take place, it seemed important to choose an environment that could physically accommodate the study (e.g., a quiet room for observations that was not foreign to the children).

It also was important to select a setting in which the staff was excited and cooperative about the prospect of an ongoing study. After locating a day-care center that met these demands, I spent 2 months as a participant observer and teacher's aide before actually starting the study. This was in accordance with an agreement worked out with the day-care staff. In addition to lending a hand at supervising activities, changing diapers, and cleaning spilled juice, I used the time to plan out the study. The children also had the chance to become familiar with me and my role at the center. I attended staff meetings to keep up with the range of problems confronting the children and had the chance during such meetings to develop rapport with the staff. During this period, I kept field notes on activities that elicited talk between peers and piloted activities based on notes made from scanning transcripts of the longitudinal studies reported earlier. Many of the procedures used were based on those outlined by Corsaro (1985). Once subjects were selected, specific tasks were piloted to test attention span and interest. At this point, I began keeping diary notes on the subset of children who would participate in the study, while they were engaging in ongoing activities at the day-care center with their peers and with adults. I continued to participate at the day-care center on a regular basis throughout the duration of the study, using the time to continue with diary observations, attend staff meetings, and keep in contact with the children's parents.

DESIGN OF THE STUDY

Subjects

Six children who attended the center on a regular basis participated in the study. These children were selected from a larger pool of children whose parents had indicated interest in participating in the study. All parents were informed by letter of the study and were asked to return a permission form if they were interested in having their children participate. They were notified that one caregiver would also be involved once a month in the study and that either the mother or the father could participate. Decisions concerning which children were to be included in the study were based on a number of factors. First, the children all had to be monolingual speakers of English. One caregiver had to be willing to participate once a month for a video recording session. It was important the children selected could be paired with a familiar playmate whom they interacted with on a regular basis and who attended the day-care center at similar times during the day. It was hoped that all children would be firstborn; but in order to meet the other requirements, it was necessary to include one child (Megan) who had a 7-year-old sibling. Sex of the children was not taken into account in selecting participants; the study included two girls and four boys. Subjects were not systematically selected on the basis of socioeconomic status or race. Nevertheless, due to demographic characteristics of the center, the group was rather homogeneous. All children were Caucasian and they came from middle-class families. Because the center was connected with a university, all of the children's parents were connected with the university either as students or as staff. None of the subjects' parents held teaching positions at the university.

The children participating in the study ranged between 20 and 32 months of age at the onset of the study. Because age is not always the best indicator of linguistic development, the selection of subjects was not based on chronological age alone. During the pilot phases of the project, samples of speech data were collected from the children and MLUs were calculated. The youngest dyad included the two girls, Megan and Grice, who rarely used grammatical morphemes and were just beginning to combine words into utterances. The two other dyads consisted of boys: Jeffrey and Keith had begun to use functors; and Eric and Thomas were well beyond the two-word stage, having begun to employ tense markers and modal auxiliaries, for instance. More details concerning the children's ages and levels of linguistic development at the start of the project are documented in chapter 4. With regard to the issue of intelligibility of the children's speech, good articulation was not a requirement for participation in the study. One child, Megan, was at times rather difficult to understand, whereas Grice pronounced words very clearly. Given the recent findings concerning the relation between intelligibility of children's early utterances and the nature of early grammatical development, it seemed important not to exclude subjects because their utterances might be difficult to transcribe (see Bates, Bretherton, & Snyder, 1988, for further discussion).

Setting

The study took place in a quiet room located next to the main playroom of the day-care center. This room was typically used by the teachers as a staff room where they gathered during nap time. It also housed gymnastic equipment used on rainy days. The children occasionally were allowed in this room to carry out special projects under the supervision of one of the teachers. One of the advantages to using this room was that the children always looked forward to being allowed to play there. The room was simply furnished with a couch and a low table where the children could play while standing. A desk was located nearby where the teachers often worked while the children played. In the present study, the children played primarily around the table area.

Tasks

Four tasks were presented each month. This allowed for developmental comparisons to take place between various children and within particular children across development. These four tasks were as follows:

Watering Plant. This task was included as a way of drawing the children into the playroom. During the piloting phase of the project each of the six children planted seeds in a cup that they had decorated with crayons and a sticker. Upon entering the room, the children were asked to check the small end table where the plants were kept. Specifically, the instructions of the researcher were as follows: "Show each other what is on the table" (peer situation) or "Show your mom what is on the table" (caregiver situation). A small pitcher of water was placed on the table so the children could water their plant. The plant task also provided children the chance to negotiate the various participants' involvements in watering the plant. In the caregiver-child situation, the question became one of how much responsibility the child could obtain—all children wanted to water the plant by themselves, but the caregivers often were afraid that the children might spill water and thus attempted to monitor the situation. It can be noted that the amount of water placed in the pitcher differed depending on the situation. For instance, less water was placed in the pitcher during the peer situation, whereas in the caregiver-child situation slightly more water was given to help provoke negotiation. In the peer situation, the pitcher itself became an object of negotiation, because both children wanted to control the pitcher first.

Semistructured Manipulative Play. The idea behind this task was to involve the children in manipulative play with toys that were thematically related. Piloting had revealed that thematically related toys led to extended discourse in both the peer and the caregiver-child situations; in contrast, giving children unrelated toys led to lots of naming, but little interaction. In addition, piloting revealed that the size of toys that interested the youngest and oldest subjects varied, and thus the two youngest subjects were provided with larger toys to manipulate. The older children were presented with a large cookie sheet tray of toys that had been arranged like a small village. The tray included two large mirrors that were partially covered by dried peas, giving the appearance of a lake surrounded by grass. On top of the peas stood several cars, two playmobile figures, two bicycles, several toy houses, and plastic trees. The figures could be attached to the bicycles, and helmets could be snapped on and off their heads. The cars ranged in size and moved in various ways. For instance, some of the cars had to be pushed, whereas others moved on their own if pressed in particular ways. This provided an opportunity to see how children talk about objects that move by virtue of effort on the part of a human agent versus those that move on their own. A few small bowls and spoons were placed next to the village so that the children could scoop dried peas from one container to another. To encourage negotiation in sharing control of goods, only one large scoop was placed next to the spoons.

The motoric development of the two youngest children was not advanced enough to allow them to manipulate the small objects. Furthermore, they tended to place objects in their mouths, which meant that objects like dried peas would be too dangerous. Therefore, the younger children received larger objects, including an egg carton; several large nuts (walnuts, filberts, etc.); the same spoons, bowls, and scoop noted earlier; a small teapot stuffed with cupcake papers; and several containers of various sizes. The containers were selected so that some of them had no tops, others had tops that the child would be unable to open without assistance, and others closed when the container was held in a certain way. The containers, like the cars noted earlier, were included to elicit talk about one's own and others' role in carrying out kinetic actions. The teapot and the scoop encouraged discussion about control of goods. The sorts of toys given to all the children not only elicited commentary about physical manipulation but also allowed the communicative partners to plan cooperative activities (e.g., having a tea party, making a cake, going to the hospital, going swimming).

Block Play. In this task, the children were presented with a tray of large building blocks in assorted shapes and colors. Also included on the tray was a large toy helicopter. Halfway through the task the children were given a second tray of smaller blocks, also of various shapes and colors. Blocks were selected because this sort of activity elicits not only talk about previous actions but also goal-directed behavior. The children talked not only about the colors and shapes of the blocks but also about what they were doing with the blocks, or what they planned to do with them. The helicopter was added because it provided a guaranteed way of getting children to talk about social control. The second tray of blocks was added because in piloting phases, presenting the children with too many blocks at once limited the amount of talk and shortened the length of time they were willing to engage in block play.

Photo-Book. The final task involved having the children and their partners look through a photo-book containing pictures of the children taken at the day-care center in the months just prior to the study. The photo-book included pictures of the six children interacting with their peers and the day-care staff in the full range of activities that took place over the course of the day. Some portrait pictures of the children, as well as some more action-oriented pictures, were included. In addition, pictures were included in which the children were depicted in various phases of a particular action—for instance, climbing up a slide, sitting at the top, sliding down, and reaching the bottom.

When looking at the photo-book the communicative partners sat on the couch next to one another, with the book placed across their laps. The point of the photo-book task was to elicit talk about self and other in depicted action. Would the children mark depicted actions similarly to ongoing actions? Previous research concerning the acquisition of pronominal forms has also involved a task in which children looked at pictures (Charney, 1980). In these studies, though, the photos were presented individually in a testlike situation. The decision to make a photo-book that was theme oriented was based on pilot results that indicated that by presenting children with single photos one got little more than referential labeling, whereas when the photos were presented in a storybook format, the children's talk was more centered on relating various persons depicted to action frames.

Procedure

The children were observed twice each month for a 4-month period. Once a month, each of the six children visited the playroom with his or her caregiver, and once a month the children participated with a peer. The children were paired off into three dyads from the start of the study and always participated with the same peer. The peer sessions and caregiver-child sessions were always within a week of each other and never occurred on consecutive days. The order in which the sessions took place varied such that in the first and third months, the peer dyads were observed first, whereas in the second and fourth months, the caregiver-child dyad was observed first.

The caregiver-child sessions usually took place on the day when the caregiver assisted in the day-care center. The peers were scheduled at a time of day when they both were present. The researcher would approach the participants a few minutes before the observation was to start, telling them that it was almost time to go water their plants. Right before the dyads entered the observation room, they were given the instruction to show their mother or peer what was on the table. After watering the plant(s), the dyad moved over to the table by the couch, where either the manipulative toys (Months I and III) or the blocks (Months II and IV) were set up. The children always stood at the table while they played, whereas the caregivers opted to sit on the couch. I was the only other person present at all of the sessions; and after the participants began playing, my role was primarily that of a participant observer. I intervened when introducing new tasks or when a specific question was directed toward me, but I did not initiate dialogue except when approaching the dyads to distribute toys or in cases of extreme disputes among peers.

The sessions lasted approximately 45 minutes. After watering the plants the dyads played at each of the other tasks for about 15 minutes. On occasion, the children returned to whatever task was last set up on the table at the completion of the study, if time was remaining. When the observation sessions were over, the children and caregivers were escorted back to the classroom.

Recording Equipment

All sessions were recorded in three ways. First, the interactions were video recorded from the time that the children entered the observation room until the time they left. Because the participants remained in one area after the plants were watered, the camera could be left unattended in the corner. Although the camera was introduced to the children during piloting, it largely went unnoticed by the children. To a large extent the caregivers also seemed unaware of the fact that they were being video taped, though they had been informed that video taping would take place. In fact, one parent asked in the third month of the study when the video sessions would begin. In addition to video recordings, two kinds of audio tapes were made. Wireless microphones were clipped to the participants. A stereo audiodeck was used as well, which had a built-in microphone.

TRANSCRIPTION

Because all coding was to be carried out in conjunction with simultaneous viewing of the video tapes, the primary purpose of transcription was to account for the verbal behaviors of the participants. After watching a video at least one time through, actual transcription started. Transcriptions were based primarily on the audio tapes from the wireless microphones. Segments of speech were transcribed and checked against the video in a second pass. Alternative interpretations were noted and checked in another pass. The transcription of the verbal material largely followed the conventions outlined by Ochs (1979). Each transcript started at the point at which the dyad entered the observation room and ended when the dyad exited. Modified orthography was used. Phenomena such as turn overlaps, pause length, and latching were recorded using symbolic notation.

Orientation Points

The present chapter serves as an orientation point on the basis of which more precise research questions can be put forth and a coding scheme can be developed. My point of departure is a series of distributional analyses of linguistic forms of the sort carried out by the American structural linguists (cf. Harris, 1951). The present chapter reports some preliminary findings and describes the coding, but a further aim is to outline a methodology for working with data that is by no means limited to the issues of agentivity and control, nor to the analysis of the particular linguistic forms analyzed here. The present methodology could easily be extended to the analysis of other linguistic forms.

The starting point of this sort of analysis is an examination of the child's distribution of particular forms. The goal is then to deal with the data in such a way that one can ultimately arrive at the child's organizational scheme governing the contrastive use of related linguistic forms. An assumption underlying such a paradigm is that the child's use of individual forms is not random but, rather, is guided by form-function pairings. Such pairings do not merely combine individual forms and their functions but instead are viewed as parts of larger systems organized around multiple form-function units. The challenge in analyzing data in such a way is to develop a coding procedure that begins with a set of well-defined categories and yet is flexible enough to capture regularities constructed by the child. The approach adopted here is similar to related approaches developed by others (Bamberg, 1987; Berman & Slobin, 1994; Ervin-Tripp, 1989; Gerhardt, 1983, 1990; Pike, 1982; Savasir, 1984). According to this approach, particular forms are coded in terms of several interrelated dimensions so that one can find bundles of linguistic and nonlinguistic factors that co-occur with the use of different forms.

I begin my analysis of the children's linguistic marking of agentivity and control with a consideration of such issues as who the children refer to and what forms are used in such references. After these preliminary analyses are presented in the first section, I move on in the second section of this chapter to refine the specific research questions. In a third section, a coding scheme for the subsequent analyses is outlined.

PRELIMINARY ANALYSES

Mean Length of Utterance (MLU)

The MLU (in morphemes) has been calculated for all children so as to provide a general index of the six children's various levels of linguistic maturity at the onset of the study, as well as across its duration. Although the use of the MLU has serious shortcomings, such an index allows us to compare the six children not only with one another but also with other children discussed in the literature.

The procedures adopted for calculating the MLU follow those outlined in Brown (1973). The index is based on the first 100 fully transcribed utterances of each session. Nursery rhymes and songs were excluded from the analysis; full names (i.e., first and last name) and compound words were counted as single units. Separate indices were calculated for each video session; thus for each child at each month of the study two indices were calculated: one for the caregiver-child session, and one for the peer session. In addition to the two separate MLUs for each child at each month, a mean score was calculated for each child at each month. Table 4.1 shows the MLUs of all six children at Month I. Table 4.2 outlines the developmental changes in MLU over the course of the study for the three youngest children.[1]

Looking first at the mean scores presented for each child in Table 4.1, we see that the two youngest children (Megan and Grice) were just beginning to combine words. Jeffrey was at a slightly more advanced phase; his utterances consisted of two to three morphemes each. Finally, three of the children (Eric, Keith, and Thomas) were beyond a two-word phase.

A closer examination of Tables 4.1 and 4.2 points up an important finding that comes up again in subsequent chapters. This concerns the differences found in the data from the video sessions involving the peers and the data from those involving caregiver-child interaction. Many of the children made

---

[1]Because there is general agreement that MLU is an even less reliable measure beyond the early phases of grammatical development, it was decided that the MLU would not be calculated for each month for the three children in the study (Eric, Keith, and Thomas) who were already regularly using multiword utterances at the onset of the study.

TABLE 4.1
Mean Length of Utterance: Month I

Child	Age in Months	Caregiver Session	Peer Session	Mean MLU
Megan	20	1.98	2.15	2.07
Grice	22	1.50	1.94	1.72
Jeffrey	30	2.88	2.75	2.82
Eric	28	3.84	3.12	3.48
Keith	31	2.70	3.73	3.22
Thomas	32	4.08	3.74	3.91

greater use of linguistic resources in the peer sessions. This could in part be attributed to the fact that when the children interacted with their caregivers, they often made use of ellipses in question-answer routines. An extreme instance of this pattern was displayed by Keith. Had I collected only the caregiver-child data I would have concluded that Keith was at Brown's Stage II (approaching Stage III), whereas 2 days later the same child, when interacting with his peer, could be placed at Brown's Stage IV. In addition to pointing up a problem in relying on MLU indices collected at single time intervals, this analysis also reveals the importance of considering grammatical development in contexts outside the caregiver-child situation. This point is especially important to keep in mind when drawing comparisons between children from different studies, in particular in cases of cross-linguistic comparisons where researchers have collected data not only from mother-child pairs and similar-aged dyads, but also from sibling pairs and other mixed-aged dyads.

TABLE 4.2
Mean Length of Utterance: Month I-IV
(Megan, Grice, and Jeffrey)

Month	Session	Child		
		Megan	Grice	Jeffrey
	Caregiver	1.98	1.50	2.88
I	Peer	2.15	1.94	2.75
	Mean	2.07	1.72	2.82
	Caregiver	2.36	2.08	3.34
II	Peer	2.24	2.38	3.69
	Mean	2.30	2.23	3.52
	Caregiver	2.54	2.76	3.65
III	Peer	2.46	2.80	3.92
	Mean	2.52	2.78	3.79
	Caregiver	3.04	3.22	3.48
IV	Peer	2.11	3.80	3.87
	Mean	2.58	3.51	3.68

Distribution of Reference to Self and Other

As a first step in my analysis of the relation between form and function in children's talk about agentivity and control, it seems essential to consider not only what sort of participants children talk about, but also the distributional patterns that emerge across development. To what extent does children's early talk about agentivity go beyond self as agent? This question is raised in light of some of the studies reported in the second chapter that suggested that children only gradually develop a conceptual category involving global agency and at first work with a narrower category involving personal agency.

In the following analysis focus has been placed on all references occurring in subject position.[2] Are the children equally likely to refer to self and to others as agents of goal-directed actions or experiencers of internal states? To answer such a question, all forms occurring in subject position were coded in terms of a three-way distinction based on whether the child's reference was: (a) *self* (*I gonna make a tower*), (b) *other* (*You needa make it real big, Gramma buy cookies*), or (c) *joint* (self and other: *We blowing bubbles*).[3]

Figure 4.1 reveals the distribution of self, other, and joint references (in subject position) for all six children during the first month of the study. The children can be divided into two groups: First, three of the children referred primarily to themselves as main participants at the onset of the study. More than 75% of their references were of the sort *My take it home* or *Grice ride bicycle*. These children who referred primarily to self are called ego-anchored.[4] A second group of children (Eric, Keith, and Thomas) regularly referred not only to themselves but also to others as main participants. These children are collectively referred to as nonego-anchored. As is shown in Fig. 4.1, only about 50% of their references were to self, and the remaining instances were to other or were joint.

Based on the analysis presented here, one can ask whether the self/other distribution represents a developmental pattern. Support for the position that children travel a route leading from ego-anchoring to nonego-anchoring can be found in Fig. 4.2. Here we find that as the three ego-anchored

---

[2]References in object position tended to be concrete and inanimate for all children across all sessions. Only occasionally did the children refer to more abstract objects (e.g., *my turn*) or animate beings (e.g., *you, Daddy*).

[3]If the child repeated or rephrased parts of an utterance, only the self reference form in the final version was included. Thus the utterance: *I I hafta I hafta I hafta do something* was coded only once as a reference to self. Rephrasings were treated similarly. All repetitions and rephrasings received an extra code so they could be pulled out at a later point for separate analysis.

[4]The label *ego-anchored* is not to be confused with Piaget's notion of egocentric speech (Piaget, 1926). Instead, the term ego-anchored as used here implies that the child's linguistic references to main participants tend to refer to self.

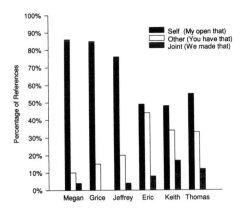

FIG. 4.1. Distribution of references in subject position at onset of study.

children developed, their distribution of references to self and other converged in the direction of that of the nonego-anchored children. Jeffrey's distribution shifted dramatically in Month III such that he could be classified as nonego-anchored, whereas the two youngest girls remained ego-anchored throughout the duration of the study.

The findings from the present distributional analysis, taken together with the review of research on self and other reference discussed in chapter 2, imply that it is indeed important to question whether children's early notions of agentivity and control extend beyond the self. Furthermore, given the findings of Deutsch and Budwig (1983), which suggested that children construct a form-function contrast between *own name + noun* (e.g., *Adam pencil*) and *first person possessive pronoun + noun* (e.g., *My pencil*) that is not matched by a contrast with regard to second or third person reference, it seems important to consider self reference forms as a kind of subsystem. In the section that follows we take a closer look at the distribution of children's self reference forms across the span of the study.

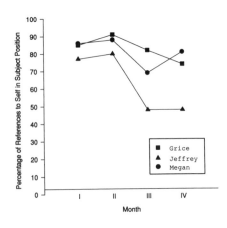

FIG. 4.2. Percentage of references to self in subject position: Months I–IV (Megan, Grice, and Jeffrey).

Distribution of Self Reference Forms

The goal of the present analysis was to find out what self reference forms the children used at each month of the study and, in addition, what the relative distribution was of the various forms. Did all the children make use of similar forms when referring to themselves? Did their usage reflect common distributional regularities?

The distributional analysis of self reference forms was conducted as follows. All utterances (clauses) containing a form that referred to the self were isolated.[5] If more than one self reference form was used in a given clause, then such forms were noted (see, though, footnote 3). Each form was then further coded as nominal (e.g., *Own Name*) or pronominal. Each pronominal form was further coded as *I*, *Me*, *My*, or *Other*, where *Other* included: (a) less frequently used first person forms (e.g., *myself, mine*); (b) self-created forms of self reference (e.g., *meself*); and (c) forms that adult speakers of English would use for other reference but that the children used when referring to self, as in the following example:[6]

(1) Keith (K) and his mom (KM) are looking through the photo-book.
 a. KM: Who are these two silly guys?
 b. K: Um Thomas and Keith.
 c. (K and KM discuss whether K and Thomas fight sometimes.)
 d. K: I see Keithy talking. (pointing to photo)
 e. KM: And Keithy is talking.
 f. K: Yeah. They bumped heads. (pointing to same photo of self and peer)

The results of the distributional analysis of self reference forms can be found in Tables 4.3 and 4.4. Table 4.3 reveals the distribution of self reference forms for the six children at the onset of the study. We find that all six children made use of a variety of nominal and pronominal forms of self reference, although the relative frequency of use differed among the children. Two of the ego-anchored children relied primarily on three forms (Grice: *I,*

---

[5]Null forms were not included in the analysis, due to problems of interpretation. It was not clear whether the child was referring to self or others. It should be noted that the three ego-anchored children at times employed a form *ma* that was pronounced quite similarly to *my*. Because the two forms were so close in pronunciation and it was often difficult to distinguish between them, such uses have been grouped together under the heading *my* in the present analysis. Finally, all proper names of the children have been altered, and the pseudonyms have been substituted in examples in which the children referred to themselves using their own names.

[6]The less frequently used forms (e.g., *myself* and *we*) were originally coded under separate headings, but because the children used them so rarely, they later were grouped together under the general heading of *Other*.

TABLE 4.3
Distribution (%) of Self Reference Forms: Month I

Child	Form					Subtotal*
	I	My	Me	Other	Own Name	
Megan	33	23	10	2	32	(91)
Grice	25	36	28	1	10	(72)
Jeffrey	38	46	6	7	3	(125)
Eric	65	6	3	17	8	(116)
Keith	56	7	1	28	9	(162)
Thomas	60	10	3	22	4	(178)

* (Raw numbers).

Me, My; Megan: *I, My, Own Name*), whereas the remaining ego-anchored child, Jeffrey, showed a preference for two forms (*I* and *My*). The nonego-anchored children all used primarily one self reference form (*I*). A further distinction between the two groups of children is that the ego-anchored children freely employed various self reference forms in subject position, often in ways that deviated from standard English. Thus, they said things like: *My did it, Me jump, I like peas*, and *Megan count.*[7]

Although the ego-anchored children all employed several self reference forms in a fairly even distribution at the onset of the study, we found that by the end of the study, these three children looked like their nonego-anchored peers to the extent that they relied primarily on the form *I* (cf. Table 4.4). It can also be noted that over time, the creative uses of *My* and *Me* in subject position faded out. In the final session Megan never used such forms in subject position, and Grice and Jeffrey each did so only once or twice.

Summary

In this section I have reviewed findings from some preliminary analyses. These findings justify the division of the children into two groups. Three of the children began the study with MLUs of about 2.2; that is, they were just beginning to combine words. These children made use of several self reference forms, and two or three of these forms were employed regularly in subject position, often in ways that deviated from adult input. This group of children has been referred to as ego-anchored. A second group of children, who are referred to as nonego-anchored, had MLUs of about 3.54. They also regularly used several self reference forms, but a distributional analysis of such forms revealed that these children relied primarily on the form *I*

---

[7]One nonego-anchored child, Keith, used *My* (alone) in subject position one time (*My don't know*).

TABLE 4.4
Distribution (%) of Reference Forms: Month I-IV
(Ego-Anchored Children)

Child	Month	Form					Subtotal*
		I	My	Me	Other	OwnName	
	I	33	23	10	2	32	(91)
Megan	II	59	9	6	2	24	(87)
	III	55	12	7	8	28	(76)
	IV	61	13	6	10	9	(77)
	I	25	36	28	1	10	(72)
Grice	II	30	41	24	1	3	(90)
	III	65	16	6	10	4	(280)
	IV	67	11	12	6	5	(212)
	I	38	46	6	7	3	(125)
Jeffrey	II	41	41	5	9	2	(164)
	III	52	9	7	30	2	(148)
	IV	53	13	8	23	3	(183)

* (Raw numbers).

when referring to self, and their use of self reference forms did not deviate from adult input in the way noted for the ego-anchored children. These findings are summarized in Fig. 4.3.

The findings of the analyses summarized here reveal that the two groups of children can best be viewed along a developmental continuum. Over the course of the study, the ego-anchored children's MLUs approached those of the nonego-anchored children (see Table 4.2), their references to self de-

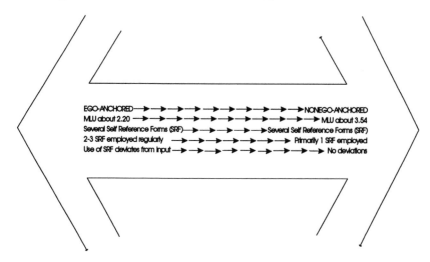

FIG. 4.3. Pictorial summary of transition from ego-anchoring to nonego-anchoring.

creased (see Fig. 4.2), and by Month IV the distribution of self reference forms by the ego-anchored children looked quite similar to the distribution noted for the nonego-anchored children at Month I (see Tables 4.3 and 4.4). The proposed developmental course can be described as follows: The children went from a phase of almost exclusive reference to self, employing several self reference forms, to a later phase of self and other reference, employing several forms but relying primarily on the form *I*. The transition from one phase to the other included the gradual disappearance of the use of self reference forms in subject position in ways that deviated from adult input.

REFINEMENT OF RESEARCH QUESTIONS

We are now in a position to refine the general research questions raised in chapter 1. The first question that arises from the distributional analyses reviewed here concerns whether the ego-anchored children were contrastively employing the various self reference forms. I start from the assumption that the nominal and pronominal forms were employed in a principled manner. One might want to claim instead that the children were simply confused about the distinctions between various self reference forms and thus might use them in free variation. Evidence that the children were not using these forms in free variation lies in numerous examples of what Karmiloff-Smith (1979) referred to as hesitations and spontaneous corrections. The following example illustrates the sort of wavering between forms often found in the children's utterances:[8]

(2) Jeffrey is playing with blocks.
   a. J: M;/ M-/ I want;/ I want-/ My-/ I want;/ I want the little ones.

In examples such as this, the child seems to hesitate over which form to employ. One might want to argue that the child's hesitation is a reflection of competition between similar or equal forms. As we see, though, the direction of repair can be accounted for. Thus I claim that such hesitations can be taken to indicate a motivated choice.

   In Part II of this book, I consider in detail the basis upon which the children selected the various self reference forms. The central claim is that at a time when children rarely refer to others, they contrastively employ self reference forms to mark various degrees of agentivity and control with regard to their own involvement in action frames. Before turning to such a discus-

---

[8]The distinction between the dash (-) and semicolon (;) in the examples can be read as follows: The dash indicates that what follows is a reformulation, whereas the semicolon indicates that what follows is a repetition. Often what precedes the semicolon has been repeated numerous times, though in the example it is listed only once.

sion, I first consider previous studies dealing with the acquisition of self reference forms, with the aim of developing more specific predictions concerning the contrastive use of self reference forms by children in the present study. Such a review is not meant to be exhaustive but, rather, is directed toward the refinement of research questions for the present study. I will then be in a position to consider the coding rationale and procedures employed in the present study.

Previous Research Related to Development of Self Reference Forms

The literature concerning the development of self reference forms either has focused on issues related to nominal and pronominal forms or has specifically investigated issues concerning the acquisition of pronominal forms. I first review some studies suggesting that nominal and pronominal self reference forms go through a phase in which they co-exist. Next, I consider the development of first person pronominal forms.

The Simultaneous Use of Nominal and Pronominal Forms. Lewis and Brooks-Gunn (1979), in one of a series of studies concerning the acquisition of self-knowledge, considered the relationship between language development and self-recognition. In this study they provided children with a series of photos of the child and other children. Of relevance here are the findings with regard to the use of self reference forms by the verbal infants ranging between the ages of 21 and 36 months. Although Lewis and Brooks-Gunn were not specifically interested in the contrastive use of nominal and pronominal forms, they nevertheless noted that the children tended to use nominal forms of self reference when labeling the photos. Fifty-eight percent of all references involved the use of the child's own name, whereas in only 18% of the cases did the children employ pronominal forms. Although age changes were not noted with regard to the use of nominal forms, Lewis and Brooks-Gunn reported dramatic changes with age for pronominal forms. They documented a steady increase in pronominal usage—pronominal forms were used by only one child before the age of 2, by 20% of the 30-month-old children, and by 42% of the 36-month-old children.

Four other studies also touched on the contrastive use of nominal and pronominal self reference forms. As mentioned earlier, Deutsch and Budwig (1983) documented that young children contrastively employed their own name and the first person pronominal form *my* in reference to possessions. The use of *Own Name* was found in the context of assertions about possessions where control was not at issue, whereas the pronominal form was found in possessive constructions in which control was under dispute. In another study, Cooley (1908) examined diary records of his daughter's references to self until the age of 33 months. He reported that the use of nominal and pronominal forms linked up with different "self ideas" (Cooley, 1908, p. 341). The child was said to use her own name or the word *baby* when referring to her physical body, as when labeling photos or referring to her body parts. In contrast, the child used *I* when expressing a "feeling of self assertion" (Cooley, 1908, p. 341), linked up with action in most cases. Taken together, these studies lend support to the idea that the children in the present study might contrastively employ nominal and pronominal forms of self reference. Further evidence for the contrastive use of nominal and pronominal forms stems from the detailed case study of Emmy's narratives as reported by Nelson (1989) and Gerhardt (1988). These researchers trace Emmy's use of distinct self reference forms, and how such forms were used both to realize distinct discursive intentions and to construct a notion of self in time.

The Acquisition of Pronominal Forms. Studies of children's early use of pronominal forms have considered three related issues: contextual variation in the use of pronominal self reference forms, deixis, and case marking errors. I briefly consider each of these areas of study.

Several developmental psychologists have noted that pronominal forms link up with different social contexts. For instance, Goodenough (1938), in a study of 30-month-old to 66-month-old children, noted that the youngest children in that study used a variety of pronominal self reference forms in different contexts. Based on observational records of children interacting in what was referred to as a controlled situation (involving adult supervision) and in a free play situation (involving peers), Goodenough reported that the first person pronominal forms were far more frequent in the free play situation. She suggested that the first person pronominal forms link up with a general sense of "ego-consciousness" and this feeling is enhanced in competitive situations involving peer play. Goodenough did not distinguish between the various first person pronominal forms.

Ames (1952) also examined the child's developing sense of self during the toddler and preschool years by observing and recording children's verbalizations about the self. At the age of 21 months, Ames noted that the use of possessive pronouns appeared in disputes over control of objects among peers. By 30 months, other pronominal forms of self reference (e.g., *I*) appeared in conjunction with naming completed or intended action.

A third study that sheds light on the use of first person pronominal forms documented the early use of nonnominal expressions in children's language. Gopnik (1980) reported that the possessive terms *my*, *mine*, and *mines* were among the most frequent expressions used by the children she studied. These words were used primarily when the child wanted to claim an object. Gopnik noted that the objects linked with the possessive expressions often did not belong to the children, and "in some cases the children had no contact with the objects in the past that might lead them to believe that they belong to them" (Gopnik, 1980, p. 200). In addition, Gopnik suggested that *my* was often used to refer to an intention to act, as in the utterance *My do it.* Because Gopnik's study was limited to the investigation of nonnominal expressions, it is not clear what the function of proper names was for her subjects, if in fact they used them.

Deixis. Several other researchers focusing on personal pronouns have studied them in reference to the general issue of shifting reference. Several developmental hypotheses have been offered (Charney, 1980; Clark, 1978; de Villiers & de Villiers, 1974; Huxley, 1970; Loveland, 1984; McNeill, 1963; Shipley & Shipley, 1969). Although the specific hypotheses and conclusions may not be so relevant to the present discussion, what such research does point up is that some children may confuse speaker/addressee referencing some of the time. Loveland, for example, in a series of production and comprehension studies, pointed out that 11 of the 27 2- to 3-year-old children in her studies mixed correct and incorrect use and comprehension of the same pronouns, which she took as an indication of a gradual phase of sorting out issues governing proper use. The children not only exhibited case errors in production but were also noted, in both production and comprehension, to have difficulty at times with shifting reference. The question remains: Why is it that usage is correct only some of the time? Could it be that the child's use is guided by a different set of assumptions that at times leads to responses that look adultlike? (see Bamberg, 1987, for an illustration of this point with regard to older children's nominal/pronominal contrasts in narrative productions). The basis of such mixed responses in the various studies has not been fully examined. There is the possibility that the children are guided by different assumptions about these forms, which in turn have been interpreted by researchers as reflecting correct and incorrect usage.

Case Marking Errors. A final set of studies related to the use of pronominal forms concerns the acquisition of case marking. Such research indicates that children between the ages of 2 and 3 years make case marking errors, often, for example, employing accusative forms where nominative forms would be expected (cf. Bellugi, 1971; Brown, 1973; Leopold, 1939; Park, 1971; Radford, 1990). For instance, children have been noted to say things like *Why me sitting on it?* or *What me do?* It has been suggested that such errors should be expected, given the complex network of rules involved in case selection (see Maratsos, 1979, for a discussion of this point). Although one might anticipate such errors, the question remains why such errors occur and not others. Why, for example, do children replace nominative forms with accusative forms but not vice versa? Very little theorizing has focused on this issue.

More recently, Radford (1990) argued that in early child English there is no case system. At this stage children "have not acquired the morphosyntax of nominatives" (p. 177) and thus often misuse pronouns. Radford did not claim that the child does not occasionally make use of nominative forms early on. Rather, he claimed that such sporadic occurrences appear in set phrases, that is, in nonproductive utterances. In chapter 9 I compare Radford's position with that based on the findings of this study. For now, the important point is that the children I studied also were noted to use accusative pronouns in place of nominative ones in early child English.

Predictions

Though none of the studies reviewed here attempted to identify specific ways in which self reference forms might be contrastively employed by young children acquiring English, taken together, the studies begin to point toward some systematic uses of particular forms. I now consider three specific predictions that stem from this review. The first two are as follows:

> *Prediction 1*: Nominal and pronominal self reference forms will serve contrastive functions. Nominal forms will be employed referentially, whereas pronominal forms will be used in more dynamically charged interactive situations.

> *Prediction 2*: The various pronominal forms of self reference will link up with the expression of different ways of perceiving the self in relation to action.

Our review of previous research concerning pronominal forms leads to two more specific predictions concerning the forms *I* and *my*:

> *Prediction 2a*: *My* will link up with the expression of control.

> *Prediction 2b*: *I* will be used in asserting inner beliefs of the self.

Evidence for Prediction 2a stems from the studies of Deutsch and Budwig (1983); see also Kolodziej, Deutsch, and Bittner (1991), Goodenough (1938), and Gopnik (1980), where it was noted that this form appeared in the context of free play situations in which the children attempted to gain control over objects. Prediction 2b is based on the findings of Cooley (1908), who noted that *I* appears in contexts in which the child makes self assertions.

With regard to the other pronominal self reference forms no specific predictions are forwarded. Rather, a further research question to be addressed by the present study is whether the children employ the other pronominal forms and, if so, on what basis.

Although there seems to be some indication in the literature that different children link the use of particular forms with a similar set of functions, a certain amount of individual variation is to be expected. In recent years, growing attention has been given to the different pathways children find in acquiring grammatical systems. In addition, children have been noted to differ in the sorts of pragmatic functions conveyed in their early utterances (cf. Bates, Bretherton, & Snyder, 1988, for a thorough review of the individual differences literature). Findings from such studies lead to the following prediction:

> Prediction 3: Some variation will be found in the ways various children employ the different pronominal forms, though all children are expected to relate form and function systematically.

The idea here is that before children regularly refer to others, they will make use of self reference forms to take different perspectives on the way they situate themselves in fields of action. If children are using the forms as predicted, one would expect the forms to show up in particular activities or junctures of children's play. For example, one would expect that nominal forms should be the most frequent in the context of the photo-book task, and *my* should appear frequently in the peer sessions in instances where the children attempt to gain control of objects. Likewise, if the children are using first person pronouns as predicted, one would expect errors of particular kinds both with regard to marking case and when shifting reference. Within the framework of the present predictions, one could question whether case errors can be related to children's budding hypotheses about the functions of particular forms. This sort of account might help explain why case errors occur only some of the time. Similarly, one could check so-called errors in shifting reference to see whether the child might be marking a slightly different notion. For instance, when children refer to experimenters' toys as *my toy*, it may well be that the children are attempting to claim the toy rather than having difficulty shifting perspective with the forms *my* and *your*. With these predictions in mind, I can now present the coding procedures for the present investigation.

CODING RATIONALE, CATEGORIES, AND PROCEDURES

Coding Rationale

The central claim in the last section concerns the expectation that the ego-anchored children's use of various self reference forms systematically links up with issues of agentivity and control. The coding scheme must be one that taps both semantic dimensions of agentivity and pragmatic features of control. As the discussion in chapter 2 pointed out, the notion of agentivity has been viewed as including a number of interrelated dimensions, suggesting that the coding of agentivity needs to take into account several different factors. A further challenge in developing a coding scheme concerns a problem raised in the review of the functionalist literature in chapter 1. The challenge is one of coding in terms of a fixed number of dimensions but simultaneously keeping in mind the child's own categorization scheme. The decision in the present study has been to work from two ends. First, based on the review presented in Part I of this book, a multilayered code has been designed. A second approach has been more qualitative in nature. Here the starting point of analysis has been the examination of minimal pairs, hesitations, and self-corrections. Such an approach assists in keeping the child's systematization in mind by allowing the researcher to develop new categories that may not have been included in the original coding.

It can be noted that the distributional analysis used in the present investigation goes beyond that set out by the American structural linguists (cf. Harris, 1951). My focus here includes various dimensions of the activity context in which forms appear. I am interested not only in the possible clustering of the individual forms not only around a particular dimension on any given level but also in the relationship between the forms across the different levels of analysis. The method adopted here is similar to that documented in Gerhardt (1983), Gee and Savasir (1985), and Pike (1982).

Coding Categories

The coding scheme consists of six different broad levels of analysis and several sublevels. These levels include: form, surface-level characteristics, semantic characteristics, pragmatic characteristics, nonlinguistic/contextual characteristics, and causality coding. I now describe briefly each of these individual levels of analysis.

Form. This level of coding has already been introduced in the discussion of the distribution of the children's use of self reference forms. The basic idea here was to examine all instances of self reference forms. These were coded as nominal (*Own Name, Other* [e.g., *baby*]) or pronominal (*I, My, Me, Other* [e.g., *meself, myself*]). Findings of this analysis appear in Tables 4.3 and 4.4.

Surface-level Characteristics. At this level of analysis, each use of a self reference form was further coded in terms of its relation to the rest of the utterance. The first decision was whether the form appeared in an utterance with a verb or in a verbless context (e.g., *My did it* vs. *My airplane*). If the form appeared in an utterance with a verb, it was further categorized as to whether it (a) occurred in subject or object position, and (b) appeared alone with the verb or with other arguments (e.g., *I jump* vs. *I saw the ball*). If the form appeared in a verbless context, it was further coded as appearing alone (e.g., *Me*), with a noun only (e.g., *My book*), or in some other construction type.

Semantic Characteristics. The semantic level of coding captured the degree of agentivity expressed in clauses containing self reference forms. The coding drew upon research in transitivity, agentivity, and prototype semantics discussed in chapter 2. Given a definition of prototypical transitivity as involving "a direct causation scheme with proximate and ultimate cause both residing in the same volitionally acting causer" (DeLancey, 1984, p. 185), one can see the close connection to agentivity. Prototypical agents are volitionally acting causers.

To code for agentivity, a subset of Hopper and Thompson's (1980) transitivity parameters were included, namely, those thought to be most relevant to the assessment of agentivity. The five parameters selected included: Participants, Kinesis, Aspect, Volitionality, and Affirmation. Each utterance containing a self reference form and a verb was given a ranking for each of the five parameters. The ranking include three degrees: high, mid, and low; an *uncoded* category was also adopted. The central question raised at this level of analysis was whether particular forms linked up with particular levels of agentivity. It should be noted that in Part II of this book, findings are reported based on a collapsed semantic rating. Those particularly interested in the semantic level of analysis are encouraged to examine the findings in Budwig (1986), where the data were presented in a noncollapsed format. The collapsed rankings were as follows: All utterances were given individual rankings of high (score of 1), medium (score of 2), or low (score of 3) for each of the five semantic parameters. The scores were added and mean scores for each example were calculated. For the purposes of the presentation of the data in Part II of this book, only the collapsed scores are used; thus uses of self reference forms with mean scores greater than 1.5 were ranked high in agentivity, and scores of 1.5 or lower were ranked low in agentivity. I briefly review the five separate parameters coded.

The first parameter coded is labeled *Participants*. Clauses containing two participants were coded as high, whereas those containing only one were coded as low (e.g., *I built the castle* vs. *I jump*). A mid ranking was assigned to clauses containing self-reflexives and to clauses containing a second participant, reflecting a deviation from the prototypical causation scheme (cf. Givón, 1984a), as in the case of locative direct objects that are not acted upon by agents. An example of a sentence with a less prototypical object would be *I rode the horse.*

The second parameter coded is referred to as *Kinesis*. A high ranking was given to clauses containing highly kinetic verbs (e.g., *blow, hit, knock down*). Clauses containing statives were given a low ranking. A mid ranking was assigned when reference was to actions that required minimal effort (e.g., *look, read*).

The third parameter coded is referred to as *Aspect*. The coding of aspect is restricted to a consideration of the telic/atelic distinction. Clauses referring to telic situations, or what Vendler (1967) referred to as accomplishments, received a high ranking. A low ranking was assigned to clauses referring to atelic situations. A small class of clauses where both a telic and an atelic reading could be given were assigned to a mid category. It should be noted that assignment was based not on verbs alone but, rather, on situations (cf. Comrie, 1976). Thus the utterance *I am singing* would rank low for aspect, whereas *I am singing a song* would rank high.

The fourth parameter of agentivity is labeled *Volitionality*. The distinction here is between volitional acts and happenings. Clauses referring to willed or purposeful action received a high ranking, whereas reference to happenings where responsibility was not assigned were ranked low. Thus the reporting of nonintentional acts and states received a Low ranking. To assign the clauses to one or the other category often involved careful observation of the video data. The utterance *I knock it down*, said as the child gazed at the tower he had just built up, while curling his hand into a fist, would have been coded as high. In contrast, the same utterance said after the child had swiftly turned around to look at the door, in the process knocking over the tower with his elbow, would be ranked low. Ambiguous cases were assigned a mid score.

The final parameter of semantic agentivity is labeled *Affirmation*. Coding for this parameter is relatively straightforward. Utterances that were stated in the affirmative were ranked high, whereas those that were nonaffirmative ranked low. There is no mid value for this parameter. The idea behind this level, as explained by Hopper and Thompson (1980), is that affirmative clauses are more likely to express transfer of action than nonaffirmative ones. For instance, the utterance *I hit Billy* ranked high, whereas the utterance *I did not hit Billy* ranked low.

To summarize, the coding of semantic characteristics proceeded in two stages. First, each clause containing a self reference form was coded on five levels for different parameters of agentivity. For each parameter, a decision was made about whether the agentivity ranking was high, mid, or low. After all the levels were coded, a global decision was made for the clause as a whole such that the coded clauses were ranked as either high or low in agentivity. In Part II of this book the focus is purely on the global agentivity rankings, though, as mentioned earlier, the findings of the individual parameters of semantic agentivity across development are reviewed elsewhere (see Budwig, 1986, 1989).

Pragmatic Characteristics. The purpose of the pragmatic function coding was to assess the potential relationship between the specific forms of self reference and the pragmatic functions they served. All utterances containing a self reference form (those with and without verbs) were coded in light of the broader discursive context. Three broad categories of pragmatic function were used; in addition, a fourth category was added for all utterances that were considered uncodable.

The basic distinction guiding the analysis of pragmatic function was a split between utterances that function to bring about a change in the world (control acts) and utterances that function to express an existing state (noncontrol acts). The notion of *control acts* is based on the use of the term by Ervin-Tripp and her colleagues (cf. Ervin-Tripp, 1981; Ervin-Tripp & Gordon, 1986; Gordon & Ervin-Tripp, 1984). Control acts, utterances by which we attempt to bring about change (i.e., requests, directives, warnings) can also be related to Searle's (1979) discussion of word-to-world direction of fit. Such utterances function to bring about change in the world so that the propositional content of the speech act and world match.

All utterances with self reference forms coded as control acts have been further categorized into one of three subcategories: as utterances that attempt to influence (a) the *hearer's action* (i.e., directives, prohibitions, invitations, and warnings), (b) the *speaker's action* (soliciting permission, claiming ownership, or controlling goods not in use or actions in progress), or (c) both *speaker's and hearer's action* (ownership and enactment disputes). Targeted utterances coded as control acts could also be further subcategorized as other or as a combination of (a)–(c).

In contrast to control acts, utterances falling under the heading of *noncontrol acts* do not attempt to bring about a change in the environment but, rather, match an existing state. Utterances coded as noncontrol acts have what Searle (1979) referred to as world-to-word direction of fit. Each utterance coded as a noncontrol act was further classified into one or more of the following categories: (a) identify/name, (b) describe, (c) assert, (d) comply. Utterances falling in the assertion category were further categorized as reports of (a) previous happenings or timeless events, (b) ongoing/immediate future intentions, or (c) long-range plans and intentions occurring outside the scope of the video session.

A third category of pragmatic function coding is referred to as *multifunction*. It should be clear that one utterance may at the same time function as an assertion about the world and as a request to perform some action (i.e., the familiar *It sure is cold in here*, uttered not only as a statement but also in hopes of getting someone to close the window). The multifunctional category was included for utterances that seemed to fall under both of the first two categories. When possible, instances falling under this category were further categorized in terms of the subcategories outlined earlier (i.e., an utterance might be further coded as a combination of a directive and a statement of future intention).

The final pragmatic category included all utterances that were considered *uncodable*. These included (a) utterances containing self reference forms that were interrupted or stopped midway (e.g., *I hafta-*), (b) cases where video view was obscured and the pragmatic function was unclear, and (c) self reference forms that occurred in a nursery rhyme or song.

We can work through one example to help clarify the coding categories reviewed here. Take the simple example of a child saying *I want the red blocks*. If while saying this the child is tugging on his or her mother's leg and, after getting the mother's attention, points to the blocks that are out of reach, such an utterance would be a good candidate for a control act. If the same utterance is said while the child is en route to and just about to pick up two red blocks, and the caregiver neither seems to be called upon to intervene nor intervenes independently, then this would most likely be coded as a noncontrol act, an assertion. The combination category might be used had the mother intervened to assist the child though the child had not made eye contact with her, or in other ambiguous cases.

Nonlinguistic/Contextual Characteristics. The fifth level of coding focused on nonlinguistic aspects of the use of self reference forms. Three dimensions of the nonlinguistic context taken into account were: (a) interactive partner, (b) activity task, and (c) nonverbal behaviors and gestures. The first two levels could be coded without the use of the video tapes. The coding of interactive partner specified whether the utterance occurred during the session involving the caregiver or the peer. The activity task coding accounted for whether the child was playing with manipulative toys, building with blocks, looking through the photo-book, or engaging in some other activity. An extra symbol was added to indicate that at the time of the utterance the researcher was either bringing over or removing toys. Such instances, as we later see, are rich in control acts and could be analyzed separately for form-function pairs.

The third aspect of nonlinguistic coding involved noting what behaviors or gestures co-occurred with utterances containing self reference forms. These included: (a) pointing, (b) being en route to object, (c) taking control of an object, (d) holding an object, (e) relinquishing control of an object, (f) showing signs of distress (stomping feet, waving hands, crying, etc.), and (g) showing signs of excitement (clapping hands, swinging feet, etc.). If the child was not in view, this was also noted. In addition, an extra code was placed after (c), (d), and (e) to indicate that the nonverbal behavior occurred in conjunction with a related action on the part of the partner. For example, it might be noted that relinquishing control of an object was due to the partner's attempts to take control of it.

The nonlinguistic coding puts us in a better position to assess whether particular self reference forms tended to occur in conjunction with particular communicative partners, with particular activity tasks, or even at particular junctures, as, for instance, when the researcher brought over additional toys. In addition, we can examine the potential relationships between the employment of particular forms and specific gestures (for instance, use of a nominal form with a pointing gesture).

Causality Characteristics. The final level of coding examines the sort of causal chains accompanying the use of various self reference forms. In chapter 2 it was noted that languages often draw a grammatical distinction between agents who are part of a direct causal scheme and agents who do not necessarily act as both proximate and ultimate agent. The coding at this level has been designed to examine the relation between the use of particular self reference forms, causation schemes, and the development of notions of agency and control. The question of concern here is whether the various self reference forms link up with particular kinds of causation schemes.

To code for causal chains, each use of a self reference form was coded in terms of a three-category coding scheme involving a consideration of causality surrounding the targeted form:

1. The child acted independently of others, either with direct physical effort or referring to and attributing previous action to internal states.
2. The child and other are jointly involved (i.e., mediated causation), whereby other can act as (a) coagent, (b) counteragent, or (c) instrument for child (the rare instances of the child acting as an instrument for the other were included here).
3. Other acts independently of child, where other might be a person, a contextual or task-related cause, an object, or a natural force.

Coding Procedures

All utterances containing self reference forms were listed on coding sheets. If two forms appeared in one utterance containing two clauses, then each form was listed with the clause in which it appeared. If two forms appeared in a single clause, then the clause was listed twice, though these instances were infrequent. The coding proceeded in numerous rounds. At each pass, one level of coding took place. Coding for form, surface level considerations, and the semantic agentivity parameters was carried out with reference to the written transcripts. The remaining levels of coding were conducted while viewing the video tapes. Any given utterance on the code sheet was followed by a series of code symbols. In addition, space was left to add comments concerning deviations from input, hesitations, self-corrections, and other comments thought to be useful at a later point of analysis.[9]

---

[9]It can be noted that at the time the original coding took place, computer programs were not available that would allow for the sophisticated cross-tier analysis now available through the CHILDES CLAN programs (see MacWhinney, 1991). Computer analysis would have greatly facilitated the process and is highly recommended for those undertaking a multilevel analysis such as the one proposed here.

SUMMARY

The purpose of this chapter has been threefold. First, I have considered the results of a series of preliminary analyses; second, I have refined the research questions and developed a series of predictions based on the findings from the preliminary analyses and an examination of the literature concerning children's use of self reference forms; and finally, I have outlined the multilevel coding scheme that has been used in coding the data reported in Part II of this book.

The results of the preliminary analyses suggest that the children fell into two groups at the onset of the study. The first group of children, referred to as ego-anchored, had an MLU of under 3.0; and these children rarely talked about others. All three children used a variety of self reference forms, and these forms were also used in ways that differed from adult usage. A second group of children, referred to as nonego-anchored, had an MLU that exceeded 3.0; and these children divided their references between self and other fairly equally. Although these children used a variety of self reference forms, they relied primarily on a single form, and their usage did not deviate from adult usage. I reviewed several pieces of evidence that suggested that the distinction between ego-anchored and nonego-anchored children is best viewed as falling along a developmental continuum. By the end of the study, the ego-anchored children looked very much like the nonego-anchored children.

The preliminary analyses have been revealing in the following ways. First, given the youngest children's almost exclusive focus on the self, one could question whether the marking of agentivity might be limited to the self. Second, the creative use of self reference forms, as well as the reliance on several different forms of self reference, leads one to question whether at an early phase the children employed such forms to mark their role as prototypical agent and various deviations from the prototype. My review of studies that touched upon children's acquisition of nominal and pronominal self reference forms has led to the development of several specific predictions about how children might link particular forms with functional clusters concerning agentivity and control.

In the next section of the book, I review findings from analyses that test out these predictions. First, in chapters 5, 6, and 7, I consider the individual findings of each of the ego-anchored children. The findings, though leading to some general conclusions, point up some intriguing individual differences; and therefore the decision has been made to report individual case studies of the children. In chapter 8, I consider the way the nonego-anchored children organized the use of self reference forms across the period of the study. Because significant individual variation from the general patterns to be reported was not observed, I discuss the findings of the nonego-anchored children as a group. After laying out the organization of the ego-anchored and nonego-anchored systems, I proceed in Part III to consider factors that might lead children to organize and reorganize their systems as they do.

PART TWO

CASE STUDIES

Jeffrey

MONTH I

Jeffrey, linguistically the most sophisticated of the ego-anchored children, had an MLU of 2.82 at the onset of the study. He referred to self in 76% of his references to main participants (see Fig. 4.1). As was also noted in chapter 4, his use of self reference forms often deviated from adult usage. Because of these characteristics, he was grouped with the other ego-anchored children.

When referring to himself in the first month of the study Jeffrey relied almost exclusively on two forms (see Fig. 5.1). Jeffrey's use of *I* and *My* accounts for 84% of the distribution. In this discussion of Jeffrey's use of self reference forms, I first focus on the core contrast between *I* and *My*. I then turn to consider briefly his use of other self reference forms.

The Core Contrast: *I* and *My*

The distinction between Jeffrey's use of *I* and his use of *My* is by no means obvious. The following examples illustrate this point:

(1) I like Anna.

(2) I show.

(3) I'll hold this.

(4) My like vanilla.

(5) My taked it off.

(6) No my build a tower.

(7) My blew the candles out.

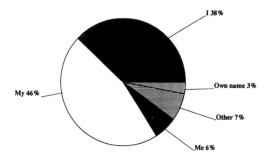

FIG. 5.1. Distribution (%) of self reference forms: Jeffrey Month I (n = 125).

(8) My read another book.

(9) I no want that one. My want the little ones.

(10) I want my put the tower.

As these examples illustrate, the two forms often occurred in consecutive utterances (see example (9)), as well as in the main and subordinate clauses of a single utterance (see example (10)). These examples might lead one to believe that the forms were not used contrastively but, rather, were randomly distributed by a child who was confused about the use of personal pronouns. One might take as further evidence for their random distribution the observation that the two forms were used with similar frequency. *I* was used in 38% of all utterances, whereas *My* occurred in 46% of all utterances involving self reference. The central aim of this chapter is to show that by working through the various coding levels, one can arrive at a systematic contrast between Jeffrey's use of the form *I* and his use of *My*. The central claim is that a full understanding of the use of these forms depends on simultaneous consideration of semantic and pragmatic information.

Surface Characteristics. Table 5.1 outlines several aspects of the surface characteristics of Jeffrey's use of self reference forms. Three trends in particular are worth noting. First, we find that *I* and *My* both are found primarily in utterances with verbs. In contrast, *Me* and *Own Name* were used solely in utterances without verbs. Second, the uses of *I* and *My* also look quite similar when considering sentence position and argument structure. *I* was used exclusively in subject position and primarily in multiargument utterances. *My* was used primarily in subject position and, as examples (1)–(10) show, not as part of a possessive construction, in multiargument utterances. Third, when forms were used in contexts without verbs, both *My* and *Me* appeared in utterances coded *Other*, primarily in predicate structures.

One last point regarding surface characteristics concerns the contrast between uses of *My* in subject position and those in object position. *My* in object position was always part of a possessive construction, whereas *My* in subject position was not. Compare, for instance:

TABLE 5.1
Distribution of Individual Forms (%) According to Surface Characteristics
(Jeffrey Month I)

(a) Verb / Verbless Context

FORM	With Verb	Without Verb	Uncoded	Subtotal*
I	85	6	9	(47)
My	62	34	3	(58)
Me		100		(7)
Other	56	44		(9)
Own Name		100		(4)
Subtotal*	(81)	(38)	(6)	(125)

(b) With Verb: Position

FORM	Subject	Object	Uncoded	Subtotal*
I	100			(40)
My	86	8	6	(36)
Me				
Other	60	20	20	(5)
Own Name				
Subtotal*	(74)	(4)	(3)	(81)

(c) With Verb: Argument Structure

FORM	Single Argument	Multiargument	Uncoded	Subtotal*
I	28	73		(40)
My	19	81		(31)
Me				
Other	33	67		(3)
Own Name				
Subtotal*	(18)	(56)		(74)

(d) Without Verb: Context

FORM	+Noun	Alone	Other	Subtotal*
I		33	67	(3)
My	30	15	55	(20)
Me		29	71	(7)
Other		25	75	(4)
Own Name		50	50	(4)
Subtotal*	(6)	(9)	(23)	(38)

* (Raw numbers).

75

(11) My cracked the eggs.
(12) I like my cereal.

This suggests that the child may not have viewed these two uses as similar.

Semantic Characteristics. All utterances containing a self reference form and a verb have been coded in terms of a number of semantic parameters involving agency and transitivity (see chapter 4). In discussing the findings here it should be noted that I focus exclusively on an analysis in which each utterance was coded at the semantic level as ranking either high or low in terms of the parameters (see Budwig, 1986, 1989, for a discussion of the independent rankings on each parameter). My concern here is whether or not the two self reference forms can be distinguished in terms of the two levels (High and Low) coded.

Before considering whether particular forms link up with the high or low end of the agentivity continuum, I should first discuss how the child distributed his talk about high and low agentivity regardless of the form used. For example, if Jeffrey rarely talked about instances ranking high in agentivity, it would be hardly surprising that his forms did not contrast along this dimension. Furthermore, an examination of the developmental data shows that over the course of the study changes took place in the extent to which the child talked about events from the standpoint of high or low agentivity. For these reasons, I first consider briefly how talk was distributed between these two categories (regardless of which self reference form was used). Collapsing across forms, we find in the first month of the study that Jeffrey's utterances containing self reference forms primarily ranked low in agentivity. Of all utterances containing a self reference form, 73% ranked low, whereas 25% ranked high (2% remained uncoded). This analysis is based on the 81 uses of self reference forms coded in terms of the semantic parameters of agentivity.

Figure 5.2 illustrates the relationship between the core forms (I and My) and semantic ranking (high or low) in Month I of the study. Although I and My occurred in fairly equal proportions (I = 49%, My = 44%) these forms distributed differently along the agentivity continuum. Ninety percent of the utterances containing I ranked low in agentivity. Utterances involving I tended to refer to self as experiencer of internal states or, less frequently, self carrying out atelic activities. Consider the following examples:

(13) I like my cereal.
(14) No no no I no want the little blocks.
(15) I wear it.

In contrast, the use of My was more varied in terms of ranking along the agentivity continuum. Although more than half of the utterances containing

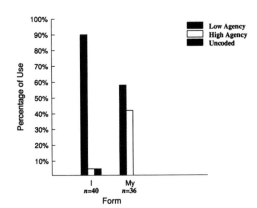

FIG. 5.2. Distribution (%) of self reference forms in terms of semantic agency: Jeffrey Month I.

My ranked low in agentivity as well (58% of all uses of *My* coded in terms of the semantic parameters), 42% of all such uses of *My* ranked high in agentivity. This finding is particularly striking if one bears in mind the finding reported earlier that in general, Jeffrey tended to talk about events ranking low in agentivity. Thus, although overall only 25% of all utterances containing self references ranked high in agentivity, 42% of all utterances containing *My* ranked high. Though Jeffrey did not talk much about self as a causer of telic action, when he did refer to telic actions, *My* was the self reference form used. For instance:

(16) My taked it off.

(17) My cracked the eggs.

(18) My blew the candles out.

It is particularly interesting to look at contrasts that revolve around the same objects. For instance, in example (15), the child was referring to a wireless microphone pinned to his outfit. The utterance in (16) referred to the same wireless microphone, though in this case the child was reporting that he just took it off. Similarly, we can compare utterances that contain two self reference forms, one in conjunction with an internal state verb and one in conjunction with an action verb. In all of these cases, the patterning is the same: *I* links up with the internal state verb and *My* co-occurs with the action verb. Thus we find instances like (19) but not like (20):

(19) I want my put the tower.

(20) My want I put the tower. (never said by child)

Although *My* was more likely than *I* to occur in utterances ranking high in agentivity, it remains to be explained why *My* also occurred frequently in utterances ranking low in agentivity. The utterances ranking low in agentivity involving the self reference form *My* took two forms. First, many of them occurred in conjunction with mental state verbs, in particular with the child's expression of his desires; and second, some of the uses of *My* in utterances ranking low in agentivity occurred in conjunction with verbs that were less kinetic. Consider the following:

(21) My read another book.
(22) My want cars.
(23) My want that.
(24) My wear it.

Comparing the uses of *I* in examples (13)–(15) to the uses of *My* in examples (21)–(24), the question remains how one can account for these differences. This is an important question that is taken up in the next section. The point to be made with regard to the coding of various semantic parameters of agentivity in terms of a continuum ranging from high to low is that the forms were used contrastively along this continuum. *My* was more likely than *I* to link up with the expression of high agentivity, whereas *I* occurred primarily in utterances ranking low in agentivity.

Pragmatic Considerations. With regard to various pragmatic functions at the outset of the study, we find that although Jeffrey used speech multifunctionally, his language functioned primarily to make assertions about the world. Over half of his utterances with self reference forms (57%) were coded as assertions, whereas only 18% were coded as control acts, and 14% were coded as multifunctional. We now consider the extent to which the core contrast co-occurred with specific pragmatic functions.

Examining how the core forms link up with the pragmatic categories, we find that distinct distributional patterns emerge (see Fig. 5.3). *I* tended to occur in utterances that functioned as assertives (68% of all uses of *I*), whereas it occurred infrequently in control acts. In contrast, *My* distributed more evenly across the function categories. Although there was a slight preference for *My* to occur in assertions (45% of all uses of *My*), *My* occurred 26% of the time in control acts, and 19% of the time it was found in utterances coded as multifunctional. In considering these distributional patterns it is important to keep in mind the overall pattern discussed earlier, under which the pragmatic function was considered independent of the form employed. This joint consideration reveals that *My* occurred more frequently than in the overall distributional pattern for control acts, whereas *I* occurred less frequently. The reverse pattern is found for assertions. This suggests that the distributional patterns were not random, but, rather, motivated in part by pragmatic considerations.

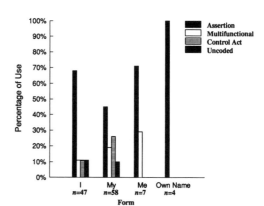

FIG. 5.3. Distribution (%) of self reference forms in terms of pragmatic function: Jeffrey Month I.

In the discussion of semantic characteristics of utterances containing self reference forms, the analysis was confined to the level of the utterance. The importance of going beyond the utterance level is revealed when one considers examples like (21)–(24). The analysis of the semantic characteristics of *My* indicated that this form often linked up with utterances that were agentive but also appeared in the context of less kinetic verbs and stative verbs such as *read* and *want*. Given that *My* generally occurred in clauses ranking high in agentivity, the question arises why *My* was also used in utterances ranking low in agentivity. The argument put forth here is that when these utterances are considered in terms of their pragmatic function within the context of the activity frame, they can be seen to function as control acts. Consider the following example:

(25) Jeff (J) and Eric (E) are looking at photo-book. Researcher (R) sits nearby.
    a. J: All done. (closing book and placing it on couch)
    b. R: Um-hmm.
    c. E: All done.
    d. J: My read another book. (looking at researcher)
    e. R: Well there is no other book. Do you guys wanna build some more?
    f. J: No. (shaking head)
    g. R: Are you all done then? Do you wanna go back to your school or do you guys wanna build one more thing for the helicopter?
    h. J: (grabs helicopter and plays with it)

Out of context one might assume that Jeffrey's utterance in line (25d) was a report of an ongoing activity. Instead, when it is viewed in the flow of discourse, we see that the child was stating his desire to carry out an activity in the immediate future. His utterance functioned as a control act by which he aimed to bring about the reading of another book. When the researcher rejected his request and suggested that the children carry out an alternative activity, Jeffrey protested (see line (25f)), though we find in line (25h) that he changed his mind, grabbing for the helicopter before his peer gained possession of it.

We can next consider examples (22) and (23) within the discursive context in which they emerged:

(26) Researcher (R) brings tray of blocks and helicopter to table while Jeff (J) and Eric (E) watch.
   a. E: Blocks. (looking at tray of blocks)
   b. J: My want cars. (pointing up in the direction in which the cars are kept out of reach of the children)
   c. R: Well there aren't cars now, there's a helicopter and blocks.
   d. J: My want that. (reaching for helicopter E holds)
   e. (J and E struggle over helicopter.)

The first use of *My* in line (26b) was directed to the researcher. At this point, the researcher was bringing over the second activity task. In line (26b) Jeffrey looked at the researcher and pointed toward the toy cars which he had been playing with previously. The use of *My* often occurred at activity junctures, when the child attempted via language to control the flow of toys. These requests for particular activities or toys often continued for several turns. In example (26), though, we find that the child switched his attention to the helicopter his peer held. In line (26d) we find a similar example of *My* with a stative verb. Although this utterance also functioned as a control act, this time it occurred in the context of an ownership dispute. Jeffrey's use of *My* in control acts was not limited to one particular kind of speech act type but, rather, cut across a range of acts that functioned as attempts to influence the hearer's actions, as well as appearing in utterances where the child's action was dominant or in ownership disputes involving both speaker and hearer.

My also occurred in utterances that were coded as multifunctional. Such uses involved stative verbs (e.g., *want, like*), as is illustrated in the following example:

(27) Jeff (J) watches his mom (JM) build with blocks.
   a. J: What's that? (pointing to JM's structure)
   b. JM: Well (.) how about (.)
   c. J: That's a house. (pointing to structure)
   d. JM: That's a house. (placing block) Is that a house? (lifting up another block and placing it on the structure)

e. J: That's no—now it's my turn to do it.
f. JM: Okay.
g. J: (whines)
h. J: (searches through pile of blocks) My want something. (still searching)
i. JM: Which would you like?
j. J: I would like -da like (.) don't. (lifting block JM has placed on structure)

In line (27h), it is unclear whether Jeffrey's utterance containing *My* functioned as an assertion, a control act (as Jeffrey's mother interpreted it in line (27i)), or a combination of both. This utterance is ambiguous because it is unclear whether it functioned to update the child's partner on his own actions (e.g., 'I'm taking my turn but I first have to find a specific block') or whether such an utterance was used to solicit his mother's help. The sort of ambiguity found in the multifunctional utterances is reminiscent of Burke's (1969) discussions of the stages of action and, in particular, his treatment of incipient acts. Burke suggested: "The concept of incipient acts is ambiguous. As an attitude it can substitute for an act—it can likewise be the first step towards an act" (p. 236). Mead (1934, 1938) discussed the sort of ambiguity involved in the expression of attitudes, suggesting (like Burke) that one can view them representationally and at the same time as "the beginning of acts" (Mead, 1934, p. 5).

Burke's and Mead's notions shed new light on the use of *My* in multifunctional utterances. I would suggest that these utterances were categorized by the child as similar to those containing *My* that functioned as control acts. When expressing attitudes, the child treated such utterances as beginnings of action sequences rather than as substitutions for action. Yet, as Mead (1934, 1938) pointed out with regard to gestures, such usage does not necessarily entail consciousness of action. This use of *My* can be viewed in terms of what Gumperz (1976, 1982) referred to as contextual cues: "Constellations of surface features of message forms are the means by which speakers signal and listeners interpret what the activity is, how semantic content is to be understood and how each sentence relates to what precedes and follows" (Gumperz, 1982, p. 131). The use of *My* then informs the partner about the contextual presuppositions.

The distinction between the expressions of attitudes that function as representational and those that function as a first step in an action sequence is clearly a subtle one. Such a distinction presents not only a problem for the researcher coding the data but also an online problem at the level of text production for the child. It is interesting to note that nearly all of the occurrences of *I* and *My* that were involved in hesitations or self-corrections were exactly the sort involving the expression of attitudes. This suggests that Jeffrey himself realized that the distinction was not all that clear. Nevertheless, the child's selection of the *My* form indicates that the utterance was viewed as part of an action sequence. Relating such uses to those involving *My* as a marker of agentivity, it is intriguing to note that direct physical action on the part of the child did not need to take place for the *My* form to be employed. The expression of internal states, when viewed as the introductory phase of an action sequence, also prompted the use of the *My* form.

Thus far, I have considered three pragmatic functions of utterances with *My*. I have noted that most frequently *My* functioned in assertions. But I have also noted that *My* appeared in conjunction with control acts; and in addition, it appeared with the expression of attitudes that marked the first step in an action sequence. Although I return to the question why the child often used the *My* form in conjunction with assertions, at this point, we can note that what the remaining two functions of *My* share is the instrumental use of language. These utterances function not so much to represent reality as to create it.

I, in contrast to *My*, has been noted to appear primarily in assertions. This contrast can account for the distinction in the minimal pair *I wear it* and *My wear it*, in examples (15) and (24). Situating these examples in the context of the child's ongoing activities, the pragmatic distinction between these utterances becomes clear:

(28) End of play session involving Jeff (J) and mom (JM). Researcher (R) is removing the wireless microphone from JM.
    a. J: No no my turn. (taking microphone from JM)
    b. R: You want me to put it on you for a minute?
    c. J: Yeah.
    d. JM: You wanna wear it?
    e. R: Okay. (begins to clip microphone on J)
    f. J: I wear it. (smiling while looking at microphone.)
    g. (R converses with JM.)

(29) Jeff (J) is looking through photo-book with Eric (E). Researcher (R) sits nearby.
    a. J: What's that? (holding microphone that was hidden behind couch)
    b. R: Oh it's just some equipment.
    c. E: That's Eric (pointing to photo in book)
    d. R: Um-hmm.
    e. J: My wear it. (gives microphone to researcher)
    f. R: You wanna wear it?
    g. J: Yeah.

h. R: Okay, I'll pin it right here. (as she is placing microphone on Jeffrey)

In example (28) the use of *I* in line (28f) was linked with an assertion. The utterance came at a point in the discourse when control of the microphone was not at issue. The child was already wearing it. Example (29) revolved around a similar event, though in line (29e) Jeffrey's utterance functioned as a control act. The child requested that the researcher place the microphone on him. Although at the level of the utterance these two examples look similar, when placed in the stream of discourse it becomes clear that they differ in terms of the pragmatic attitude expressed.

One might want to conclude that *My* occurred in discourse with future orientation, whereas *I* might occur in discourse about ongoing or previous happenings. Although this was often the case, there are instances of *I* in discourse with future orientation; and the contrast between the uses of *I* and *My* with future orientation is informative. The uses of *My* with future orientation tended to occur when the child was in the middle of another activity and anticipated what was to come next. For example, *My read the story* was uttered while the child was playing with the blocks. Jeffrey said this while looking over in the direction of the photo-book, which was resting on the desk where the researcher was sitting. In another example, the child was watering his plant at the beginning of the session; and while looking across the room at the table that had been set up with some toys, Jeffrey said, "My play with the helicopter." In such cases of *My* with future orientation, the child did not have sole control over the instigation of the event he wanted to take place—he alone could not bring the activity about.

Utterances involving *My* with future orientation contrast with similar utterances containing *I*, because the utterances with *I* always took place when the child presupposed control. In such cases the partners had often negotiated a joint activity, and the child's utterance elaborated on an established plan. In one example, Jeff and his mother decided to "make food" by filling containers with dried peas. In the process of the activity Jeffrey suggested, "I'll make breakfast for you," and he continued to "prepare food" on his own. With regard to the cases of *I* with future orientation, the child did not wait for the partner's intervention to begin carrying out the activity referred to in the future-oriented utterance.

Presupposition also plays a central role in the contrast between *I* and *My* with reference to control of objects. Many cases of *I* with future orientation occurred when Jeffrey discussed how he planned to distribute toys he considered himself to be in control of, as in the following example:

(30) Jeff (J) and mom (JM) are building with blocks.
   a. J: And/ And you have that. (giving JM a block from the block pile)

b. JM: Okay.
c. J: And I'll have this. (takes block for himself)

The utterance in line (30c) contrasts with that containing *My* in example (26d). Although *I* was used when Jeffrey presupposed control, he switched to *My* when his partner (most often his peer) was in control of the objects he would like to possess. Thus the child expressed his desire to play with an object differently, depending on whether his partner had claim to it or the object was not in use.

In summary, the results of the analyses of pragmatic function reveal that the two self reference forms appeared in utterances serving distinct communicative functions. *My* occurred more frequently than *I* in control acts or when Jeffrey expressed the first step in a causal sequence in which he used language to get others to act in particular ways. *I*, in contrast to *My*, appeared most frequently in assertions that were descriptive in nature. The pragmatic analyses have helped account for examples that could not be accounted for by the semantic analyses reviewed in the previous section. The question remains: To what extent are the semantic characteristics and pragmatic factors that link up with the use of the particular self reference forms interrelated? This question is pursued in the section that follows.

Core Field of Use and the I/My Contrast. Thus far, I have focused on two separate layers of analysis. Do the findings reviewed so far reflect two different meanings of each of the self reference forms, or can they be brought together under some broader categorization scheme? I claim that the co-occurrences between the individual forms and parameters at the semantic level of analysis are in certain ways similar to the connection between the self reference forms and the co-occurrences at the pragmatic level. The semantic and pragmatic features cluster together and are best viewed as falling under one broad categorization on the part of the child.

If the uses of *I* and *My* are linked up with meaning clusters that cut across semantic and pragmatic boundaries, one can formulate predictions for a combined analysis of agentivity and control. When simultaneously considering semantic and pragmatic factors, *My* should be the preferred form in utterances that rank high on the agentivity scale and function as control acts. Similarly, *I* should be the preferred form in utterances that rank low in agentivity and function as assertives. No predictions can be made about the ways the forms would link up with utterances that, for instance, rank high in agentivity but function as assertives, or utterances that rank low in agentivity but function as control acts. An analysis of these instances would reveal what Jeffrey did when the semantic and pragmatic factors were in conflict.

The findings of the joint analysis support the predictions. *My* was found in 100% of the instances in which the utterance ranked high in semantic agency and functioned as a control act. In addition, 77% of all utterances ranking low in semantic agency and functioning as assertions included *I.* The fact that 85% of the utterances ranking high in semantic agency that functioned as assertives included *My* suggests that Jeffrey seemed to place more weight on semantic components than pragmatic ones in selecting a form when the semantic and pragmatic levels were at odds.

By way of summary, the reader can reconsider the set of utterances listed as examples (1)–(10). At the beginning of this chapter they were put forth to illustrate what has been referred to as Jeffrey's core contrast. Although at first glance these forms did not appear motivated, a series of distributional analyses that took into account semantic and pragmatic function indicated that the two forms did not occur in free variation but, rather, linked up with broader activity types. Based on these analyses, we are in a better position to return to Jeffrey's use of the other self reference forms.

Other Self Reference Forms

The distributional analysis of self reference forms reveals that 84% of all of Jeffrey's references to self involved the core contrast discussed here (see Fig. 5.1). The remaining instances involved *Me* (6%), *Own Name* (3%), and *We* (3%), as well as a small array of *Other* forms (5%) including *meself, mine,* and *let's.* Because the use of *We* appeared to be nonproductive at this point (occurrences were either direct imitations, incomplete utterances, or uses with another self reference form, e.g., *We my hide*—for which no pattern could be found), I do not discuss it further here. In addition, because the combined occurrences of *Other* forms made up only 5% of all self reference forms, these examples are also not discussed. Rather, the discussion briefly focuses on the use of *Me* and *Own Name*, specifying how these two forms contrast with one another as well as with the other self reference forms discussed earlier.

To a certain extent, the uses of *Me* and *Own Name* look quite similar. Neither of these forms occurred in utterances with verbs, and thus they are distributionally distinct from *I* and *My.* These forms then have not been coded in terms of agentivity, because they were not involved in utterances overtly marking agent-action relations. In addition, both forms at first glance appeared to serve a similar function. They both appeared in assertives involving naming and identifying:

(31) Jeff (J) and mom (JM) look through photo-book.
    a. JM: Who's that? (pointing to picture of J)
    b. J: Jeffrey.

(32) Jeff (J) and Eric (E) have been playing with manipulative toys. Researcher (R) is clearing off table.
   a. J: This/ This for you. (holding bowl of dried peas)
   b. R: Who made it?
   c. J: # Me.

Although both *Me* and *Own Name* occurred when the child was looking through the photo-book, *Own Name* is limited to this activity context, whereas Jeffrey used *Me* in other activity tasks. Although both forms occurred in utterances that functioned to name and identify, a subtle difference can be found in their use. *Own Name* seemed to be limited to instances of a labeling game played by communicative partners. In such sequences, action was backgrounded and focus was placed on giving names to pictorial representations. The naming game was not restricted to references to the self; the child also attached names to other pictures (e.g., *That's Anna*). In contrast, *Me* occurred in discussions of who carried out various actions. In such contexts, naming was less relevant than was supplying information that allowed the partner to distinguish objects and people from one another. Because the numbers are low, I do not discuss further how *Me* and *Own Name* were employed. Instead, I turn to a general summary of Jeffrey's system of self reference.

Summary of Month I

In the discussion of Jeffrey's use of self reference forms I noted that Jeffrey relied on a number of forms to refer to self in a systematic way. The distinction between the different forms was said to be based on the view of self in a given activity context. The core contrast, that between *I* and *My*, marked a contrast between self acting as volitional agent to bring about a change in the world either by direct physical effort or via language (*My*) and self as experiencer of inner states or doer of less agentive actions (*I*). Notions of degree of agentivity and pragmatic function both played a central organizing role in such a contrast. The use of *Me* represented a perspective in which the self or items related to the self were identified without necessarily focusing on the self's agentive role in action frames. Finally, *Own Name* was employed in acts of naming, particularly in labeling games where names were given to people and things. In such cases no reference was made to the self's role in action.

MONTH II

During Month II, Jeffrey continued to be categorized as an ego-anchored child. Although his mean MLU jumped to 3.52 during this month, his references to self constituted 80% of all references to main participants (see Fig.

4.1). In addition, we see later that many of Jeffrey's uses of self reference forms continued to deviate from adult usage. Despite the fact that he continued to be ego-anchored, I note some aspects of his self reference system that were developing during the second month of the study.

During Month II, Jeffrey continued to rely on two core self reference forms, *I* and *My*. As is shown in Fig. 5.4, these two forms occurred at similar levels and together represented 82% of all self reference forms during this month of study. I now consider whether Jeffrey contrastively employed these two forms in Month II and how such usage compares to that in Month I. I do not consider aspects of Jeffrey's usage of the other forms of self reference because there were few interesting developmental changes in these forms during Month II of the study. The only change worth noting is that *Me* began to be used in utterances with verbs, in subject and object position. Because such usage was infrequent, however, I do not discuss these changes further.

The Core Contrast: *I* and *My*

Surface Characteristics. Table 5.2 shows distributional characteristics of the various self reference forms. I restrict my analysis here to an examination of differences between Month I and Month II for the two core self reference forms. Here we find minimal differences from Month I of the study. In Month II, Jeffrey used all of the forms more frequently than in Month I in utterances with verbs. Although *I* was used more frequently than *My* (94% vs. 71%), both forms typically occurred in a context with a verb. In addition, both forms continued to be used in similar positions in utterances with verbs. *I* continued to occur exclusively in subject position, and *My* was used primarily in subject position (alone) but occasionally appeared in object position with a noun. And both *I* and *My* tended to appear in multiargument structures.

Semantic Characteristics. I begin to investigate whether the core self reference forms link up with particular degrees of semantic agency by considering the overall distribution during Month II of talk about high and low agency, regardless of form employed. Here we find that in Month II, there was

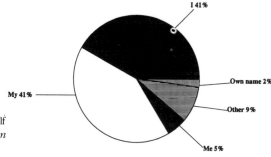

FIG. 5.4. Distribution (%) of self reference forms: Jeffrey Month II (*n* = 64).

TABLE 5.2
Distribution (%) of Self Reference Forms According to Surface Characteristics
(Jeffrey Month II)**

(a) Verb / Verbless Context

FORM	With Verb	Without Verb	Uncoded	Subtotal*
I	94	2	5	(65)
My	71	29		(68)
Me	44	56		(9)
Own Name	25	75		(4)
Subtotal*	(14)	(29)	(3)	(146)

(b) With Verb: Position

FORM	Subject	Object	Uncoded	Subtotal*
I	100			(61)
My	85	8	6	(48)
Me	50	50		(4)
Own Name	100			(1)
Subtotal*	(105)	(6)	(3)	(114)

(c) With Verb: Argument Structure

FORM	Single Argument	Multiargument	Uncoded	Subtotal*
I	15	82	3	(61)
My	13	88		(48)
Me	50	50		(4)
Own Name	100			(1)
Subtotal*	(18)	(94)	(2)	(114)

(d) Without Verb: Context

FORM	+Noun	Alone	Other	Subtotal*
I			100	(1)
My	5	10	85	(20)
Me		60	40	(5)
Own Name			100	(3)
Subtotal*	(1)	(94)	(23)	(29)

* (Raw numbers).
** This table excludes 15 instances of other.

an overall increase in the proportion of talk about high agency and a simultaneous decrease in talk about low agency. In Month II, 35% of all uses of self reference forms ranked high in agency, whereas in Month I only 25% did. In contrast, during Month II 63% of all uses of self reference forms ranked low in agency, whereas in Month I 73% ranked low. Thus we see that during this month of the study, Jeffrey showed an increase in his interest in talking about self as agent, though he continued to talk about himself primarily in a nonagentive way.

The analysis of *I* and *My* during Month I revealed that Jeffrey systematically distinguished between these two forms, in part on the basis of the degree of agentivity expressed. *My* tended to be employed in utterances ranking both high and low in agentivity, whereas *I* occurred in utterances that ranked low. In Month II we also find that *I* dominated the low end of the agentivity continuum, although this difference was less pronounced than in Month I (see Fig. 5.5). In Month I, 90% of all uses of *I* ranked low, whereas in Month II only 66% of all uses of *I* ranked low. The use of *I* linked up with utterances ranking high in agentivity 34% of the time.

With regard to the use of *My*, we find that the trends were similar to those in Month I, though they were less pronounced (see Fig. 5.5). Thus although *My* continued to be used in utterances ranking both high and low in agentivity, in Month II *My* (like *I*) appeared primarily in utterances ranking low in agentivity. We find that 67% of all uses of *My* ranked low, whereas 31% of utterances containing *My* ranked high in Month II. In Month I, 58% of the uses of *My* ranked low, whereas 42% ranked high. Thus in Month II, both forms were used not only in utterances ranking low in agentivity but also in utterances ranking high. The following examples illustrate that both forms occurred in what appeared to be similar semantic contexts ranking high and low in agency:

(33) I'll make a cake all by meself.

(34) My make a house with/ with these/ these blocks.

(35) I want that.

(36) My want that.

I return to further distinctions in such minimal pairs. For now, I simply note that there no longer appeared to be a semantic distinction between the two core self reference forms.

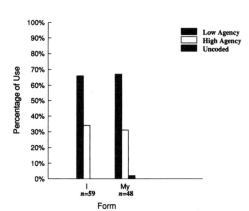

FIG. 5.5. Distribution (%) of self reference forms in terms of semantic agency: Jeffrey Month II.

Pragmatic Characteristics. Turning to a consideration of pragmatic function, we can first note that there was no real change in the second month with regard to how Jeffrey's language functioned. Without considering the use of particular forms and generalizing instead across all self reference forms, we find that Jeffrey continued to divide his use of language functions much as he did in Month I. In utterances containing self reference forms, his language functioned primarily to make assertions about the world (60%), whereas his use of control acts was less frequent (17%). The general distribution of pragmatic function (regardless of form) looked quite similar to that in Month I.

Taking into account how Jeffrey linked the core self reference forms with the various communicative functions, we also find a pattern similar to that described in Month I (see Fig. 5.6). Jeffrey continued to use *I* in utterances that functioned as assertions, though in Month II the link between *I* and assertive function was even stronger. With regard to *My*, the distributional patterns remained primarily unchanged. *My* continued to be favored in utterances that functioned as assertions (41%) but was used more frequently than *I* in utterances that functioned as control acts (25% of all instances of *My*). The only major change in Month II with regard to Jeffrey's use of *My* along pragmatic dimensions was his increased use of *My* in utterances coded as multifunctional. Thus in Month II, there were some distributional differences in terms of how Jeffrey linked the use of *I* and *My* with various language functions, though there were no major developmental differences in such use between the first two months of the study.

Core Field of Use and the I/My Contrast. In Month I I noted that Jeffrey used *I* and *My* in utterances that differed in terms of their semantic and pragmatic functions when these were considered as separate layers of analysis. Moreover, when both terms were considered together, one could make predictions about which form would appear in utterances that, for

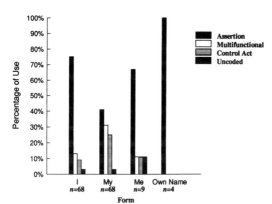

FIG. 5.6. Distribution (%) of self reference forms in terms of pragmatic function: Jeffrey Month II.

instance, ranked high in semantic agentivity and functioned as control acts (e.g., *My*) or ranked low in semantic agentivity and functioned as assertives (e.g., *I*). The combined analysis revealed that Jeffrey's use of such forms matched the predictions, suggesting ways in which the forms linked up to broader meaning clusters that cut across semantic and pragmatic dimensions.

Considering the findings from a similar analysis that combined the semantic and pragmatic dimensions in Month II, we find that *I* continued to dominate to about the same extent in utterances ranking low in semantic agentivity and functioning as assertives. In contrast, in Month II we do not find that *My* tended to dominate in utterances that ranked high in agentivity and functioned as control acts. First of all, we find that Jeffrey rarely produced utterances with these semantic and pragmatic characteristics (there are only two examples involving self reference forms), and *My* never occurred in Month II in these cases. Thus, a change that took place between Month I and Month II was that *My* no longer was best characterized in terms of a semantic and pragmatic prototype in which utterances ranked high in agentivity and at the same time functioned as control acts.

The most dramatic change from the first to the second month of the study for Jeffrey involved his incorporation of *I* into utterances ranking high in semantic agentivity. The question remains: On what basis did Jeffrey employ *I* or *My* in such instances? Can the instances of *I* be distinguished from those involving *My*? If one looks at the broader discursive context, one finds that the new use of *I* with some clauses ranking high in agentivity during Month II was of a very restricted sort. Such utterances appeared within a framework of joint activities, whereas *My* tended to occur as the child introduced new plans or attempted to bring about new activities. The following example illustrates the contrast:

(37) Jeff (J) and his mom (JM) are playing with a helicopter and blocks. They pretend to drive the helicopter to the grandparents, who J says (incorrectly) live in Berkeley.
    a. J: They live in Berkeley.
    b. JM: In Berkeley? Oh okay # that would be nice and close # wouldn't it?
    c. J: No. My make a house with/ with these/ these blocks.
    d. JM: Okay with these big red # blocks we'll make a house.
    e. J: Yeah.
    f. JM: Okay.
    g. J: No we'll// I'll put these.
    h. JM: xx And xx put these out of the way. (moving small blocks)
    i. J: No no I/ No I need the chimneys. (chimneys = small cylinder shaped blocks)
    j. JM: Oh okay. You need the chimneys.

In line (37c), Jeffrey suggested a plan to make a house with big blocks. His mom agreed in line (37d) and turned Jeffrey's plan into a joint endeavor. Jeffrey offered no protest. It was at these junctures that Jeffrey no longer used *My* in references ranking high in agentivity. In these instances, Jeffrey switched to the use of *I*. Thus Jeffrey took a different stance on the same event sequence (e.g., placing a block, making a house) depending on whether it was part of a jointly agreed upon activity frame or was independently motivated.

Most of Jeffrey's uses of *I* in Month II that ranked high in agentivity were accompanied by a modal form (80%). In my previous discussion of Jeffrey at Month I, I noted that modal forms were used with *I* but not with *My* when referring to future-oriented actions. This pattern became more pronounced in Month II. In addition, in 5% of the cases when *I* was not followed by a modal form, it was used in utterances employing the pattern *I + My + verb + object*, for instance, *I my make Daddy*. In Month II we find that *My* was integrated into a position other than subject position more frequently and in some of these cases was preceded by *I*.

Taken together, these findings lead to two conclusions about the use of the core self reference forms during Month II. First, *My* no longer occurred in conjunction with reference to self as prototypical agent. Rather, the child restricted the use of *My* to an activity scene that was guided by personal motives. As soon as his actions became contextualized as part of a shared plan, the *I* form was employed. Thus the contrastive use of *I* and *My* must go beyond a semantic level of analysis to include a consideration of discursive context.

A second conclusion to be drawn regarding developmental differences in the contrast between *I* and *My* during Month II is as follows. As the *My* form was employed more restrictively in subject position, the child began to reinterpret this form as being more similar to modal forms. Thus during Month II, Jeffrey seemed to have called into question his neat contrast between *I* and *My* noted during Month I, and he seemed to be experimenting with alternative form-function pairings. I reconsider these conclusions in light of what we find in our subsequent discussion of Jeffrey's use of the core self reference forms in Months III and IV.

MONTH III

During Month III, Jeffrey's self reference system underwent radical reorganization. First of all, we find a change toward several characteristics noticed in the nonego-anchored children's use of self reference forms. As in Month II, Jeffrey's MLU was above the 3.0 mark—his mean MLU during Month III was 3.79. Second, we find for the first time that his overall proportion of references to self as main participant dropped below 50%; 48% of all of Jeffrey's references to main participants were about himself. Third, as I later note in more detail (see Fig. 5.7), Jeffrey no longer contrasted between multiple self reference forms but, rather, primarily used *I* when referring to himself. Finally, there were relatively few instances of self reference form usage that deviated from the adult system. I briefly consider these various changes in more detail.

I begin our consideration of changes with a more complete analysis of the distribution of various self reference forms during the third month of the study. In Month III, as is shown in Fig. 5.7, Jeffrey primarily used *I* to refer to himself. Most of his use of self reference forms (52%) involved the use of *I*. We can also note the dramatic decrease in the use of the form *My* at this point. Although in Month II Jeffrey used *My* in 41% of all instances of self reference, in Month III *My* appeared in only 9% of all instances of self reference. A third change to be noted in the use of forms involves the category *Other*. In contrast to Month II—where this category made up only 9% of all usage—in Month III *Other* accounted for 30% of all self reference forms. A closer examination reveals that this was in part due to a single form, *We*, which accounted for 18% of all self reference forms. Thus we have further evidence that Jeffrey's system was organized during Month III in a way similar to that to be described for the nonego-anchored children. They too drew a greater contrast between *I* and *We* than between any other pair of self reference forms.

The Core Contrast: *I* and *My*

As was noted earlier, *I* and *My* no longer represented the core contrast for self reference forms in Month III. Nevertheless, from a developmental perspective it is interesting to follow up on the relationship between these forms during the third month of the study. Several questions emerge. First,

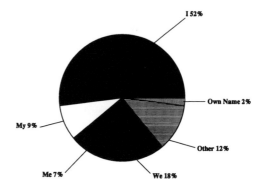

FIG. 5.7. Distribution (%) of self reference forms: Jeffrey Month III (*n* = 148).

when *My* was no longer contrastively employed in subject position, do we find *I* now used multifunctionally? Similarly, when *My* was used as in the adult system, do we find it in multifunctional contexts? We turn to a brief consideration of these issues.

Surface Characteristics. The discussion of surface characteristics is brief, because I have already noted that Jeffrey no longer employed the various forms with any regularity in subject position. *I* appeared in utterances with verbs, as did *We*. Both forms appeared in subject position. *My*, with rare exception, appeared in conjunction with a noun. It occurred in a variety of sentence contexts. *Me* often appeared alone, but it also appeared in object position in sentences with verbs. There were no longer any uses of *Me* in subject position of the sort noted in Month II. From the standpoint of surface characteristics, Jeffrey's system looked similar to the target language.

Semantic Characteristics. I begin the analysis of semantic characteristics of the various self reference forms by noting that there were no important changes in the overall distribution of the various degrees of semantic agency for the combined analysis of self reference forms. As was the case in Month II, Jeffrey continued to refer to himself primarily with utterances that ranked low in agency (61%), whereas only 34% of all utterances containing a self reference form ranked high. This is interesting in that when Jeffrey gave up his special usage of pronominal forms he might have simultaneously begun using *I* more multifunctionally to refer equally to both high and low agency. This was not the case.

Looking more specifically at the issue of the relation between individual forms and the degree of agency, we find a pattern similar to that of the overall distribution. Both *I* and *We* tended to be found in utterances that ranked low in agency (*I* = 59%; *We* = 75%). There were only four instances of *My* used with a verb, and such usage was split equally between high and low agency. Thus it was not the case that when *My* was no longer used in subject position, Jeffrey began using *I* to refer to self as prototypical agent more frequently. Furthermore, it was not the case that when *We* was introduced into the system, it appeared in utterances ranking high (i.e., new form, new function). Rather, all forms referred to the same degree of agency, and thus there were no form-meaning patterns developed at this point.

Pragmatic Characteristics. During Month III we find that Jeffrey continued to use roughly the same proportion of assertions with self reference forms (59% in Month III vs. 60% in Month II). His use of control acts increased slightly from 17% for Month II to 25% for Month III. The question is whether the specific forms took on new distributional patterns as the system underwent major reorganization. Figure 5.8 reveals these distributional patterns.

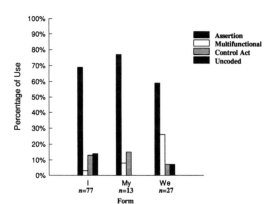

FIG. 5.8. Distribution (%) of self reference forms in terms of pragmatic function: Jeffrey Month III.

We find that *I* continued to be used as in Month II with assertions. *My* was used more frequently in assertions than in Month II, and as *We* was introduced into the system we find that it was used primarily with assertions but was found 26% of the time in multifunctional contexts in instances where Jeffrey was asserting a plan with a simultaneous attempt to change the environment. Thus although many of the instances of *I* and *We* appeared in similar pragmatic contexts, one distinction was the more frequent use of *We* in multifunctional utterances.

Core Fields of Use. We can now consider the core fields of use of each of the self reference forms. In Month III we find a dramatic shift in the way *My* was used. It no longer linked up with the notions of agency and control but, rather, was employed almost exclusively in possessive constructions. *I* was found primarily in assertions ranking low in agency, as was the form *We*, which was introduced into the system at this time. The question then becomes: On what basis did Jeffrey employ one or the other form? We might suppose that the distinction was that joint reference was made with *We* and reference to self alone was made with *I*. A closer examination, though, of the examples involving *I* and *We* shows that the difference was not so straightforward. Often we find that Jeffrey used *I* when he and his mother were jointly negotiating action sequences, and likewise we find *We* employed when there was no clear joint reference.

(38) Jeff (J) and mom (JM) are playing with manipulative toys. J announces that he is making ice cream. J and JM discuss their favorite flavors of ice cream and then J says:
    a. J: I could dump it in here. (referring to pretend ice cream)
    b. JM: Okay. Great.
    c. J: And then we could make some more.
    d. JM: Okay.

One might want to argue that once the plan was agreed on, Jeffrey switched to the *We* form in line (38c). This account, though, does not hold for other sequences:

(39) Jeff (J) and mom (JM) continue to play with manipulative toys. They are negotiating a new sequence:
   a. JM: This is a big car isn't it? (lifts car)
   b. J: No no I mean that's the ambulance.
   c. JM: Oh is that the ambulance?
   d. J: Yeah.
   e. JM: Is there a fire?
   f. J: No.
   g. JM: No? What's the ambulance doing?
   h. J: Uh;/ uh we should; we should get this bowl instead of that bowl. (reaching for another bowl)

In this example we could argue that Jeffrey and his mother were negotiating a scene involving an ambulance, though by line (39g) they still did not have a joint focus. One would have expected that Jeffrey would have used *I* in line (39h) because he was working on his own plan. Because the examples are few it is difficult to determine how Jeffrey contrastively employed *I* and *We*. One important distinction is that the two forms appeared in utterances with different modal forms: *I* usually appeared in conjunction with *wanna*, whereas *We* appeared with *needa* and *hafta*. I return to this contrast when I consider Jeffrey's self reference system during Month IV.

Other Self Reference Forms

Because Jeffrey's use of other self reference forms accounts for only 21% of all occurrences, the discussion is brief. Here I note that *Own Name* appeared exclusively in the context of picture labeling. *Me* accounts for 7% of all occurrences of self reference forms. Jeffrey used this form with his peer to claim actions he would like to carry out and when commanding the other to allow him to act. For instance, Jeffrey said, "No no me," as a command to his peer to allow him a chance at turning the page of the photo-book. There was only one instance of *Me* in object position in a construction with a verb. This too was a command: *And watch me*. Thus *Me* appeared in a limited range of activity contexts.

   What is particularly interesting about Jeffrey's use of other reference forms is that several new forms were added to the system this month, and they appeared in contexts in which *My* appeared in previous months. Most notably, he used the word *mines* to claim or try to maintain control of objects. Thus we see that as an old form faded out, new forms were integrated into the system to take on the old function. The reorganization, though, cannot be described simply in terms of a new form taking on an old function, because we find hierarchical integration at the same time as differentiation. Not only did Jeffrey now use *mines* to gain control of objects, but he also used a distinct form, *me*, to claim rights to actions. Furthermore, in this month we find new joint self reference forms such as *let's*, which was found in directives as a way to bring the partner into a shared plan. Thus, in Month III Jeffrey no longer relied on *my* as a global form of control but, rather, distinguished several different kinds of control with separate forms.

In sum, Jeffrey was not simply working toward multifunctional usage of each individual self reference form. He had a rather complicated system that underwent changes at the level both of form and of function. Old functions were expressed in more differentiated ways by the introduction of new forms, and old forms took on functions that were previously associated with separate forms. New contrasts were introduced into the system as well. We turn now to a brief discussion of the further developments in Jeffrey's system during Month IV of the study.

MONTH IV

In the final month of the study, Jeffrey's use of forms continued to look similar to that in Month III. His MLU stabilized with a mean of 3.68. His proportion of references to himself as main participant remained at 48%, and he relied on *I* in 53% of all his uses of self reference forms. These characteristics, combined with the fact that there was only one example of *My* appearing in subject position in a way that deviate from the target language, suggests that Jeffrey's system was more like those of the nonego-anchored children at this point in time.

Considering Jeffrey's overall distribution of self reference forms, we find few differences from Month III. As is shown in Fig. 5.9, Jeffrey primarily used one self reference form, *I*. The use of *My* increased slightly in Month IV, from 9% in Month III to 13% in Month IV. The use of the other self reference forms do not show any distributional differences between Months III and IV. I now consider briefly the way such usage links up with various other characteristics, focusing exclusively on differences between Months III and IV rather than providing a complete analysis.

Surface Characteristics. In Month IV, we can note the following changes in surface characteristics of the various self reference forms. First, *I* and *We* both appeared in subject position, whereas *My* occurred only once as a subject pronoun that was not part of a possessive construction. It is of interest that this use (*My have my mommy*) occurred in a moment of urgency,

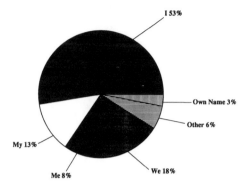

FIG. 5.9. Distribution (%) of self reference forms: Jeffrey Month IV (n = 182).

when the child stated he needed to go to the bathroom and demanded that his mother accompany him rather than the researcher. It is possible that in such cases where the child quickly attempted to make his point, he fell back on previously exercised pairings. The only other change in surface characteristics that ought to be noted was that during Month IV, *Me* began to be used regularly in object position. Recall that in Month III, *Me* appeared almost exclusively in utterances without a verb.

Semantic Characteristics. With regard to semantic characteristics, there was very little in the way of change. Jeffrey continued to refer to self primarily in terms of low agency throughout this session. What is interesting is a contrast between the use of *I* and that of *We* at the semantic level (see Fig. 5.10). Although *I* continued to refer to low agency 69% of the time, we now find *We* referring to high agency 41% of the time. Thus we see a shift from *My* referring to high agency in Month II, to no form referring to high agency in Month III, and an increased use of *We* referring to high agency in Month IV. Though both *I* and *We* appeared in utterances rating low in agency, *We* was more likely than *I* to refer to self as prototypical agent.

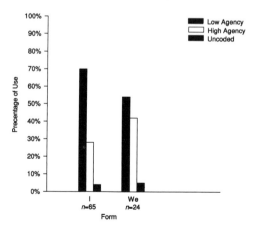

FIG. 5.10. Distribution (%) of *I* and *We* in terms of semantic agency: Jeffrey Month IV.

Pragmatic Characteristics. The overall use of language in Month IV resembled that in Month III. Jeffrey used language primarily to make assertions about self. There were two form-function patterns worth noting, though, in Month IV. First, *I* appeared more frequently than in previous months in utterances coded as control acts. We find that 23% of all uses of *I* in Month IV were control acts. This compares with 9% in Month II and 13% in Month III. One reason for this increase is that Jeffrey began using conventional requests like *Can I have x* rather than relying on his earlier strategies of *My + desired object* in Month II or *mines* in Month III. Another interesting pattern was the increased use of *We* in assertions; although in Month III, 59% of all uses of *We* were coded as assertions, in Month IV we find 78% of all uses of *We* coded as such. The question to be raised is: What is the distinction between the assertions with *I* and those with *We*? In part, the answer to this requires a combined analysis of various coding levels, so we turn to that in the next section.

Core Fields of Use. The primary change in Jeffrey's system that we have seen over the four months of the study is the gradual deterioration of the special *I/My* contrast. At the beginning of the study I noted that *I* was typically used in assertions that ranked low in agency and, in contrast, *My* was used by Jeffrey to talk about self as a prototypical agent acting to bring about change or control his environment. By the end of the study the core use of *My* no longer marked prototypical agent or control. This form instead took on its target usage as a possessive pronoun—occasionally in control acts, though primarily in assertions. This, though, is not to say that *I* became the only pronominal form used in subject position in a multifunctional context. Over the course of the study, Jeffrey introduced a new form into the system, namely, *We*. As the special use of *My* faded away, *We* began to be used contrastively with *I*. Both typically appeared in assertions, though *I* appeared in requests as well. My statements concerning the function of *We* during Month III hold for Month IV as well. That is, at this early point, *We* did not seem to mark the notion of joint agency per se. In fact, in Month IV it seemed more likely than in Month III to be used when the child described aspects of his personal plans. That is to say, *We* was even less likely than before to refer to a notion of joint subjecthood. Most frequently, when Jeffrey used *We* he was referring to his own independent actions he was about to carry out en route to a broader goal. It appears that in such cases *We* was employed to mark a less volitional kind of agency rather than a kind of agency based on personal motives. Consider example (40):

(40) Jeffrey (J) and mom (JM) are playing with blocks. Researcher (R) brings over more blocks.
    a. J: Now look (calling to researcher)

b. R: Oh look how colorful.

c. (pause)

d. JM: Should we put some little chimneys on? (no action)

e. J: Yes. But not the ones with—we need another green. (picking up blocks)

f. JM: Another green one? (J and JM discuss shapes and colors of blocks for the next five turns.)

g. J: Yeah a square like these.

h. JM: Okay. Where you gonna put the chimneys?

i. J: Now we hafta get the lights. (picking up and placing more blocks)

j. JM: The lights. Oh right. (J continues building.)

Although at first glance one might assume that Jeffrey was contextualizing his own actions as joint, several factors lead one to doubt this conclusion. First, in the video the dyad was positioned in such a way that the child was acting independently with his mother providing guidance from the side. Second, Jeffrey never checked for his mother's approval along the way. Third, we find in line (40h) that even his mother referred to his actions as his own, though in other cases (see line (40d)) she referred to joint agency when she suggested a plan. What is common to these uses of *We* by Jeffrey is that they typically occurred in sequences in which Jeffrey was building an already announced structure. It seems that what Jeffrey was indicating with the *We* form was a switch in attitude. The uses of *I* are found in the contexts in which personal motives guided action, whereas *We* indicates a more depersonalized agency—the motive for the child's action involved a broader plan, namely, to build that kind of structure. This finding fits with those reported for Month III regarding the use of distinct modal forms with *I* and *We*. If *We* was used to mark a more depersonalized agency, it would make sense that it would be found more often with forms like *needa* and *hafta*. Likewise, it makes sense that if *I* expressed a kind of personalized agency, it would co-occur with *wanna*. I conclude this discussion of Jeffrey's contrastive use of *I* and *We*, because the examples are few. I return to a similar discussion in chapter 8 when we turn to an analysis of the nonego-anchored children, which lends further support to the sort of argument being developed here.

Over the span of only 4 months, Jeffrey's self reference system underwent major changes. I have noted not simply the addition of new forms but also a change in the distribution of various forms at the syntactic, semantic, and pragmatic levels. What remained constant over the course of the study was that Jeffrey organized the use of various self reference forms to situate the self in distinct ways. What changed was the kind of stances that received linguistic marking. Early on in the study, Jeffrey was concerned with the issues of prototypical agency and control. Later on, he became more interested in marking the various kinds of motivations of his actions (i.e., personal, social norms, joint agency). As he developed additional linguistic means (for instance, the use of modal forms) these marked distinctions previously indicated by self reference forms. The changes that were described were gradual. Although we saw dramatic changes in the system in Month III, we nevertheless found important developments in Months II and IV, suggesting that the transitions were both sudden and slow. Jeffrey appeared to make small shifts in his hypotheses concerning the relationship between linguistic forms and the functions that they served. I now consider the developmental findings of the other children to see whether these patterns can be generalized.

Grice

MONTH I

Grice, a 22-month-old girl, was the second youngest participant in the study. At the onset of the recordings, she was also the child who had the least advanced MLU; her mean MLU for Month I was 1.72 (see Table 4.1). Thus at the beginning of the study Grice was just beginning to combine words. With regard to her distribution of reference to self and other, Grice referred primarily to herself as main participant at the onset of the study; 85% of all such references were to herself (see Fig. 4.1). Even by the end of the study, we see that she continued to refer to herself as the main participant in her utterances. Like the other ego-anchored children, Grice used multiple self reference forms throughout the course of the study. The major developmental changes involved her reorganization of the relationship between such forms and the contexts in which they appeared. I now consider Grice's organization and reorganization of this self reference system across the 4 months of the study.

In contrast to Jeffrey, who relied primarily on two self reference forms, Grice relied on three distinct forms when referring to herself at the beginning of the study. As is shown in Fig. 6.1, 36% of all uses of self reference forms involved *My*, whereas *Me* was used in 28% and *I* was used in 25% of all utterances containing self reference forms. The only other major form used was her own name, which she used only 10% of the time. The discussion first focuses on the core contrast between *I*, *Me*, and *My* and then turns to her use of other forms of self reference during the first session.

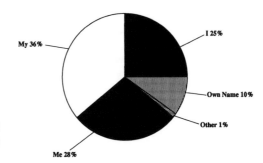

FIG. 6.1. Distribution (%) of self reference forms: Grice Month I (*n* = 72).

The Core Contrast: *I*, *Me*, and *My*

Grice's use of self reference forms, at first glance, looks similar to Jeffrey's use. First, we find that Grice also used the various self reference forms in subject position in ways that deviated from adult usage (see examples (4)–(5)). In addition, we find that one utterance often included multiple self reference forms (see example (8)). Grice often used different self reference forms in similar verbal contexts (compare examples (1) and (4)).

(1) I want nuts.

(2) I soup pour.

(3) My teapot.

(4) My want nuts.

(5) Me jump.

(6) Me to do!

(7) Me in there.

(8) I want my the blocks.

Surface Characteristics. At the first level of analysis I consider whether there are distributional regularities in the surface characteristics of the individual self reference forms used by Grice at the onset of the study. Four findings are revealed in Table 6.1. First, the three core forms can be contrasted in terms of whether they regularly appeared in utterances with or without verbs. One of the forms, *I*, regularly appeared in utterances with a verb (see example (1) and Table 6.1a). *My* typically occurred in utterances without a verb (see example (3)), and *Me* was used in utterances both with and without verbs.

Looking more specifically at the use of self reference forms in utterances with verbs, we can note that two of the forms (*I* and *My*) were used exclusively in subject position, whereas *Me* is found in both subject and object position (see Table 6.1b). Grice was more likely than the other two ego-anchored children to use *Me* in subject position in utterances with verbs (see

TABLE 6.1
Distribution of Individual Forms (%) According to Surface Characteristics
(Grice Month I)

(a) Verb / Verbless Context

FORM	With Verb	Without Verb	Uncoded	Subtotal*
I	100			(18)
My	15	85		(26)
Me	45	55		(20)
Other	100			(1)
Own Name	14	86		(7)
Subtotal*	(35)	(39)		(72)

(b) With Verb: Position

FORM	Subject	Object	Uncoded	Subtotal*
I	100			(18)
My	100			(4)
Me	56	44		(9)
Other			100	(1)
Own Name	100			(1)
Subtotal*	(28)	(4)	(1)	(33)

(c) With Verb: Argument Structure

FORM	Single Argument	Multiargument	Uncoded	Subtotal*
I	11	89		(18)
My		100		(4)
Me	100			(5)
Other	100			(1)
Own Name		100		(1)
Subtotal*	(8)	(21)		(29)

(d) Without Verb: Context

FORM	Subject	Object	Other	Subtotal*
I				(19)**
My	73	9	5	(11)
Me		36	64	
Other				
Own Name	33	67		(6)
Subtotal*	(18)	(10)	(8)	(36)

* (Raw numbers).
** Three uses of My are uncoded; one use of Me is uncoded.

example (5)). A further distributional pattern concerns the relationship between the various forms and the argument structure of clauses with verbs (see Table 6.1c). Both *I* and *My* (when used in clauses with verbs) appeared in multiargument clauses; in contrast, *Me* appeared in clauses with a single argument (compare examples (1), (4), and (5)). Finally an analysis of the uses of core self reference forms in utterances without verbs reveals that only *My* and *Me* appeared in clauses without verbs, and these showed distinct distributional patterns: *My* usually (but not always) appeared in connection with a noun (see example (3)), whereas *Me* appeared either alone or in some other context (see example (7)).

There are two points to be noted with regard to the analysis of surface characteristics of these forms. First, these findings indicate that the children did not seem to be using the various forms randomly. Decisions about which form was employed seem at least partially related to aspects of surface characteristics of the utterances in which they appeared. A better understanding of how one is to interpret these findings—in particular, why certain nonadult patterns might exist—is possible after an examination of the other levels of analysis.

Semantic Characteristics. As was noted in the discussion of surface characteristics of Grice's use of self reference forms, the majority of such forms occurred in utterances without verbs. As was shown in Table 6.1a, less than half of Grice's uses of self reference forms involved a verb. This is central, because forms appearing in verbless contexts were not coded in terms of semantic characteristics. One should therefore keep in mind that only 15% of Grice's uses of *My* were coded in terms of the semantic characteristics. In this section, I report the findings of our analysis in terms of whether the utterances containing particular self reference forms ranked high or low in agentivity (see Fig. 6.2).

Examining the uses of the core self reference forms in utterances with verbs, we find that in general such utterances tended to rank low in agen-

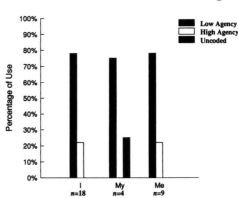

FIG. 6.2. Distribution (%) of self reference forms in terms of semantic agency: Grice Month I.

tivity. Of all utterances coded, 79% ranked low, whereas 18% ranked high. With regard to particular forms, we find that all three of the core forms followed this pattern. Of all uses of *I* coded for semantic agentivity, 78% ranked low, whereas 22% ranked high:

(9) I want nuts.

(10) I want read more book.

(11) I want Thomas.

(12) I put it in.

In contrast, all uses of *My* coded for semantic agentivity took the same form. They all involved utterances with the verb *want*:

(13) My want nuts.

Although similar contrasts can be found in Jeffrey's data, what is different is that Grice never used *My* at the onset of the study in utterances ranking high.

Grice's use of *Me* often occurred in subject position with verbs ranking low in agentivity. The following examples reveal, though, that such uses involved a different kind of verb:

(14) Me to do.

(15) Me jump.

(16) Me read book.

Although the verbs in (14)–(16) typically rank low in agentivity, they are action verbs, in contrast to the state verbs so frequently associated with the uses of *I* and *My* ranking low in agentivity. The verbs linking up with *Me* were verbs that referred to actions that deviated from prototypical agentivity, to the extent that an agent did not bring about a change in some physical object.

Summarizing the semantic characteristics of Grice's system and comparing that system to Jeffrey's, we find that for Grice, all three of the core forms tended to appear in utterances ranking low in agentivity. Only 18% of the uses of these forms ranked high in agentivity, and such uses involved *I* or *Me* but never *My*. Thus at the level of semantic characteristics, at the onset of the study Grice's system differed from Jeffrey's. In contrast to Jeffrey, in whose system we noted a form-meaning pairing, Grice did not seem to use particular self reference forms with a particular degree of semantic agentivity. One factor contributing to this finding could be that she so rarely used *My* in utterances with a verb.

Pragmatic Characteristics. We can now consider how Grice's use of self reference forms relates to pragmatic aspects of the utterances in which they appeared. It is first helpful to consider pragmatic aspects of Grice's use of self reference forms in general, apart from a consideration of specific linguistic forms. Such an analysis reveals that Grice used language to serve a variety of functions. Control acts made up 38% of all utterances involving self reference forms, whereas noncontrol acts made up 32% of all these utterances, and 22% of utterances containing a self reference form were coded as multifunctional. With these distributional regularities in mind, we can consider whether the particular forms linked up with specific function categories.

As is shown in Fig. 6.3, an examination of the three core self reference forms reveals support for the claim that Grice's use of self reference forms bore a relationship to particular pragmatic functions. Looking across the forms, we find that *I* tended to link up with utterances coded as multifunctional (76% of all uses of *I*), *My* linked up primarily with control acts (70% of all uses of *My*), and *Me* was used with both control acts (55%) and noncontrol acts (40%). I now consider the individual forms and the relations between them, in light of the communicative context.

Grice typically used *I* in conjunction with the verb *want* in utterances such as *I want that*. These utterances were primarily multifunctional, to the extent that the child stated her desires with what appeared to be the hope that others would respond to them:

(17) Grice (G) and mom (GM) have been building with blocks. Researcher (R) brings over a second tray of small blocks.
   a. R: Look at these.
   b. G: (disappears under table)
   c. R: You want more Grice? You like these little ones?
   d. G: I want nuts (standing up)
   e. R: What?
   f. G: I want nuts. (nodding head yes)
   g. R: (explains to G that she can play with nuts later)

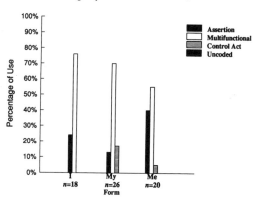

FIG. 6.3. Distribution (%) of self reference forms in terms of pragmatic function: Grice Month I.

The use of *I* typically occurred in situations where the child wanted to bring about a change but was physically unable to do this without assistance. It is important to note, though, that at the time the child stated her desire to bring about such a change, the change was not the focus of dispute. The use of *I* in examples (17d) and (17f) contrasts with the remaining 24% of the uses of *I* that occurred in utterances coded as noncontrol acts. In these instances, the child indicated her desires but did not do so with the intention of getting others to help bring about the change:

(18) Grice (G) and Megan (M) play with manipulative toys while the researcher (R) sits nearby.
   a. G: Soup. (placing nut in spoon, then in mouth)
   b. R: Just pretend. Take that out of your mouth.
   c. G: (complies)
   d.   (Peers play independently.)
   e. G: I want that. (en route to and lifting nut)
   f.   (Peers continue to play alone.)

In example (18e), Grice was already moving in the direction of the object she desired, and she took control of it without external assistance. In the utterances in which *I* functioned as a noncontrol act, the child seemed to be either informing her partner about motives for her actions or regulating her own behavior with these utterances.

Grice's use of *My* appeared in quite different pragmatic contexts. These uses are found in particular kinds of control acts, namely, when focus was placed jointly on speaker's and hearer's ongoing actions. These uses surfaced primarily in disputes over objects, and often (as was noted in the previous section) the child used *My* simply in conjunction with a noun referring to the object she desired:

(19) Grice (G) and Megan (M) are having a tea party.
   a. M: (approaches G, who plays with teapot and then places spoon in teapot G is using)
   b. M: Do want some Meggy's. (taking teapot from G)
   c. G: My teapot! (pulling teapot back from M)
   d. G: My teapot!
   e. M: Wait! (Both girls tug on teapot.)
   f.   (G lets go, stamps feet, and shows signs of distress.)

(20) Researcher (R) is setting up block activity for Grice (G) and Megan (M).
   a. R: Here are these things. (bringing over helicopter and toy car)
   b. M: Me airplane. (both children reaching for helicopter)

c. G:　My helicopter. (both holding and tugging)
d. R:　You guys share.
e.　　(M holds plane; G yells, then begins to build.)

As is shown in these two examples, Grice typically used *My* in disputes over toys, in particular those introduced by the researcher that were salient and in limited supply. It is of interest that she did not use *My* in other kinds of control acts, in contrast to Jeffrey (see chapter 5). Although Grice's use of *My* in (18c) and (19c) conformed to adult English, this was not always the case. For instance we find examples like *I want my the blocks* (see (21h)), revealing that the child was using *My* not simply in standard possessive constructions but also in other utterances in which she attempted to gain control over objects.

Me appeared in utterances that functioned either as control acts or as assertions. The following examples reveal that the context of *Me* in some respects compared with that of *My*, to the extent that both forms appeared in control acts.

(21) Grice (G) and Megan (M) are finishing their play with the manipulative toys. The researcher (R) approaches to clear away the toys and to introduce the block activity.
a. G:　# Read bo(ok).
b. G:　Me read bo(ok).
c. R:　Do you guys wanna play with the blocks?
d. M:　Yeah.
e. R:　Let's put all these on here.
f. R:　Put everything # (R and children clean up toys.)
g. R:　Great and I'll give you guys the blocks.
h. G:　I want my the blocks.
i. R:　You want the blocks?
j. G:　The blocks.
k. R:　Okay I'll get the blocks.

(22) Grice (G) and Megan (M) are playing with blocks. Researcher (R) sits nearby.
a. G:　Tower. (placing one block on another)
b. G:　Tower. (placing block, which then falls)
c. G:　Oh I want read book. (looks to R)
d. G:　Tower. (continuing to build)
e. G:　Me to do! (looking at helicopter in M's hand, with her own hand open)
f.　　(M ignores G, G leaves table.)

These examples reveal that the uses of *Me* in control acts in examples (21b) and (22e) were similar to some of the uses of *My*. Both of these core self reference forms were used when the child wished to gain control of objects or sought to carry out certain activities. A major distinction between these forms is that *My* was used when the child was actually involved in an ongoing dispute over control, whereas *Me* appeared when Grice attempted to get others to give her control when actual struggles were not involved. Example (22e) contains the only use of *Me* in an utterance that came close to a dispute. The other uses of *Me* functioned as directives to others to help the child achieve particular objects or goals.

Finally, we can consider Grice's use of *Me* in utterances coded as non-control acts. In these utterances the child announced her ongoing activities to others. Such uses never appeared with stative verbs such as *want*; rather, *Me* was used in conjunction with the expression of change of state or location, or with activity verbs (see example (23a)). To this extent, *Me* contrasted with the examples of *I* also described as associated with noncontrol acts.

(23) Grice (G) and Megan (M) have finished all the activity tasks. G looks through the photo-book again, while M builds with the blocks.
    a. G: (climbs off couch) Me in there. (walks towards door leading back to main playroom of day-care center, voice tone of an announcer)
    b. R: (takes children back to playroom)

This analysis of the pragmatic function of utterances containing particular self reference forms indicates that the three forms can be distinguished in terms of pragmatic considerations. Even the use of *Me*, which seemed to overlap at a general level with that of both of the other forms, can be distinguished when one examines more specific aspects of the kinds of control and noncontrol acts with which it was linked.

Core Field of Use and the I/My/Me Contrast. Thus far, I have focused on two separate levels of analysis. In this section, I consider the interrelationship between these different layers of analysis in order to arrive at a fuller understanding of the dimensions along which these different self reference forms can be contrasted. We find that one can thus arrive at a rich definition of the way in which individual self reference forms were used by Grice. In contrast to the approach in the discussion of Jeffrey, I do not emphasize a combined analysis of the semantic and pragmatic dimensions because, as I noted earlier, Grice so rarely used *My* in conjunction with verbs at this phase of development. Instead, I consider each form in terms of a variety of verbal and nonverbal features that co-occurred with its use.

I first examine the contexts in which *I* was used. Thus far, I have noted that *I* was used primarily in utterances with a verb, and that such utterances ranked low in agentivity. Typically these utterances appeared in contexts in which the child stated desires in order to get others to bring about change. On some occasions, Grice used *I* when making assertions about actions she was carrying out; thus *I* was used with utterances ranking high in agentivity. The core use of *I* for Grice seemed to be to inform others about the child's states or plans, often, but not always, with the intention of getting others to alter the environment in ways desired by the child.

I have noted that *My* often occurred in utterances that did not have verbs. When *My* appeared in utterances with verbs, the utterances ranked low in agentivity. At the semantic level, such uses look similar to uses of *I*, though I have noted that differences between these two self reference forms can be found at the pragmatic level. When *My* occurred in utterances without a verb, the child typically named objects she would like to control. What held the various uses of *My* together was pragmatic function. The function of utterances containing *My* was to obtain or maintain control of objects, most often those in limited supply and desired by others. In contrast to the case for Jeffrey, the notion of agentivity was not central to the use of *My*.

In comparing the uses of *I* and *My*, one might question what the difference was between the use of *I* in utterances in which the child attempted to gain the help of others to carry out particular plans, and the use of *My* in utterances to gain control of objects. One major difference involves the role of the other in such activity scenes. For Grice, *I* was used in events where the other was more of an instrument, a coagent acting on the child's behalf in order to bring about desired goals of the child. In contrast, Grice used *My* in scenes where the other was more of a counteragent, in particular when self and other were in dispute over the control of objects. Thus, although both of these forms were used to talk about the desires of the self, this analysis reveals that different perspectives were taken on self and other when using these forms.

The use of *Me* was more complex than that of the other two self reference forms. I have noted that it appeared in utterances that included verbs as well as in utterances that did not. When *Me* was used in utterances with verbs, these utterances typically ranked low in agentivity, though they occasionally ranked high as well. The pragmatic level of analysis revealed that *Me* tended to be used in utterances functioning as control acts, though it also was found in assertions. Thus, this form cannot be linked to a particular functional cluster. Nevertheless, when one begins piecing together separate aspects of the use of this form, a coherent meaning cluster becomes apparent. When *Me* occurred in utterances without a verb, it was often used in conjunction with a locative expression (*Me in there*). When *Me* was used with a verb, this was an activity verb or a verb that expressed a change of state (*Me jump, Me done*). What holds these different uses together is that in all cases the child acted as an instigator of actions that were directed back onto the self. The child not only was the first link in a causal sequence that brought about change but also was referring to events in which she would be affected by the action described. This description can account equally well for uses in scenes describing object transfers in which the child wished to receive particular objects, and events in which the child both initiated and was affected by actions. Grice's use of *Me* appears quite similar to the linguistic marking of the notion of affected agent in some languages (see Saksena, 1980).

What is particularly interesting is that rather than marking a notion of prototypical agency (a scene in which an agent acts to bring about a change of state in some external object), as in Jeffrey's use of *My*, we find Grice using *Me* to mark a scene in which the self instigated action that was directed back onto the self. I have noted that Grice did not mark the notion of prototypical agency with the form *My* as Jeffrey did but, rather, reserved this form to refer to a scene involving maintaining or the obtaining of control over desired objects.

Other Self Reference Forms

Thus far, the discussion of Grice's use of self reference forms has focused on the core contrast of *I*, *Me*, and *My*. Such uses account for 89% of Grice's use of self reference forms during Month I. As can be seen in Fig. 6.1, the remaining self reference forms consist primarily of instances of *Own Name* (10%), with only 1% of all instances falling under the category of *Other*. Given these distributional figures, my discussion of Grice's use of self reference forms that are not considered part of the core contrast focuses simply on her use of *Own Name*. Such usage usually occurred in a verbless context. As was the case with the discussion of *My*, it is not particularly helpful to examine the usage of *Own Name* in terms of the semantic agentivity coding, because it so rarely occurred in utterances with verbs. I focus instead on a consideration of the pragmatic function of utterances containing *Own Name*, as well as the nonlinguistic features associated with its use.

With regard to pragmatic function, we find that all uses of *Own Name* functioned in a similar way. All instances appeared in assertives that named or identified. This usage is illustrated in the following examples:

(24) Grice (G) and mom (GM) look through photo-book.
    a. GM: Can you find yourself? Where's Grice? Is Grice in any of these pictures?
    b. G: Yeah.
    c. GM: Where's Grice?
    d. G: (points to wrong picture)
    e. GM: Look under your arm. (pointing to other page) Who's that?
    f. G: Grice.

g. GM: What are ya playing with?
h. G: Truck. (patting picture)
i. GM: A truck.

(25) Grice (G) and Megan (M) are looking though photo-book naming
     pictures. Researcher (R) is holding book.
     a. G: Meggy.
     b. M: Meggy. (hitting page)
     c. R: Mm-hmm.
     d. M: Meggy.
     e. G: Grice. (pointing to picture of herself)

In these examples we find that Grice used *Own Name* not only when
responding to her mother's questions (see example (24f)), but also in spontaneous namings taking place with her peer (see example (25e)). It is particularly interesting to note Grice's mother's use of forms to refer to her
child. In example (24), Grice's mother used the following forms to refer to
Grice: *you, yourself, Grice, your,* and *ya.* In this same stretch of discourse
Grice used one form: *Own Name.* Most of Grice's uses of *Own Name* occurred in the context of the caregiver-child interactions, though instances
such as that in example (25) can be found in the context of peer play. This
most likely has to do with the fact that for the mother-child dyad, the
photo-book activity centered primarily around labeling photos, whereas for
the peers the major task was one of negotiating who would hold the book
and turn the pages. As would be predicted, the peer session involved more
use of pronominal forms than of *Own Name.*

It should be noted that although Grice tended to use her own name in
labeling photos of herself, use of *Own Name* was not restricted to the
photo-book activity. Occasionally Grice used her own name to refer to her
ongoing activities while playing with other toys:

(26) Grice (G) and Megan (M) are playing separately with manipulative
     toys at different corners of the table.
     a. G: (looks across the table at plate of nuts)
     b.   Grice wants some. (intonation of announcement)
     c.   (reaches across table towards nuts)

Although such instances were not frequent, they are nevertheless revealing.
They show that *Own Name* was not reserved solely for pictorial representations of the self. In example (26), Grice appealed to the sort of labeling
genre linked with the use of *Own Name.* She used the form as a contextual
cue (Gumperz, 1982). In contrast to her uses of *I* in somewhat similar
contexts where she asserted a desire, in this context Grice called up a

different frame. By using *Own Name*, Grice focused more on the naming of her state, as in the referential frame called upon in the photo-book task. The central use of *Own Name*—namely, to adopt a referential perspective-could be extended to other situations in a metaphorical manner. This sort of extension outside the photo-book session was not found in Jeffrey's references to self.

Summary of Month I

Grice's use of self reference forms involved the contrastive use of four forms. Three of the forms (*I*, *My*, and *Me*) were used fairly equally and accounted for 89% of all instances of self reference. The remaining form, *Own Name*, was employed 10% of the time. According to Grice's system, all forms could appear in subject position, though two of the forms (*My* and *Own Name*) tended to appear in a verbless context. Although *I* often occurred in conjunction with a verb, *Me* occurred in both verbless and verb contexts.

In comparing the use of the various forms along a number of dimensions, we find the forms appeared in conjunction with slightly different kinds of activity types. No one level of analysis could account for the contrastive use of the self reference forms. Rather, the use of these forms was related to an interconnected set of semantic, pragmatic, and nonlinguistic factors having to do with agentivity and control. It can be noted that the semantic level of analysis was not as revealing a level as it was in examining Jeffrey's use of the various self reference forms. Two reasons for this have been suggested: First, the self reference forms often appeared in clauses without verbs, and thus the semantic coding took place only for a limited subset of utterances. Second, when Grice did employ self reference forms in clauses with verbs, she rarely referred to events ranking high in agentivity, so several of the forms were noted to link up with low agentivity. For these reasons the other levels of analysis, in particular the examination of pragmatic function, were more central.

MONTH II

During Month II of the study, Grice showed an increased use of two-word utterances. Her mean MLU for the two video sessions this month was 2.23 (see Table 4.2). As was noted in Fig. 4.2, Grice continued to refer primarily to herself as the main participant in utterances, and she rarely referred to others. In addition, she continued to use multiple forms to refer to herself, and she continued to use these forms in ways that deviated from adult input. During Month II, Grice continued to display several of the characteristics that distinguished her as ego-anchored in Month I.

Figure 6.4 shows the distribution of Grice's self reference forms during Month II. We find that in the second month of the study, the distributional pattern was roughly the same as for Month I. Grice continued to rely on three forms of self reference: *I*, *My*, and *Me*. *My* was the form that was used most frequently—its use accounted for 43% of all uses of self reference forms. *Me* was used least frequently, accounting for only 22% of all self reference form usage. During Month I, we noted that the three forms were employed in almost equal proportions, except that *My* occurred most frequently. In Month II, Grice used *My* much more frequently than the other two forms, and she used *I* more frequently than *Me*. In addition, we find that Grice used her own name even less frequently during this session. Its usage accounts for only 3% of all self reference forms. I now consider the various co-occurrence patterns associated with the use of the core self reference forms, which accounts for 95% of all uses of self reference forms during this session.

The Core Contrast: *I*, *Me*, and *My*

Surface Characteristics. We can begin our analysis of the core self reference forms by analyzing various distributional patterns associated with surface characteristics of their usage. Table 6.2 reveals findings concerning the sentential contexts in which such forms appeared. Table 6.2a indicates whether the various forms appeared in utterances with or without verbs. As in Month I, a good number of Grice's self reference forms appeared in utterances without verbs. The same basic trend reported for Month I continued, namely, that *I* appeared in utterances with verbs, whereas nearly all of the instances of *My* appeared in utterances without verbs. In contrast to Month I, we find that Grice began to use *Me* in utterances with verbs more frequently than she did in Month I.

Looking more specifically at the uses of self reference forms in utterances with verbs, we find that the major developmental change from Month I is the growing conventionalization of the system. Here we find *My* in object position (with a noun) rather than occurring exclusively as a subject pronoun in utterances with verbs, as in Month I. An even bigger trend is shown in Table 6.2b with regard to the growing use of *Me* in object position. Thus,

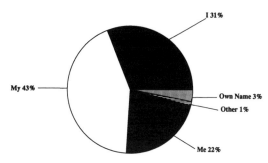

FIG. 6.4. Distribution (%) of self reference forms: Grice Month II (*n* = 87).

TABLE 6.2
Distribution (%) of Self Reference Forms According to Surface Characteristics

(a) Verb / Verbless Context

FORM	With Verb	Without Verb	Uncoded	Subtotal*
I	100			(27)
My	30	70		(37)
Me	58	42		(19)
Other				(1)
Own Name		100		(3)
Subtotal*	(50)	(37)		(87)

(b) With Verb: Position

FORM	Subject	Object	Uncoded	Subtotal*
I	100			(27)
My	82	18		(11)
Me	18	73	9	(11)
Other	100			(1)
Own Name				
Subtotal*	(39)	(10)	(1)	(50)

(c) With Verb: Argument Structure

FORM	Single Argument	Multiargument	Uncoded	Subtotal*
I	22	78		(27)
My	9	90		(11)
Me	45	55		(11)
Other		100		(1)
Own Name				
Subtotal*	(12)	(38)		(50)

(d) Without Verb: Context

FORM	+Noun	Alone	Other	Subtotal*
I				
My	50	46	4	(26)
Me		50	50	(8)
Other				
Own Name		67	33	(3)
Subtotal*	(13)	(18)	(6)	(37)

* (Raw numbers).

we find that the most significant change in Grice's system was that she used multiple self reference forms in subject position less often. With regard to utterances without verbs, there are no noteworthy changes to be discussed.

Semantic Characteristics. In this session we find that there is a slight increase in the overall use of the core self reference forms in utterances with verbs. That is, although in Month I we found that less than half of all core uses were in utterances with verbs (46%), in Month II 54% of all core uses occurred with verbs. Furthermore, looking at all core self reference forms to see whether they occurred in utterances coded as high or low in agentivity, we see that the general finding for Month I holds in this session as well. In Month I, 79% of all Grice's core self reference forms coded for semantic agentivity ranked low in agentivity; and in Month II, 71% of those utterances coded also ranked low.

In addition, we find a similar pattern in the proportion of individual forms coded in terms of semantic agentivity during Month II (see Fig. 6.5). That is, in Month II—as was the case in the first month of the study—Grice tended to use all three core self reference forms in talk about low agentivity. This differs from the pattern noted for Jeffrey, in that when Jeffrey talked about high agentivity early on in the study he was more likely to link *My* with high agentivity.

Although Grice tended to talk about events ranking low in agentivity, the question remains whether she reserved a particular self reference form for utterances that ranked high on the agentivity scale. In keeping with the first month of the study, this was not the case. Looking at the distributional patterns for all three core forms, we find that each form occurred only occasionally in utterances ranking high in agentivity. In particular, we find in Month II that *My* linked up with high agentivity in one example that actually involved the use of *Me* as well. When *I* and *Me* were used in utterances that ranked high in agentivity, the utterances differed from one another in terms of a range of semantic characteristics, as is illustrated in the following examples:

(27) I wanna put in.

(28) I ride that one. (question intonation)

(29) I'll came. (said with announcer intonation while walking from office to classroom)

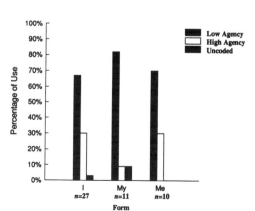

FIG. 6.5. Distribution (%) of self reference forms in terms of semantic agency: Grice Month II.

(30) Put me in there.

(31) You put me in there Mama.

(32) Want me read my book. (as a command to read photo-book)

One central distinction between the use of *I* and that of *Me* in these examples is that *Me* appeared as object of a verb, whereas *I* occurred regularly in subject position. In keeping with this, *I* expressed actions the child desired to carry out, questioned carrying out, or was in the process of carrying out, whereas *Me* referred to actions that would be carried out by others on the child.

Considering the contrastive use of the three core forms at the low end of the agentivity scale certain distinctions can also be found. For instance, *Me* continued to be used in utterances in which the child wanted to elicit action from another (e.g., *Show me, Help me Mama*), but Grice also used *Me* to refer to actions that she undertook without external help (e.g., *Me drinking*)—situations in which she initiated and was affected by the action. In contrast, *I* linked up with the expression of states (e.g., *I don't know, I don't like that one*, and *I have it*). Finally, the few instances of *My* in utterances coded for semantic agentivity (mainly ranked low) appeared with the verb *have* (e.g., *My have it*). The one instance that ranked low was of the form *verb + possessive pronoun + object* (*Play my toys*). Comparing such uses to those of *I* and *Me*, we find that when *My* ranked low it often appeared in contexts semantically similar to those of *I*. Thus the central finding is that during Month II, although certain semantic distinctions can be found between the various forms, there is no evidence for a form-meaning mapping with regard to Grice's use of various self reference forms.

Pragmatic Considerations. Considering the overall distributional patterns for language function during Month II, we find that during this month Grice began to use language much more to make assertions. This leads to an almost equal division between control acts (44% of all uses of self reference forms) and assertions (41% of all uses). Control acts increased only slightly from Month I to Month II: They accounted for 38% of all core uses in Month I and 44% in Month II. Multifunctional utterances decreased during this period from 22% (Month I) to 13% (Month II). We can now consider whether there were any changes in the ways the particular core forms linked up with these language functions.

During Month I we noted that Grice linked the various self reference forms with distinct functions. The basic change during Month II is that each form became more multifunctional (see Fig. 6.6). The use of *I* was split between assertions and control acts, that of *My* was split between control acts and multifunctional acts, and that of *Me* was split between assertions and control acts. The question then becomes: Are there differences between

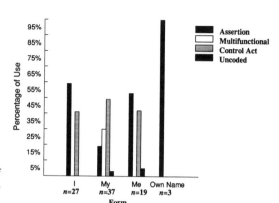

FIG. 6.6. Distribution (%) of self reference forms in terms of pragmatic function: Grice Month II.

the kinds of assertions that involve *I* and *Me*, and are there differences between the kinds of control acts involving the three core self reference forms? I now examine such potential differences.

At the level of the pragmatic analysis, the uses of *I* and *Me* in assertions look quite similar. Most often these forms were used to announce or describe ongoing aspects of the situation. For instance, in one situation Grice described her actions with a block by saying, "I rolling it." Somewhat later in the same session, while playing with pretend teacups, Grice stated "Me drinking." At the level of pragmatic function, both of these utterances look quite similar in that the speaker was informing the listener of the ongoing contextualization of the play. Both statements are assertions. In the next section, though, we see ways these two forms can be distinguished.

Turning next to the contrastive use of the various self reference forms in control acts, we find the following distinctions. First, when used in control acts, *I* was most often found in utterances reflecting an attempt to influence the hearer's actions. In particular, *I* was found in requests or directives for the partner to act in particular ways. For instance, several times Grice uttered "I want books," as a directive to her mother or the researcher to allow her to look at the photo-book. Similarly, as the researcher cleaned up the blocks and began to set up the tea party toys, Grice requested the teapot by saying "I want teapot." Such usage contrasts with the use of *My*. *My* was typically used in control acts in disputes over mutually desired objects. In such situations, the child attempted to claim control of objects the other possessed. For instance, trying to grab the same teapot from her peer, who was using it, Grice uttered "My have it" or "My had it." At times *My* was used to claim available objects that no one was using but that the child had access to. For example, playing with her mother, Grice picked up a large spoon sitting on the table and said "My souper," clutching the object. Notice how this contrasts with the directive use of *I* in situations where the other acted to help the child obtain goods. Finally, we can consider the use of *Me* in the context of control acts. *Me*, as I noted earlier, now appeared in object position as well as subject position. These occurrences resemble the directives involving *I*, except that the child was requesting that others perform actions that would bring about some change of state or location for the child. Thus we find examples like *Put me in there* and *Help me in there* in situations where the child wanted to change location. In sum, then, we find that the forms showed subtle distinctions at the level of pragmatic function. Although we no longer find a simple form-function mapping of the sort outlined in Month I and we see multiple forms linking up with the various functions, upon closer examination distinctions can be found.

Core Field of Use and the I, Me, and My Contrast. We can briefly summarize the major developmental changes in the core fields of use of each of the various self reference forms as follows. First, with regard to the form *I* we find that on the whole, characteristics of its use remained unchanged. It was used with verbs in subject position, and it typically linked up with verbs ranking low in agentivity. With regard to pragmatic function, it continued to be used primarily in assertions about intentions of the self when disputes were not involved, though during Month II *I* also appeared in control acts in which the child requested others to act in light of her own intentions.

My shows a bit more developmental change. First, we see it occurred more frequently in utterances with a verb; and in addition, it appeared in subject position of such utterances more frequently than in Month I. Nevertheless, in Month II, as in Month I, semantic agency was not central to its usage; instead it linked up with the pragmatic function of claiming control of objects. The basic change was that although in Month I Grice would say, "My teapot," as a claim to obtain and maintain possession of the teapot in a dispute with her peer, in Month II she was more likely to use *My* in subject position, saying, "My have teapot" or "My want teapot."

The form *Me* also underwent some changes in Month II. The most significant change involved surface characteristics. Like *My*, *Me* also appeared more frequently in utterances with a verb; but now when Grice used *Me* with a verb, she was more likely to use it in object position than in subject position. The semantic and pragmatic aspects of its usage remained the same as in Month I. The form tended to be employed to describe actions the child carried out that impacted back on the self or actions she wished others to perform that would cause a change in her. Thus we find *Me* with both activity and accomplishment verbs and in assertions as well as in control acts. What at first glance appeared to be a multifunctional use was, on closer examination, a cluster of related uses. Therefore we find in Month II that the core cluster associated with *Me*, namely, affected agency, did not change, though structural aspects of its use looked more like those of the target system.

MONTH III

Forms of Self Reference

In Month III, Grice's system of self reference underwent major changes. We can begin our analysis with an examination of general characteristics of her language development. First, we find that Grice's MLU jumped to a mean of 2.78 in Month III. Her references to self as main participant continued to dominate her talk (see Fig. 4.2). These findings suggest that she was still primarily ego-anchored. Aspects of her use of various self reference forms nevertheless underwent massive reorganization in this month. In terms of a purely quantitative analysis, we find in this month an explosion in the frequency with which she referred to herself. Grice now employed three times as many self reference forms as in the previous month. In terms of the distribution of the various forms, we find a major change in the frequency of occurrence of the various self reference forms (see Fig. 6.7). Although in the first and second months of the study Grice relied primarily on three forms, in this session we find a dramatic change in terms of both the forms that were regularly employed and the relative distributions of these forms. For instance, *I* was now used most of the time (65%) when referring to the self; and in contrast to the case in previous months, *My* was significantly less common (at 16%, compared to 41% for Month II). In addition, *Me* was no longer the third most common form; instead, Grice now employed forms coded as *Other* 10% of the time. Thus in this session, Grice began to use a variety of new forms to refer to herself (e.g., *we, mines*). We can also note that although *I* was now the dominant self reference form—as was charac-teristic for the nonego-anchored children—Grice continued to employ *My* and *Me* in subject position in ways that deviated from adult usage. In the sections that follow, I continue to focus the discussion on Grice's use of what was previously referred to as the core contrast in Months I and II, because the *Other* category comprised a variety of forms that were yet to be used with more frequency than *I, My,* or *Me.*

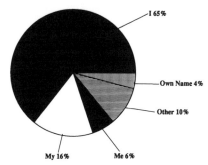

FIG. 6.7. Distribution (%) of self reference forms: Grice Month II (*n* = 280).

Surface Characteristics. Table 6.3 reviews the distributional aspects of Grice's use of self reference forms in Month III in terms of surface characteristics of the utterances. We find that one major developmental shift involved the substantial increase in overall proportion of self reference forms found in utterances with verbs (see Table 6.3a). Table 6.3b also reveals that *My* continued to be used in more conventional ways-not only did it appear more regularly in object position, but also when Grice used it in subject position it only rarely appeared alone. It is of note that Grice continued to

TABLE 6.3
Distribution (%) of Self Reference Forms According to Surface Characteristics
(Grice Month III)**

(a) Verb / Verbless Context

FORM	With Verb	Without Verb	Uncoded	Subtotal*
I	97	1	3	(181)
My	36	50	14	(44)
Me	75	25		(16)
Own Name	56	44		(9)
Subtotal*	(208)	(31)	(11)	(250)

(b) With Verb: Position

FORM	Subject	Object	Uncoded	Subtotal*
I	100			(175)
My	63	38		(16)
Me	33	67		(12)
Own Name	60	40		(5)
Subtotal*	(192)	(16)		(208)

(c) With Verb: Argument Structure

FORM	Single Argument	Multiargument	Uncoded	Subtotal*
I	7	93		(175)
My	13	88		(16)
Me		100		(12)
Own Name		100		(5)
Subtotal*	(14)	(194)		(208)

(d) Without Verb: Context

FORM	+Noun	Alone	Other	Subtotal*
I			100	(1)
My	68	5	27	(22)
Me		50	50	(4)
Own Name	50	50		(4)
Subtotal*	(16)	(6)	(9)	(31)

* (Raw numbers).
** This table excludes 28 instances of other.

use *Me* regularly in subject position in ways that deviated from adult usage. The only other major trend to be noted with regard to surface characteristics concerns the argument structure of clauses containing various self reference forms. In contrast to earlier months, in which the forms could be distinguished in part by their use in single-argument or multiargument structures, we now find that nearly all of Grice's self reference forms appeared in multiargument clauses (see Table 6.3c).

Semantic Characteristics. As was shown in Table 6.3a, most of the uses of the self reference forms occurred in utterances with verbs. This implies that our analysis of semantic agentivity could take into account a greater number of uses of self reference forms. An analysis of the utterances containing self reference forms (regardless of form) reveals a substantial decrease in the amount of such talk focusing on low agentivity. That is, 58% of all uses of self reference forms occurred in utterances that ranked low in agentivity features. Thus from the first month of the study to the third month, we see a gradual increase in Grice's use of self reference forms in utterances that ranked high in agentivity (compare 18% in Month I, 29% in Month II, and 38% in Month III). The question remains whether Grice linked the use of particular forms with the degree of agentivity expressed. In weighing such a question it is important to keep in mind that although a majority of the uses of *I* and *Me* occurred in utterances with verbs, only 36% of all uses of *My* were coded for semantic agentivity, because many of the utterances in which *My* appeared contained no verb. This implies that our assessment of how *My* linked up with semantic agentivity is based on only a small proportion of the total use of *My*.

An analysis of the examples involving the particular forms points up some important differences between Grice's previous use of the core forms and their current usage (see Fig. 6.8). Although we continue to find no simple form-meaning mapping between the specific self reference form and the

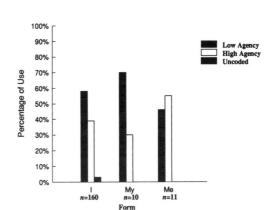

FIG. 6.8. Distribution (%) of self reference forms in terms of semantic agency: Grice Month III.

degree of agency expressed, some trends can be noted. The basic finding is that a large proportion of uses of any given form occurred in utterances ranked at the low end of the agentivity scale; this was especially true for *My*. This is in direct contrast to what I noted for Jeffrey. Furthermore, both *I* and *Me*, but not *My*, were used by Grice in utterances ranked at the high end of the agentivity scale. In general, though, no single form appeared primarily in utterances ranked at the high end of the scale.

With these comparisons in mind we can more carefully examine the three core self reference forms in terms of semantic agency. First, we can consider the use of *My*, keeping in mind that the analysis here is based on a small proportion of all Grice's uses of *My*. What changed in Grice's use of *My* during the third month was the frequency with which it was employed in combination with a noun in utterances with a verb. Grice typically employed *My* in utterances ranking low in agentivity (e.g., *My mommy play, My giant one fell down*), though one also finds examples of *My* in conjunction with a noun in utterances ranking high in agentivity (e.g., *Want I pour it in my cup*). In such examples, the use of *My* does not seem to be linked up with a particular degree of agentivity.

One also finds, though, examples of *My + verb*, as in previous sessions; and the question can be raised whether Grice used such constructions any differently. Again one can find instances ranking both high and low in terms of semantic agentivity. For instance:

(33) My put it on me.
(34) My put this on.
(35) My have tups (=cups).

Thus we find no reason to believe that the use of *My*, whether alone or with a noun, can be linked to the degree of semantic agency expressed. In comparing the use of *My* in utterances with verbs in this session to that in the previous months, though, two changes can be noted. First, Grice more regularly used *My* now in conjunction with a noun; and second, we now find instances of *My* with action verbs. This use is reminiscent of Jeffrey's special usage of *My*, though we see later that important differences can be found in their usages at the semantic level of analysis. This becomes clear later when we turn to a discussion of the use of *I*.

The coding of agentivity for Grice's use of *I* during Month III looks very similar to that in Month II. We find that *I* linked up primarily with utterances ranking low in agentivity, though it could also appear in utterances ranking high. What is different now is that one also finds *My* in a similar set of examples. That is, although in Month II we found only *I* in conjunction with high agentivity, examples (33)–(35) now reveal *My* in similar semantic contexts. I later discuss further the basis for this comparison; the main point here is that both forms can be found at both ends of the agentivity continuum, suggesting that agentivity is not a major factor in the contrastive use of *I* and *My*.

With regard to the form *Me*, in this session the major change involved the increased incorporation of this form into utterances that ranked high in agentivity. In particular, we find that Grice used *Me* more often in conjunction with prepositions indicating that the self was either a benefactor, or a receiver, or indicating location of action:

(36) I'm putting this on there for me.

(37) Give them to me.

(38) My put it on me.

Grice continued, though, to use *Me* in subject position with activity verbs in contexts in which she acted in ways that affected the self rather than some external object:

(39) Me drinking tea.

What remains unclear are the following two uses of *Me* in subject position, for which an affected agent reading is less feasible:

(40) Me open it.

(41) Me stir around.

In example (40), Grice was requesting that a container be opened for her by the researcher, a request that the researcher rejected. Note that Grice changed to the form *I* when she announced that she herself was able to open the container by saying "I did it Nancy," showing Nancy (the researcher) the container. Thus it seems that Grice was extending the form *Me* to subject position to imply the benefactive reading, though what remains unclear is why, when she made a similar request to her mother in that video session, she said, "Want you to open that for me." Another interesting contrast is between example (41) and Grice's utterance *I stir that for you*. Both examples appeared in apparently similar agentivity contexts, though, as we later see, what distinguished them were aspects of the pragmatic context in which they were embedded.

Taken together, the findings for Grice's use of *I*, *My*, and *Me* indicate that for Grice, semantic factors of agency do not explain how these forms were used. At best, they help provide a partial account of the use of *Me*, to the extent that Grice used this form to express a view of the self that received or was affected by action.

Pragmatic Characteristics. Turning to the analysis of language function, we find a dramatic change in distributional properties of Grice's language in terms of its pragmatic function. Although in Month II, Grice divided
her use of language between assertives (41%) and control acts (48%), in
Month III Grice relied far more on assertives (62%), than on control acts
(23%). Over the course of the study, Grice began to use language less and
less as a means to control her world and simultaneously began to use
language to comment and question about ongoing happenings.

The question remains whether Grice continued to align specific forms
with particular functions during Month III of the study. It can be remembered
that in Month II Grice distributed her use of the core forms differently across
the various language functions. *I* was divided between assertions (59%) and
control acts (41%), whereas *My* was divided between control acts (49%) and
multifunctional acts (30%). *Me* showed a distributional pattern similar to that
of *I*, that is, a slight preference for assertions (45%) over control acts (36%).
What this points up is that in Month II, no single form was noted to link
up with control acts, although *My*, when it was used, typically occurred in
control act contexts. In Month III the distributional regularities look different
(see Fig. 6.9). *I* was rarely found in control acts anymore (21%) and was
instead employed in assertives (67%). *My* was now rarely used in control
acts (18%) and instead typically occurred in assertions (57%); and the use
of *Me* seemed to follow a similar distributional pattern as in Month II, showing
a preference for assertives (53%) over control acts (41%). These findings
indicate that no single form linked up with a single function, though clear
patterns can be found. In the final section of the discussion of Month III, I
clarify the grounds on which these three forms can be distinguished.

Core Fields of Use and the I, My, and Me Contrast. Although I have
noted that the use of the core forms in Month III does not line up neatly with
semantic distinctions or pragmatic distinctions, an analysis that cuts across

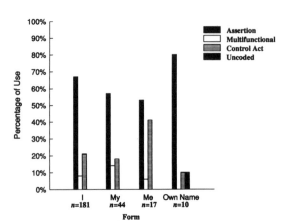

FIG. 6.9. Distribution (%) of self
reference forms in terms of pragmatic function: Grice Month III.

boundaries reveals some subtle ways in which these forms can be contrasted. In order to illustrate the contrastive use of the core forms, I now consider examples that provide minimal pairs with respect to usage. First, consider the distinction between *I* and *My*. Recall that at the semantic level of analysis, both forms were noted to occur with both action and state verbs. With state verbs, both forms occurred in subject position followed by the verb, although the same range of verbs was not used in both cases. *My* occurred only in conjunction with the verb *have*, whereas *I* was used with a range of verbs such as *want* and *like* but never with *have*. Both forms were at times used with the same action verbs:

(42) Grice (G) and Megan (M) are playing with blocks. G is building a block tower, trying to place two blocks together, when her peer (M) approaches with a block in her hand.
   a. G: My put this on!
   b. G: I putting this one there.
   c. G: I'm putting this on there (.) for me.

In this example, Grice was concentrating on getting the two blocks together. It was when her peer approached that she looked at her peer and exclaimed (42a). Her peer immediately moved away. At this point, Grice again attempted to connect the blocks, uttering (42b). The distinction between *I* and *My* has to do with control over doing. When Grice was simply informing her listeners of her ongoing activities, she used *I*. But when she felt challenged or when another intruded on her ability to carry out actions, she switched to *My*. It is important to note that Grice typically used *My* in conjunction with a noun, and in such contexts neither semantic agentivity nor pragmatic control played a role in its use. At this point there is no evidence that the child drew a connection between these two different uses of *My*.

Turning next to the connection between *I* and *Me*, we also find a distinction that cuts across semantic and pragmatic boundaries. Consider the contrast noted earlier, in which both forms occurred in subject position:

(43) Grice (G) and mom (GM) are playing tea party. G has just prepared a cup of "juice" for GM.
   a. GM: Um very good.
   b. G: I stir that for you.
   c. GM: Thank you.

In this example, Grice was stirring pretend juice when she uttered (43b). This example contrasts with the following:

(44) A few minutes later Grice (G) and mom (GM) are still playing tea party. GM has offered G "sugar" and "milk" to place in her tea. G then approaches GM and grabs cup GM is using, saying:

a. G: Me stir around.
b. G: # Me stir it around.
c. GM: Yeah stir it up.

A comparison of these two examples reveals that *I* was used in the less dynamic context when Grice was reporting her ongoing actions to her mother, whereas *Me* was used when Grice was attempting to gain control of the action in particular ways. This, though, cannot account for all examples with similar contexts involving *I* and *Me*:

(45) Grice (G) and mom (GM) still engaged in tea party. Grice is showing her mom how she can drink.
   a. GM: Good!
   b. G: I drink all up.
   c. GM: You drink it all up.

In example (45), Grice used *I* when she reported completing an ongoing action. This usage is similar to that in example (42) to the extent that control was not at issue. As the following example reveals, however, obtaining control is not the only factor related to this contrast.

(46) Grice (G) is having a tea party with Megan (M) while the researcher (R) sits nearby. G approaches R, bringing her a cup of tea. R requests that she return to the play table. G pulls the cup back and pretends to drink it and then says:
   a. G: Me drinking tea.

One can question why Grice did not say something like (45b). Again the difference is one of perspective taken on the scene. The claim here is that in using *Me* Grice focused on herself as affected by the drinking rather than on her desire to complete an activity. In instances like this, an element of contrast is involved as well. Although control was not at issue, Grice was stressing that she, rather than the researcher, benefited from the tea. The notion of benefit rather than simple control comes into play in the following set of examples:

(47) Grice (G) is playing with manipulative toys with Megan (M). She struggles unsuccessfully to open a childproof container that contains an interesting object, at which point she approaches the desk where the researcher (R) is sitting.
   a. G: Me open it.
   b. G: I (wan)na open it.

As she was uttering both (47b) and (47c), she was attempting to give the container to the researcher, who rejected the offer and told the child to return to the table and try herself. What is particularly interesting about examples (47a) and (47b) is that neither of them referred to an action sequence in which the child was opening an object. In both cases the child was attempting to get the researcher to open the container. What did the child indicate in these two examples? The point put forth here is that the child was providing two distinct ways to classify the event. In example (47a), the child was signaling that she wanted the other to open it "for me" (i.e., *Open it for me*). In example (47b), the child seemed to be indicating something like *I want it to be opened.* That is, the various uses of *Me*, in either subject or object position, occurred in an activity context in which the child was referring to a scene in which she pictured herself as benefiting from the action sequence.

   At this point the question can be raised: What is the difference between the Grice's use of *Me* and her use of *My*? I noted earlier that *My* was always used in dynamic contexts in which control was at issue, and that at times the use of *Me* linked up with dynamics of control and agency. One major distinction at this point between the adultlike and the nonadultlike uses of these forms concerns an assessment of presupposition of control. In examples involving *My*, the child presupposed control—that is, the child was involved in carrying out an activity at a point where another was viewed as intruding, or the child was simply attempting to bring about a change without another becoming involved. In contrast, when the presupposition of control lay with the other, then the child was more likely to use *Me*, emphasizing the *Me not you* aspect of its use. What is extremely interesting here is that the child's selection of one form or the other is claimed to depend on fairly subtle contrasts in the ongoing sequence of events. The child was not simply drawing distinctions based on an assessment of the degree of semantic agentivity expressed or on the pragmatic function of the utterance.

MONTH IV

My discussion of Grice's use of self reference forms during Month IV is limited in that there were very few developmental changes that took place. In Month IV Grice's mean MLU passed the 3.0 mark noted for nonego-anchored children; her mean MLU during Month IV was 3.51. During Month IV, she also continued to show a gradual decrease in the proportion of self reference forms occurring in subject position (74% in Month IV vs. 82% in Month III). The fact, though, that the majority of her references to main participants were to herself distinguishes her from the nonego-anchored group.

   With regard to the distribution of various self reference forms, we find a pattern similar to that reported in Month III: Grice tended to rely on one form, *I*, and occasionally used *My* and *Me* (see Fig. 6.10). At this point Grice no longer used *My* and *Me* in subject position in ways that deviated from adult English. *My* now occurred in conjunction with nouns and, occasionally, other pronominal forms (e.g., *My this*). *Me* occurred in object position, and Grice no longer marked the notion of self as affected agent. Although Grice no longer used the self reference forms in subject position in ways that deviated from adult input, some examples reveal that she was still working on the self reference system. In several of her utterances she employed multiple self reference forms in ways that deviated from adult English. For instance, in one example Grice wanted to stir pretend tea in the toy teapot and turned to her peer, saying, "Don't do me stirring for me!" In another example, her peer had given Grice a plate, which Grice lifted up, saying, "Don't do me my this!" At times, then, Grice still seemed to mark distinct notions about the self with different self reference forms.

Because *I* was the only form used in subject position, a consideration of the way the particular forms linked up with various semantic and pragmatic functions is not helpful. Nevertheless, it is important to point out certain developments with regard to the overall distribution of self reference forms with respect to semantic agentivity ranking and pragmatic control. The changes during Month IV follow the developmental path I have reported from Month I to Month III. More specifically, over the course of the study a gradually increasing proportion of Grice's references to self were coded as ranking high in agentivity. In Month I only 18% of her self reference forms ranked high, whereas in Month IV 48% of such forms ranked high. This is particularly interesting in that the most frequently used self reference form was *I*, which in Month I was primarily (78%) linked with low agentivity. Thus we see that not only did Grice no longer link this form with low agentivity, but in general her talk about the self was fairly equally distributed between high and low agentivity.

With regard to pragmatic function, a similar developmental transition can be noted. In the first month of the study, Grice divided her use of language between several language functions, though most frequently her use of self reference forms linked up with control acts (38%). By the fourth month of the study, Grice showed a clear preference for linking self reference forms

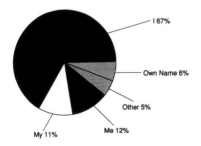

FIG. 6.10. Distribution (%) of self reference forms: Grice Month IV (*n* = 221).

with assertives (68%), whereas control acts accounted for only a small amount (20%) of the utterances containing self reference forms. Thus, although over the course of the study we see a gradual decrease in the linking of specific self reference forms with particular semantic and pragmatic functions, we nevertheless find that there are important developmental changes in the semantic meanings expressed by self reference forms and the pragmatic functions associated with their usage.

In sum, Grice's construction of a system of self reference went through tremendous changes over the course of the study. We saw a rather slow transition from the frequent use of various self reference forms in utterances without verbs to the gradual use of such forms in the context of a verb. In addition, Grice only gradually came to use these forms as in the target language. In particular, in Months I–III we noticed how various forms were found in subject position in ways that deviated from adult English. Thus Grice's construction of an adultlike system was quite gradual. Along the way, the number of units per utterance increased, allowing her greater flexibility in the kinds of resources that could be drawn on. For instance, by Month III and Month IV we see the addition of both modal forms and prepositions. The use of modal forms seemed to permit the marking of various degrees of agentivity and control, because such forms allow the speaker to qualify the intentional stance toward the action described. Also, the onset of prepositional forms provided Grice with more conventionalized resources for expressing the notion of benefactor that previously was marked with *Me* in subject position. As was the case for Jeffrey, there was a complicated web of factors interacting in the developmental reorganization of the self reference system over the course of the study.

CHAPTER SEVEN

Megan

MONTH I

Megan was the youngest child in the study. She was 20 months at the onset of the study and was just beginning to combine words (mean MLU for Month I = 2.07). As was shown in Fig. 4.1, the majority of her references to main participants were about herself at the onset of the study; 86% of references to main participants were coded as self reference. Furthermore, Megan, like the other ego-anchored children, began the study using multiple forms to refer to herself, often in ways that deviated from adult input. These factors led her to be characterized as ego-anchored at the onset of the study.

Megan's distribution of the various forms that she used to refer to herself is outlined in Fig. 7.1. Megan, like Grice, divided her use primarily between three forms. She was the only one of the ego-anchored children to draw regularly on the use of her own name. We see that *I* and *Own Name* were used most frequently, 33% and 32% of the time, respectively. *My* accounted for 23% of all usage and *Me* occurred in 10% of all her references to herself.

The Core Contrast: *I*, *Own Name*, and *My*

As in the case of the other ego-anchored children, I begin the discussion of Megan's use of self reference forms with some examples.

(1) I want that one.

(2) I wanna wear that.

(3) I cried.

(4) I knocked.

132

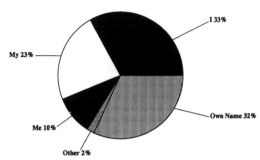

FIG. 7.1. Distribution (%) of self reference forms: Megan Month I (*n* = 91).

(5) Meggy.
(6) Meggy count.
(7) Meggy swinging.
(8) My open that.
(9) My put back.
(10) My want that.

Like the other ego-anchored children, Megan used a variety of self reference forms in subject position. She was the only child, though, who included the use of her own name in the core contrast. As in the previous chapters, I now consider whether there was a principled basis for the selection of various self reference forms or whether Megan simply employed the various forms randomly.

Surface Characteristics. Table 7.1 describes surface characteristics of the various self reference forms. I begin the analysis of the forms by noting that only 53% of Megan's self reference forms were in utterances containing a verb, whereas 42% were in utterances without a verb (see Table 7.1a). The forms differed in frequency of occurrence in utterances containing verbs. *I* was the form that most frequently occurred in such a context; 87% of all uses of *I* were in utterances with a verb. In contrast, *Own Name* occurred only 21% of the time with a verb. *My* was typically used in utterances with a verb (62%), though 38% of all uses of *My* occurred in a verbless context.

Turning to the use of self reference forms in utterances with verbs, we find that all of the instances of *I* and *My* were in subject position (see Table 7.1b–c). *I* was typically found in multiargument utterances (77%), whereas *My* was found exclusively in multiargument utterances when appearing with a verb. *Own Name* typically occurred in contexts without a verb, though when used with a verb it appeared in both subject and object position and was usually found in single-argument utterances.

Table 7.1d outlines aspects of the usage of forms appearing in utterances without verbs. Of interest is the observation that both *My* and *Me* appeared in constructions of the shape *form + noun.*

TABLE 7.1
Distribution of Individual Forms (%) According to Surface Characteristics
(Megan Month I)

(a) Verb / Verbless Context

FORM	With Verb	Without Verb	Uncoded	Subtotal*
I	87	10	3	(30)
My	62	38		(21)
Me	11	77	11	(9)
Other	100			(2)
Own Name	21	69	10	(29)
Subtotal*	(48)	(38)	(5)	(91)

(b) With Verb: Position

FORM	Subject	Object	Uncoded	Subtotal*
I	100			(26)
My	100			(13)
Me		100		(1)
Other	100			(2)
Own Name	50	33	17	(6)
Subtotal*	(44)	(3)	(1)	(48)

(c) With Verb: Argument Structure

FORM	Single Argument	Multiargument	Uncoded	Subtotal*
I	23	77		(26)
My		100		(13)
Me				
Other	50	50		(2)
Own Name	67	33		(3)
Subtotal*	(9)	(35)		(44)

(d) Without Verb: Context

FORM	+Noun	Alone	Other	Subtotal*
I	67		33	(3)
My	88		13	(8)
Me	43	29	29	(7)
Other				
Own Name		50	50	(20)
Subtotal*	(12)	(12)	(14)	(38)

* (Raw numbers).

Semantic Characteristics. From the start it should be noted that only 53% of all uses of self reference forms involved utterances containing verbs; thus, only a little more than half of Megan's self reference forms were coded in terms of the semantic characteristics of agentivity. This was also true for Grice. With this in mind we can consider the semantic characteristics of the core self reference forms.

A combined analysis of all uses of self reference forms reveals that Megan's forms tended to occur in utterances that ranked low in agentivity. Only 21% of the utterances containing these forms ranked high. Thus all three children spent most of their time talking about self in the context of low agency.

The question remains whether particular forms were employed contrastively to express particular degrees of agentivity. An analysis of the core forms in terms of their agentivity rankings can be found in Fig. 7.2. In keeping with the general trend, the use of *I* tended to link up with the expression of low agentivity; 92% of all uses of *I* were coded as ranking low. A similar pattern was found for Megan's use of *Own Name*. Of the uses of this form coded in terms of semantic agentivity, 83% ranked low. *My* was the form that was most frequently associated with high agentivity. 39% of the coded instances of *My* ranked high. In fact, of all the instances of self reference forms coded as ranking high in semantic agentivity, 50% were instances of *My*. The other 50% of the forms were scattered instances of the individual forms. Examples (1)–(4) illustrate this patterning of the data. Even when Megan employed an action verb like *knock* in example (4), it was an instance of an activity verb, and the utterance referred to an ongoing activity conducted by an actor, rather than an action conducted by an agent. Most typically, though, the examples with *I* referred to inner states of the child rather than activities.

The use of *Own Name* also has been noted to link up primarily with a low degree of agentivity. Examples like (6) and (7) are typical of Megan's

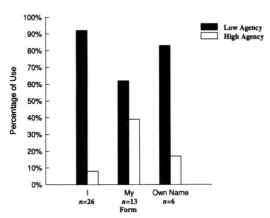

FIG. 7.2. Distribution (%) of self reference forms in terms of semantic agency: Megan Month I.

use of *Own Name*. In contrast to *I*, *Own Name* never occurred in subject position with a mental state verb. That is, we never find instances such as *Megan want some*; instead, the use of *Own Name* typically occurred with activity verbs that were neither very kinetic nor telic.

My was the self reference form that rank both high and low in terms of semantic agentivity. Examples (8) and (9) are instances referring to events involving prototypical agents. We also find instances like example (10), which ranked low in agentivity. Thus *My* was associated with both ends of the agentivity scale.

The following chart summarizes Megan's distribution of the core self reference forms along the agentivity continuum.

(11) AGENTIVITY CONTINUUM
       High   Mid   Low
       My   *Own Name*   *I & My*

In order to uncover the organising principle underlying the use of both *I* and *My* in utterances ranking low in agentivity, we need to consider other levels of analysis.

Pragmatic Characteristics. An analysis of the pragmatic function of Megan's utterances containing self reference forms reveals that Megan used such forms primarily in utterances that served an assertive function. More than half of the uses of self reference forms (54%) were coded as assertives. In contrast, only 28% were coded as control acts, and 13% were multifunctional. The function of Megan's self reference forms as a whole looks most similar to that of Jeffrey's at the onset of the study.

When one considers the core self reference forms, we find some indication that the individual forms linked up with pragmatic functions (see Fig. 7.3). For instance, the majority of uses of *I* were coded as assertives (60%),

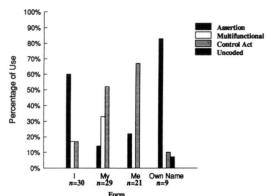

FIG. 7.3. Distribution (%) of self reference forms in terms of pragmatic function: Megan Month I.

whereas 34% of the uses were divided equally between control acts and multifunctional utterances.

The pattern is somewhat similar for the use of *Own Name*, to the extent that 83% of such uses were coded as assertives, whereas only 10% were coded as control acts. Although it appears as though *I* and *Own Name* both occurred in a similar pragmatic context, closer examination reveals that the kinds of assertives referred to with each form did differ. *I* tended to occur in conjunction with utterances that asserted plans and intentions Megan had for the immediate future when control was not at issue. In addition, these utterances referred to previous or timeless happenings. In contrast, the use of *Own Name* linked up with assertives that were coded as serving a naming or identifying function. *My* occurred most frequently in utterances that functioned as control acts (52%) or multifunctional utterances (33%). Very few instances of *My* linked up with assertives (14%).

The pragmatic contrasts between utterances containing the different self reference forms can be best illustrated through an examination of some examples in context. I first consider the use of *My* in control acts and then turn to an examination of the use of the other two core self reference forms in assertives.

(12) Megan (M) and mom (MM) are playing with manipulative toys.
    a. M: I want that one. (as lifting childproof container)
    b. MM: Oh you want that one, okay.
    c. M: (Tries to open container) My open that.
    d. MM: What?
    e. M: My open that, Mommy. (handing container to MM)
    f. MM: Wanna open that?
    g. M: Yeah.

In this example, we find the use of *My* linked up with a directive. Megan, after trying to open the childproof container without success, tried to solicit her mother's assistance. In line (12e) we find a particularly clear example of a directive. Megan not only included a vocative to elicit her mother's attention but also gave the container to her mother. In line (12g) we find that Megan's attempts were successful. In this example, Megan used *My* in a control act where she attempted to get her partner to bring about change. The following example reveals that Megan also used *My* in control acts in which her own actions were dominant.

(13) Megan (M) and mom (MM) are playing with blocks and a toy helicopter.
    a. MM: Who's in there? (looking in window of helicopter)
    b. M: (looks in window) Ba.

c. MM: Looks like a fireperson. A fireman.
d. M: Uh. (putting hand out to take helicopter) My a see the fireman. (taking hand back)
e. MM: You wanna what?
f. M: (extends hand out and then takes it back) My see the fireman. (looking at helicopter)
g. MM: You wanna see the fireman?
h. M: Yeah.
i. MM: (points to fireman and explains that he is painted on and cannot be removed)

In particular, Megan's hand movements in lines (13d) and (13f) suggest that the child was seeking permission to see (have?) the fireman. It was thus her own action that was dominant in this control act.

The most frequent occurrence of *My* appeared in control acts with joint action focus, specifically in disputes over ownership and enactment of actions.

(14) Megan (M) and Grice (G) are playing tea party with manipulative toys.
a. G: Pour it out. (pouring with teapot)
Ga saups. (=got cups)
Ga saups. (=got cups)
(takes cupcake papers M has been using)
b. M: My cups. (trying to grab back)
c. G: My! (struggling with M)
Let her share. (M is taking control of papers.)

Such occurrences took place only in the peer sessions. In these cases Megan typically coupled the use of *My* with the name of the object she wished to control. Often struggles between the peers terminated only when the researcher intervened.

The rather dynamic quality of *My* can be contrasted with the use of *I* in assertives. In example (15), Megan used *I* in conjunction with a statement of her ongoing plans.

(15) Megan (M) plays with blocks, while Grice (G) looks through the photo-book.
a. M: I 'na pick that up. (as she is leaning under the table to pick up blocks that have fallen)
(sits on floor and collects blocks, making no contact with her peer)

In such instances, the child had already begun the action named. The goal-directed nature of the utterance seems intended not only to inform others of Megan's plans but also to serve a self-regulative function. Such uses can be contrasted with similar ones in which Megan's utterance functioned more as a directive to inform her partner not to engage in the activity. In such instances we find Megan keeping eye contact with her partner. As predicted, such uses occurred in conjunction with *My* rather than *I*.

The use of *I* has also been noted to occur in the reporting of previous states and actions:

(16) Megan (M) and mom (MM) are looking at pictures of children at a pumpkin patch in photo album.
   a. MM: Did we trick or treat?
   b. M: Yeah.
   c. MM: To the door?
   d. M: Yeah.
   e. MM: (knocks on door)
              What did ya say?
   f. M: I knock.
   g. M: You knocked. And then what did you say?
   h.   (After a brief pause MM offers a prompt to M, who finally answers, "Trick or treat.")

These reports tended to take place in the context of looking through the photo-book. They were not references to depicted actions, and often what the child was reporting was a part of speech routines exercised between mother and child. The child's focus in line (16f) was less on her actual role in carrying out knocking behavior than on things one does when going out to trick or treat.

Most frequently the use of *I* appeared in statements of ongoing desires.

(17) Megan (M) and mom (MM) are cleaning up blocks. M has dropped several blocks on floor and MM has gotten angry.
   a. MM: Can you get that one that fell underneath the table?
   b. M: (M is under the table.)
   c. MM: Can you find it?
   d. M: # Yeah. (standing up)
   e. MM: There we go, okay.
   f. M: I want that block. (bending down again)

The use of *I* in line (17f) was linked to a context in which the child was already en route to the desired object and there was no indication that control was at issue. At this point we are in a better position to account for the distinction between the use of *I* and that of *My* in subject position in utterances with state verbs ranking low in agentivity. The following example involving the use of *My* received the same semantic agentivity rating as did (17f), which involved the use of *I*.

(18) Megan (M) and mom (MM) are playing with manipulative toys.
  a. M: Ah ga Mommy. (reaching for container)
  b. MM: Ah that's a container.
  c. M: My that. (touching another container near MM)
  d. MM: What's in there? (MM holds it up and M takes it.)
  e. M: My want that. (reaching for other container)
  f. MM: (switches M's focus back to clear container)

As was the case with the other ego-anchored children, the use of *My* in utterances ranking low in agentivity and expressing states linked up with Megan's attempts to get assistance. Thus the uses of *I* and *My* that ranked low in terms of semantic agentivity can be distinguished in terms of pragmatic function.

Finally, we can compare the assertives using *Own Name* in acts of naming and identifying with the assertives noted to link up with *I* and the more dynamic uses of *My*. Instances of the use of her own name often occurred in the context of reading the photo-book.

(19) Megan (M) and mom (MM) are looking through the photo-book.
  a. MM: And who's that with the red coat on?
  b. M: Meggy.
  c. MM: Is that you?
  d. M: Yeah.
  e. MM: Say, "That's me."
  f. M: That me.
  g. MM: Right!
  h. M: That a Meggy.

What is particularly interesting about example (19) is that although Megan correctly labeled the picture of herself to the extent that she was depicted in the picture, her mother was not content with Megan's use of her own name and requested that she use the pronominal form *Me*. Although the child repeated the utterance that her mother requested, note that Megan switched back to her own name one turn later.

Megan's use of *Own Name* was not limited to contexts in which she labeled photos of herself. The following example shows that she used this form when pointing out objects that belonged to her.

(20) Megan (M) and mom (MM) are playing with manipulative toys.
  a. M: Rocking chair. (pointing to chair in the corner of the room)

b. MM: A rocking chair yeah. A rocking chair. Whose car seat is
        that? (pointing to a car sear in corner)
c. M: Meggy's. (laughs)
d. MM: (laughs) Right. It's yours.

In such uses control was never at issue. The utterance served a referential
function. This kind of usage contrasts with the use of *My* in example (14b),
where Megan attempted to grab back cups from her peer, stating, "My cups."
The use of *My* linked up with issues of control where possession was up
for negotiation (i.e., centered around the toys the researcher brought),
whereas the use of *Own Name* occurred in referential contexts where reference to possessions was ongoing (see Deutsch & Budwig, 1983).

This analysis of the three core self reference forms reveals clear distinctions
between the kinds of pragmatic contexts in which they occurred. At this
point, I turn to a combined analysis of semantic and pragmatic aspects of
use of these three forms.

Core Field of Use and the I, Own Name, and My Contrast. A
combined analysis of semantic and pragmatic characteristics would not be
particularly revealing, for two reasons that have been noted earlier. First,
just over half (53%) of all references to self were coded for semantic characteristics because only these were in utterances with verbs. A second reason
such an analysis would not be particularly helpful is that Megan so rarely
referred to events ranking high in agentivity. For this reason, I simply pull
together the findings from the separate levels of analysis, considering each
of the three core self reference forms.

For Megan, the use of *I* linked up with the expression of actions ranking
low in agentivity or with the expression of ongoing states. Such utterances
functioned pragmatically as assertives that most frequently informed her
communicative partner of her intentions or plans to act in particular ways.
At times, *I* also functioned to motivate or give reasons for actions Megan
undertook. In cases involving *I* Megan typically was acting on her own.

Own Name was not typically used in utterances that received an agentivity
ranking. What was central to the use of this form was the child's labeling
of pictures or objects, either to identify them or distinguish them from others.
Neither control nor agentivity were related to these uses.

For Megan, the use of *My* (like that of *I*) often linked up with the expression of ongoing states. These uses can be distinguished from seemingly
similar examples with *I* because the uses of *My* occurred in utterances that
functioned pragmatically as control acts. When reference was made to highly
agentive acts, the *My* form was employed. Thus Megan also linked *My* with
both high agentivity and control acts. I have noted that *My* linked up with
two kinds of control acts. When interacting with her caregiver, Megan often

employed *My* when she attempted to direct her mother to play an instrumental role in helping her reach particular goals. When Megan used *My* with her peer, it tended to link up with disputes over control. What holds these distinct uses of *My* together is their role in bringing about change. In all cases Megan was attempting to use language to bring about a change in the world.

Other Self Reference Forms

As was revealed in Fig. 7.1, Megan's use of the core self reference forms accounted for 88% of all usage of self reference forms. The remaining 12% included *Me* (10%) and *We* (2%). Because the instances of *We* were few and varied they are not discussed further. In this section I focus exclusively on the use of *Me*.

Surface Characteristics. *Me*, like *Own Name*, occurred primarily in utterances without verbs. There was only one example of *Me* used in an utterance with a verb: *Let me make a tower.* The uses of *Me* in a verbless context were divided between use alone (*Me!*), with a noun (*Me airplane*), or in predicatives (see Table 7.1 for review). Because there was only one instance of *Me* coded at the semantic level, I turn to pragmatic factors guiding the use of this form.

Pragmatic Characteristics. At the level of pragmatic function, we find that *me* occurred primarily in control acts (see Fig. 7.3 above). In one of the two instances of *Me* used in an assertive, Megan's mother had actually prompted her to say, "That's me" (see example (19f)); and thus the child's use was not spontaneous. In fact this use was the only instance of *Me* that occurred in the context of the caregiver-child interactions; all the others occurred when she was playing with her peer. I also should note that 33% of the uses of *Me* centered around control of one particular object, namely, the helicopter in the block task. Such uses tended to occur as the child was en route to or just beginning to use an object. In most cases, her peer was acting on the object as well. In all instances involving *Me*, the child seemed to have a double focus: On the one hand, the child referred to her desire to be in control of an action or object, whereas on the other, focus was placed on the child as the (conscious) goal of a transaction (cf. Givón, 1984a). In the cases of both *My* and *Me*, control was at issue, though the perspective was slightly distinct. In the instances involving *My* the child viewed herself as an agent who had the right to initiate change such that she gained or maintained control, whereas with the utterances involving *Me* the child acted more as a conscious goal of or one benefiting from a transaction. The following example, when compared to the earlier examples involving *My*, illustrates this distinction:

(21) Researcher (R) is setting up the block task for Megan (M) and Grice (G). Note that (R) has left toy helicopter on the desk though usually it is on the tray with the blocks.
a. R: You guys gonna build?
b. M: Yeah.
c. R: I'll put some blocks here.
d. G: (starts taking blocks off tray)
Uh. (reaching over blocks)
Helicopter. (removing hand from tray)
e. M: Me airplane. (looking at tray)
Me airplane.
f. G: 'Copter me 'copter.
g.   (Children start to build, R returns with helicopter.)

Note in this example that the children were not actually trying to claim the helicopter in the sense that it was not present. In similar instances where the helicopter was present, they used *My*. What this implies is that they used *Me* more in the sense of 'to me the helicopter.'

MONTH II

During Month II, Megan had a mean MLU of 2.30. Even though she showed an increase in word combinations, in her references to main participants she continued to focus almost exclusively on herself; 88% of her references were coded as about self. With regard to her use of self reference forms, we find major changes in her system. Although in Month I she used multiple self reference forms to refer to herself, in Month II this pattern changed. As we see later, Megan now relied primarily on *I*. Although this was noted as one of the characteristics of the nonego-anchored children, it is significant that aspects of her use of self reference forms deviated from the target system.

Figure 7.4 illustrates the distributional pattern for the various self reference forms during Month II. Although in Month I Megan had a fairly even distribution between *Own Name* and *I*, in Month II, *I* accounted for 59% of all self reference usage. At this point *Own Name* was used only 24% of the time. Even more interesting is the dramatic decrease in use of the form *My* from 23% in Month I to only 9% in Month II. Neither *Me* nor any other forms were used with any frequency.

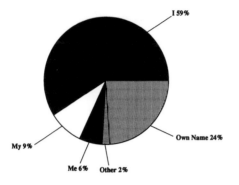

FIG. 7.4. Distribution (%) of self reference forms: Megan Month II (n = 85).

Because there were major distributional changes in the self reference forms at this point, we can question whether these forms also changed in terms of the functions associated with their use. I turn now to such a consideration.

The Core Contrast: *I*, *Own Name*, and *My*

Surface Characteristics. One of the major changes with regard to surface characteristics was that Megan now used the self reference forms more regularly with verbs (see Table 7.2a). Although in Month I only 53% of all self reference forms were in utterances with verbs, by Month II 67% of all forms occurred with verbs. Nevertheless, Megan did not use all of the forms with verbs. She had a fairly neat system: *I* was used in utterances with verbs, and *Own Name* was used in utterances without verbs. The other forms were rarely used, though when they were, *Me* was used mostly with verbs in subject position in multiargument sentences, whereas *My* occurred in utterances with and without a verb. What is interesting is that although in Month I Megan used *Me* in object position, this form appeared exclusively in subject position when used with a verb. *My* was used in subject position alone and in object position in a possessive construction, suggesting the possibility that these represented two distinct constructions for Megan at this point in time (see Table 7.2b).

Semantic Characteristics. Megan continued her pattern of talking about self as low in agency during Month II. Seventy-three percent of all her self reference forms in utterances with a verb ranked low in agency. As the following examples reveal, the use of *I* tended to occur in utterances ranking low in agentivity. These uses involving low agentivity rankings typically referred to desired states:

(22) I wan(t) another hot dog.
(23) I wanna see it.
(24) I wanna open it.

TABLE 7.2
Distribution (%) of Self Reference Forms According to Surface Characteristics
(Megan Month II)**

(a) Verb / Verbless Context

FORM	With Verb	Without Verb	Uncoded	Subtotal*
I	94	6		(51)
My	50	50		(8)
Me	80	20		(5)
Own Name	5	86	10	(21)
Subtotal*	(67)	(31)	(2)	(85)

(b) With Verb: Position

FORM	Subject	Object	Uncoded	Subtotal*
I	100			(48)
My	75	25		(4)
Me	100			(4)
Own Name	100			(1)
Subtotal*	(98)	(2)		(57)

(c) With Verb: Argument Structure

FORM	Single Argument	Multiargument	Uncoded	Subtotal*
I	15	85		(48)
My	25	75		(4)
Me		100		(4)
Own Name		100		(1)
Subtotal*	(8)	(49)		(114)

(d) Without Verb: Context

FORM	+Noun	Alone	Other	Subtotal*
I		33	67	(3)
My		25	75	(4)
Me			100	(1)
Own Name		28	72	(18)
Subtotal*		(7)	(19)	(26)

* (Raw numbers).
** This table excludes two instances of other.

Example (24) illustrates that the use of *I* could also link up with a high agentivity ranking. When *I* was used in utterances ranking high (such as example 24), it tended to be used in conjunction with the quasi-modal form *wanna*; rarely would one find instances such as example (25):

(25) I eat your foods.

Very little can be said about the semantic rankings of the other self reference forms used by Megan in Month II. The three examples of *My* that were coded for agentivity appeared in different surface contexts and show no unified semantic pattern. There was no longer evidence that *My* was used in the two semantic contexts outlined for Month I. Similarly, there was only one instance of *Own Name* coded for semantic agentivity; and thus one could conclude only that Megan no longer used her own name in conjunction with activity verbs, as was the case in Month I.

Pragmatic Characteristics. An analysis of the relation between particular self reference forms and pragmatic function reveals that during this month Megan used language primarily for its assertive function. Of all her utterances containing self reference forms, 70% were coded as assertives, whereas only 17% were coded as control acts. Thus from Month I to Month II we find a decrease in the frequency at which Megan used self reference forms in attempting to bring about changes; language took on a more representational function. With these general changes in mind, we can turn to an analysis of the particular self reference forms.

Figure 7.5 illustrates the relationship between the various forms and their pragmatic function. The distributional pattern for *I* looks fairly similar to that of Month I. Megan continued to use *I* primarily in assertives (65%), and control acts accounted for only 18% of all self reference. There were no real changes from Month I to Month II in terms of the function of utterances containing the self reference form *I*. The function of utterances containing *Own Name* also did not change; in Month II, *Own Name* continued to be used in assertives (86%), and only rarely was this form used in a control act. The functional distinction between these two forms was primarily the same as in the first month of the study. *I* linked up with the expression of ongoing states, whereas *Own Name* was found in the context of naming and identifying the self, most often in the photo-book activity.

Where we see the most substantial changes in Megan's self reference system with regard to language function is with the form *My*. Recall that in

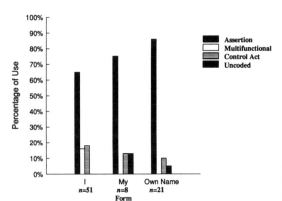

FIG. 7.5. Distribution (%) of self reference forms in terms of pragmatic function: Megan Month II.

Month I, Megan used this form primarily in control acts. Fifty-two percent of all uses of *My* during Month I were coded as control acts. In contrast, in Month II we find only one example of *My* used in a control act. First, it is important to remember that there was a dramatic decrease in the overall use of *My* during Month II; and second, Megan now used *My* primarily in an adultlike way in conjunction with a noun (i.e., *My mommy hair is blond* vs. *My see a fireman*). It is of interest that the single use of *My* in subject position occurred in a dispute over control.

(26) Megan (M) and mom (MM) are playing with manipulative toys, pretending to make food. M has said she has a cup of cottage cheese.
   a. MM: Okay. I'll have some. I'd like some please. (pretends to take some, then starts to place spoon in M's cup)
   b. M: My gonna xxput/bitexx my cottage cheese. (pulling cup back and placing spoon in it)

This example reveals that at times, *My* retained something of its previous core field of use. Nevertheless, in the same session we find *My* + *noun* combinations in utterances functioning as assertives.

Core Fields of Use. Given that neither *Own Name* nor *My* were noted to link up with particular degrees of semantic agentivity, it is not worth pursuing a combined analysis of the agentivity and the pragmatic function. We should consider, though, a distinction said to guide the contrastive use of *I* and *My* in Month I. It was noted that in Month I, Megan contrasted *I want x* and *My want x* to highlight different perspectives on her role in the action frame. When *I* was used, Megan herself was en route to the goal, and her utterance was said to provide motives for her actions. In contrast, *My* was employed in a similar utterance context when she needed assistance to achieve a goal. In Month II we find Megan making use of a different categorization scheme. *I* was now used in both of these contexts. *I* took over what was previously marked by the *I/My* contrast. The use of *My* was mixed. Megan rarely used this form, and when she did it appeared in a variety of sentence contexts and was linked neither to a particular degree of agentivity nor to a pragmatic function. What is most interesting here is that Megan's strategy seemed to be one of avoiding control acts and the form noted to be associated with them during Month II.

Other Self Reference Forms

Before concluding the discussion of Month II, I briefly consider the use of the only other self reference form to occur, namely, *Me*. Although its use was infrequent (6% of all uses of self reference forms), it reflected another view taken by Megan on action sequences. The following examples illustrate its use.

(27) Me gonna built.
(28) Me no want this xx on over xx. (whispering)
(29) Me no want xx to play here xx. (whispering)
(30) For me more nuts.
(31) Me do it.

All of these examples contrast with those containing *I* to the extent that they do not provide motives for other actions, nor do they have the self-assertive quality of many of the utterances containing *I*. In the cases containing *Me*, the child did not seem to take any responsibility for the happenings being described. Example (27) was uttered as Megan approached the table where the researcher had set out the blocks; and similarly, example (30) was uttered as the researcher brought over more nuts for the children to play with while using the manipulative toys. Examples (28) and (29) were uttered by Megan as she wandered off from the play table, expressing her lack of desire to play with the toys. Although the examples are few, one can nevertheless speculate that the child took a more distant view of her role in not wanting to continue the activities provided, de-emphasizing herself as the seat of control, and focusing more on such feelings arriving into her consciousness. In all of these examples, it appears that Megan was referring to events for whose occurrence she did not view herself as the sole responsible force. In the discussion of Months III and IV, I further consider the development of this form.

MONTH III

Megan continued to be ego-anchored in Month III of the study. Her mean MLU was 2.52; there were no dramatic increases from Month II. With regard to the proportion of her references to main participants that referred to self, we find a decrease from 88% during Month II to 69% in Month III. Thus even during Month III, much of Megan's talk was about herself. Finally, we can note that Megan's distribution of forms remained similar to that discussed for Month II. She continued to use a variety of forms, though she usually depended on *I* (see Fig. 7.6). Notable changes in Megan's distribution of the various self reference forms included a slight decrease in the use of her own name and an introduction of some new forms, *We* and *Mine*, neither of which were used with enough frequency for me to examine functional aspects of their use.

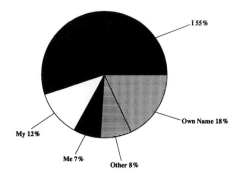

FIG. 7.6. Distribution of self reference forms: Megan Month III (*n* =
76).

Surface Characteristics. Table 7.3 depicts the distribution of the various self reference forms in terms of surface characteristics. During Month
III we continue to find an increase in the proportion of self reference forms
appearing in utterances with verbs. During Month II 67% of all uses were
in utterances with verbs, whereas in Month III 79% were. Furthermore, we
find that *I* continued to appear almost exclusively in utterances with verbs,
whereas *Own Name* typically appeared in utterances without verbs. Though
My and *Me* were not used frequently, they tended to appear in utterances
with verbs. Table 7.3a summarizes these findings. *I* appeared exclusively in
subject position in multiargument utterances. In contrast to Month II, where
Me was used in subject position, in Month III we find the few instances of
Me typically in object position, with the single exception of the utterance
Me scared. My typically appeared in object position as well and was used
as part of a possessive construction; there were only a few instances of
preverbal *My,* and one of these appeared in conjunction with *I* in a way
noted for Jeffrey: *I m'ant that. Own Name* occurred primarily in a verbless
context in which the child was referring to photos of herself. Thus the uses
of the various pronominal forms were becoming more conventionalized in
Month III.

   Semantic Characteristics. During Month III we find an increase in
the overall proportion of Megan's uses of self reference forms ranking high
in agency. In Month II, only 20% of all uses ranked high, whereas in Month
III Megan's uses ranked high in agency 30% of the time. I now consider the
way the individual forms linked up with agency.
   Figure 7.7 depicts the distribution of uses of self reference forms with
respect to the degree of agentivity expressed. Again I should point out that
there were very few instances of any of the forms other than *I,* and thus
my discussion focuses on this form only. First, note that *I* was used primarily
in utterances ranking low in agency, though we find an increase in the
number of instances of *I* ranking high. In addition, note that unlike the case
in Month II, where Megan's instances of *I* in utterances ranking high in

TABLE 7.3
Distribution (%) of Self Reference Forms According to Surface Characteristics
(Megan Month III)**

(a) Verb / Verbless Context

FORM	With Verb	Without Verb	Uncoded	Subtotal*
I	98	2		42
My	78	22		9
Me	80	20		5
Own Name	21	79		14
Subtotal*	(79)	(21)		(70)

(b) With Verb: Position

FORM	Subject	Object	Uncoded	Subtotal*
I	100			41
My	29	71		7
Me	25	75		4
Own Name		100		3
Subtotal*	(44)	(11)		(55)

(c) With Verb: Argument Structure

FORM	Single Argument	Multiargument	Uncoded	Subtotal*
I	5	95		(41)
My	14	86		(7)
Me	50	50		(4)
Own Name	33	67		(3)
Subtotal*				

(d) Without Verb: Context

FORM	+Noun	Alone	Other	Subtotal*
I		1		(1)
My	1		1	(2)
Me			1	
Own Name		73	27	(11)
Subtotal*				

* (Raw numbers).
** This table excludes six instances of other.

agency included a modal form (*I gonna open that*), in Month III there were instances of the sort *I knock it down* and *I make a cake*. In this sense *I* was becoming more multifunctional.

Pragmatic Characteristics. The general analysis of the pragmatic function of utterances containing self reference forms reveals that the patterns observed followed a developmental course noted in Month II. In Month III we continue to find a gradual decrease in the proportion of self reference forms

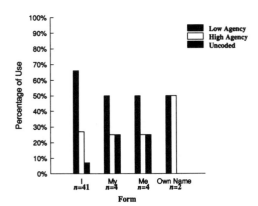

FIG. 7.7. Distribution (%) of self reference forms in terms of semantic agency: Megan Month III.

used in control acts. Although in Month I Megan's use of self reference forms in control acts accounted for 28% of all use of self reference forms, in Month III such usage accounted for only 12%. We simultaneously find a gradual increase in the proportion of self reference utterances that functioned as assertives. By Month III, 72% of all uses of self reference forms served this function.

The analysis of the relationship between particular self reference forms and specific language functions lends no evidence for the claim that Megan contrasted the forms in terms of pragmatic function (see Fig. 7.8). All forms were found primarily in assertives, and at this point no specific linkages were apparent. It is of interest that the utterance *I m'ant that,* cited earlier, occurred as the child struggled over control of a toy with her peer. Recall that in Month II, such a dispute led to the use of *My* in subject position. Although Megan no longer retained *My* in subject position and instead employed *I* in this example, we find traces of the old marker of control in this utterance. This sort of gradual fading has also been noted in the other children's systems.

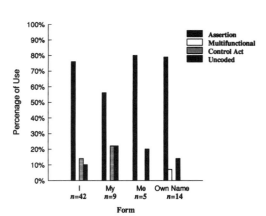

FIG. 7.8. Distribution (%) of self reference forms in terms of pragmatic function: Megan Month III.

Core Fields of Use: I conclude this section with a brief summary of the core fields of use of each form. *I* continued to be the primary self reference form, and it was used most frequently when Megan provided motives for why she or others acted or should act in particular ways. It also appeared in assertions about accomplishments. Generally, this form was used to refer to the inner feelings and evaluations of the speaking subject. *Own Name* appeared when Megan was labeling pictures of self, and *My* occurred in a variety of contexts, almost exclusively in possessive constructions. *Me* tended to appear in object position, referring to the receiver or the location of action.

MONTH IV

In Month IV Megan continued to be categorized as ego-anchored. Her mean MLU was 2.58. And though I noted a decrease in the overall proportion of references to self as main participant in subject position in Month III, references to self rose to 81% of all references in Month IV. With regard to the overall distribution of self reference forms (see Fig. 7.9), we find a pattern that looks more like that of the nonego-anchored children. *I* continued to be the primary self reference form used. In addition we find that the use of *Own Name* decreased to only 9%, and finally we see Megan beginning to add new forms into the system. Ten percent of all uses of self reference forms were coded as *Other*; 75% of these other uses involved the word *mine.*

Surface Characteristics. Table 7.4 summarizes distributional aspects of the various self reference forms during Month IV in terms of surface characteristics. There were few changes to note. The basic difference was that *I* was the only form used in subject position. Both *Me* and *My* were used in object position, and *My* was always used in possessive constructions. Thus Megan's use of pronominal forms no longer deviated from the target

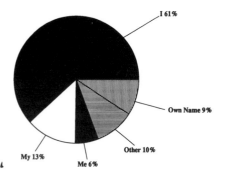

FIG. 7.9. Distribution (%) of self reference forms: Megan Month IV (*n* = 77).

TABLE 7.4
Distribution (%) of Self Reference Forms According to Surface Characteristics
(Megan Month IV)**

(a) Verb / Verbless Context

FORM	With Verb	Without Verb	Uncoded	Subtotal*
I	45	1		(46)
My	2	7	1	(10)
Me	5	1		(6)
Own Name		7		(7)
Subtotal*				

(b) With Verb: Position

FORM	Subject	Object	Uncoded	Subtotal*
I	45			45
My		2		2
Me		5		5
Own Name				
Subtotal*				

(c) With Verb: Argument Structure

FORM	Single Argument	Multiargument	Uncoded	Subtotal*
I	5	40		45
My		2		2
Me	1	4		5
Own Name				
Subtotal*				

(d) Without Verb: Context

FORM	+Noun	Alone	Other	Subtotal*
I		1		(1)
My		7		(7)
Me		1		(1)
Own Name	2		5	7
Subtotal*				

* (Raw numbers).
** This table excludes eight instances of other.

language in ways noted in previous months. *Own Name* was never used in constructions with verbs.

Semantic Characteristics. The major difference between Month III and Month IV for Megan involved the frequency with which her references to self ranked high in agency. Whereas in Month I only 21% of all uses of self reference forms coded for agentivity ranked high, by Month IV 51% of the utterances coded for agentivity ranked high. This change was most dramatic for the form *I.* In Month I, 92% of all uses of *I* coded for agentivity ranked low, whereas in Month IV only 41% ranked low and 55% ranked high. Thus in Month IV we find that Megan employed *I* most frequently when referring to herself as an agent who brought about change.

(32) I open this.

(33) I did it.

(34) I put (th)em back now.

The use of the other self reference forms in the context of utterances with verbs was too infrequent to make discussion of patterns meaningful; only 17% of all uses of self references forms coded for agency did not involve the use of *I.*

Pragmatic Characteristics. The patterns for the coding of pragmatic function did not change much between Month III and Month IV. The minor changes followed the overall pattern noted for Month III; there continued to be a small decrease in the proportion of utterances containing self reference forms coded as control acts (10%), and a slight increase in the number of utterances coded as assertives (78%). Figure 7.10 depicts the relation between the particular self reference forms and various language functions. Several forms linked up with assertives, ruling out the kind of one-to-one mapping noted earlier in the study.

Although several of the forms were now multifunctional, it is interesting to contrast how Megan expressed control acts in Months I and IV. In Month I, I noted that *I* and *Own Name* occurred in different kinds of assertives and that *My* was used primarily in control acts. What was interesting in Month IV was that Megan now recruited a full range of forms for a wide range of control acts. For instance, requests soliciting permission were used

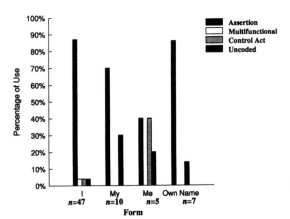

FIG. 7.10. Distribution (%) of self reference forms in terms of pragmatic agency: Megan Month IV.

with *I* (*I do a nut, okay*), and requests for assistance occurred with *Me* (*Could help me?*), whereas the newly introduced form *Mine* occurred in disputes over ownership. Control acts previously tended to co-occur only with *My*, but now several different forms were used to express different kinds of control acts. Thus, although in Month III, I noted that Megan's strategy en route to the adult system differed from Jeffrey's to the extent that she went through a phase of minimal use of control acts and avoidance of the form *My* that was said to link up with control acts, in Month IV we find exactly the sort of hierarchical integration and differentiation of forms so characteristic of Jeffrey's system. I return to this issue in the concluding section of this book.

Core Fields of Use of Self Reference Forms. By Month IV of the study, I noted that Megan had created a system of self reference in which the forms could be distinguished across multiple levels of analysis. This contrasts with her early system, in which each form linked up with a semantic and a pragmatic category dealing with agentivity and control. By Month IV, Megan no longer used a variety of self reference forms in subject position. She tended to rely on a single form, *I*; and she used this form when reporting her ongoing involvement as an agent in actions, as well as when reporting internal states. *Own Name* continued to be used in acts of labeling, primarily when referring to actions and possessions depicted in photographs. *My* was employed exclusively in possessive constructions. *Me* appeared in object position marking self as recipient of actions-at times in the contexts of requests.

In conclusion, although Megan's MLU and the proportion of her references to self categorized her as ego-anchored, other evidence indicates general signs of a burgeoning ability to talk about self in relation to other. For instance, during this month Megan began to employ regularly the prepositions *for* and *with*. *For* appeared when Megan expressed her role in carrying out actions for another's benefit (*I open this for you*). *With* was used as a marker of coparticipation (*I go to the zoo with Sandy*). Thus, Megan was slowly developing other linguistic resources to talk about her involvement in action fields in more complex ways. Such devices, though restricted to the self, represented the first steps toward being able to situate others in action fields as well. One finds a similar integration of a range of linguistic devices for talking about self in relation to other and reference forms to refer to other in the other ego-anchored children as they became nonego-anchored. I consider the three nonego-anchored children in the next chapter and return in the final section to a discussion of common characteristics of the ego-anchored children's development of systems of self reference.

CHAPTER EIGHT

The Nonego-Anchored
Children

The nonego-anchored children included Eric (28 months), Keith (31 months), and Thomas (32 months). At the onset of the study all three had a mean MLU over 3.0. Several other factors led to the conclusion in chapter 4 that this group of children was linguistically more advanced than the ego-anchored children. The nonego-anchored children could be distinguished from the three ego-anchored children in that: (a) in their utterances they referred almost as often to others as to themselves (see Fig. 4.1), (b) they relied primarily on a single self reference form *I*, and (c) their use of self reference forms did not deviate from the target language in the ways noted for the ego-anchored children. Because the findings for the nonego-anchored children were so similar, I consider the children jointly, noting along the way any major individual differences. I begin this discussion with a reconsideration of the general distribution of self reference forms for the three children at the onset of the study.

The nonego-anchored children made use primarily of one self reference form. In contrast, the ego-anchored children used several self reference forms with fairly equal frequency. For each of the nonego-anchored children one finds a second form (or set of forms) that was used with some regularity, although far less frequently than the dominant form. All three of the nonego-anchored children relied on the second most frequent self reference form, *We*. As is indicated in Fig. 8.1, Eric used *I* 65% of the time and used *We* 10% of the time, with *Own Name* being used 8% of the time. Keith relied on *I* 56% of the time and used *We* 21% of the time. Finally, Thomas employed *I* 60% of the time, whereas he used *We* 15% of the time. In the sections that follow I first examine the basis on which the nonego-anchored children

156

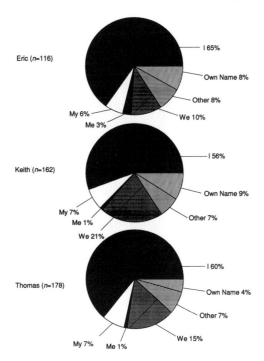

FIG. 8.1. Distribution of self reference forms: nonego-anchored children.

contrastively employed *I* and *We*. I then examine these children's use of other forms of self reference.

THE CORE CONTRAST: *I* AND *WE*

One might want to suggest that the use of *I* and that of *We* can be distinguished in terms of the conceptual distinction between singular and plural. That is, it would seem likely that when the children employed *I* they were referring to actions or states involving the self, whereas the use of *We* would link up with references that were being made to both self and other. An analysis of all instances of the use of *I* and *We* provides only partial support for this claim. All utterances containing the form *We* have been coded in terms of whether reference was made to an independent happening or a joint one. The use of the term *happening* is meant to be neutral with regard to whether reference was made to states, actions, or activities. If the children were contrastively employing *I* and *We* on the basis of a distinction involving plurality, one would expect that the use of *We* would link up with the expression of joint happenings. Figure 8.2 summarizes the findings of this analysis. We find that although the children often did employ *We* in the context of reference to joint happenings, 40% of the uses of *We* involved references to what was coded as an independent happening.

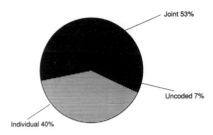

FIG. 8.2. Distribution of *We* in terms of individual or joint agency: nonego-anchored children ($n = 72$).

Given that the nonego-anchored children were not drawing a distinction between *I* and *We* based simply on plurality, the question becomes: On what basis were the children contrastively using these forms? I begin to answer this question by examining the relationship between the core forms and the semantic and pragmatic dimensions noted to guide the ego-anchored children's use of self reference forms. I do not review findings from the analysis of surface characteristics because the two core forms were used primarily in utterances with verbs, and in subject position, by all children; and the sort of deviations from the target language noted for the ego-anchored children were not found for this group of children.

Semantic Considerations

The discussion of semantic characteristics begins with an assessment of the semantic characteristics of utterances containing self reference forms, regardless of the particular form employed. We find that all three children were more likely to refer to self in utterances that ranked low in agency; 62% of all self reference forms ranked low in agency, whereas 37% ranked high. This distribution is quite similar to that reported for the ego-anchored children toward the end of the study (see Budwig & Wiley, in press).

Turning to an analysis of the individual core reference forms, we can ask whether the two forms differed in their agency rankings. Here we find support for the claim that they did differ. Figure 8.3 shows that *I* tended to rank low in agency, whereas *We* was slightly more likely to rank high than low. It is important to note that although this finding held for all three children, there were large distributional differences with regard to the form *I*. Although all three preferred *I* in utterances ranking low in agency, the frequency of occurrence ranged from 83% of the time for Keith to 55% of the time for Thomas (see Fig. 8.4).

Recall that when the ego-anchored children's use of the various self reference forms did contrast in terms of semantic agentivity, *I* was always the form most likely to occur in utterances ranking low in agentivity. It is interesting that although the nonego-anchored children did not seem to link form and meaning, as did some of the ego-anchored children, there are tendencies reflected in the nonego-anchored children's corpora suggesting

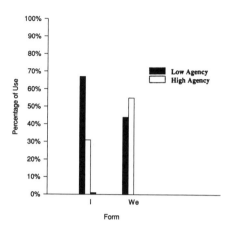

FIG. 8.3. Distribution (%) of self reference forms in terms of semantic agency: nonego-anchored children (n = 310).

that *I* was more likely than *We* to occur in utterances ranking low in agentivity. Taken together, the analyses provided here suggest that the contrastive use of *I* versus *We* was not based solely on an assessment of semantic agentivity. At best, the use of one form or the other can be viewed as related to the notion of agency reviewed here. I report further explorations into this issue after I consider the other coding dimensions.

Pragmatic Considerations

The trends with regard to the coding of pragmatic force are similar for the various nonego-anchored children. Overall, all three of the nonego-anchored children used language primarily in utterances containing self reference forms, to make assertions about the world. Two of the children (Eric and Thomas) used assertions 69% of the time. The other child, Keith, used language to make assertions about the world 80% of the time. The analysis of pragmatic force indicates that the nonego-anchored children used lan-

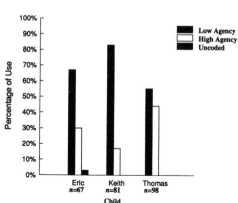

FIG. 8.4. Individual differences in use of *I* in terms of semantic agency: nonego-anchored children.

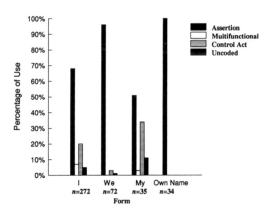

FIG. 8.5. Distribution (%) of self reference forms in terms of pragmatic function: nonego-anchored children.

guage to make assertions about the self more frequently than did any of the ego-anchored children.

The question remains whether the core self reference forms linked up with specific pragmatic functions. Figure 8.5 shows that both *I* and *We* tended to occur with assertions, though there were distributional differences between the two forms. *I* occurred with control acts 20% of the time as well, whereas *We* almost exclusively (96% of the time) occurred with assertions. Thus, as was the case for our analysis of semantic characteristics, we find that there are not any one-to-one mappings between form and function, though there are some indications that the two forms were distinguished with regard to pragmatic force.

Core Field of Use and the *I/We* Contrast

I have presented evidence that the core self reference forms *I* and *We* differed, though the two forms could not be distinguished solely on the basis of an analysis of semantic and pragmatic characteristics of the utterances containing these forms. I now attempt to unravel the core field of use for each of these forms, beginning the analysis of the contrast between these forms by appealing to some examples of the utterances containing *I* and *We*.

(1) Eric: I wanna pee.
(2) Eric: I'm gonna crash.
(3) Eric: Can I put it on?
(4) Keith: I don't know.
(5) Keith: I push it down.
(6) Keith: I want the helicopter.
(7) Thomas: I don't like that on there either.
(8) Thomas: I wanna take this off.
(9) Thomas: Can I use your thing for a minute?

(10) Eric: We gonna build a bridge.
(11) Eric: We are going to turn this on. (talking about microphone)
(12) Eric: We're riding bikes. (referring to a photo)
(13) Keith: We're gonna build big castle.
(14) Keith: Now # we should # um # put the people xx xx right put one to bed.
(15) Keith: We are playing in some grass. (referring to photo)
(16) Thomas: Yeah we should # build a little # city in here.
(17) Thomas: What we do is take some of that see # with this #.
(18) Thomas: We're putting grass in this. (referring to photo)

Rather than beginning with preestablished categories of the sort described earlier, the present analysis is guided by a form out approach. The question is framed in terms of how utterances differed from those involving the use of *I*. Four distinctions have been noted, and I briefly discuss each.

In the earlier discussion of semantic characteristics, I noted that *We* was more likely to occur in utterances ranking high in agency, though both *I* and *We* were used by the nonego-anchored children in utterances ranking low (see Fig. 8.3). Looking at the examples, though, one finds very few examples of *We* with stative verbs. Figure 8.6 reveals results from an analysis of all the instances of the forms *I* and *We* that ranked low in agency, in terms of whether they co-occurred with state or activity verbs. *I* tended to occur with state verbs; 65% of all instances of *I* coded as low in agency involved utterances with state verbs. In contrast, of all the utterances with *We* ranking low in agency only 24% occurred in utterances with state verbs; rather, most uses of *We* ranking low in agency occurred with activity verbs that were not highly agentive.

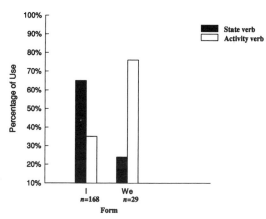

FIG. 8.6. Distribution (%) of forms coded as low agency in terms of verb type: nonego-anchored children.

Differences in the distributions of *We* and *I* go beyond verb semantics. A second important co-occurrence pattern concerns the relationship between form and activity task. Recall that the children were asked to play with manipulative toys and blocks and look through a photo-book. An analysis of the use of form by activity task reveals that 35% of the uses of *We* clustered during play with blocks. At first glance, this is surprising, because play with the manipulative toys and play with building blocks would be equally likely tasks for the form *We* to appear in. Only 22% of all uses of *We* were found in play with manipulative toys. As was mentioned in chapter 3 in the discussion of the method, the reason both play with blocks and play with manipulative toys were selected is that they elicit different kinds of talk about action. I suggested there that play with manipulative toys encourages talk about ongoing action, whereas play with blocks elicits much talk about plans and goals. We see later that this distinction plays a role in the contrastive use of *I* and *We*.

A third interesting distinction previously noted regarding the use of *We* is that it often appeared in stretches of discourse that could not be characterized as involving joint action. That is, all three children used *We* when referring to their own independent actions (see Fig. 8.2). These three levels of analysis can be linked into two predominant patterns. I now consider these clusters.

One set of uses of *We* involves utterances that referred to joint activities in the photo-book task. A second grouping consists of uses of *We* that referred to independent accomplishments in the context of block play. In essence, we have two related uses of *We*. The first use of *We*, that which tended to appear in talk during the photo-book task, appeared when the children referred to pictures describing themselves and other(s) engaged in depicted action. For instance, in example (12), Eric referred to a picture of several children (including himself) riding bicycles by saying, "We're riding bikes." Similarly, Keith referred to a picture of Thomas and himself outside in the school yard by saying, "We are playing in some grass" (see example (15)). In contrast, the second use of *We*, that found primarily in the block session, tended to occur in reference to goal-directed behaviors the children were performing independently.

The major question is how the uses of *I* and *We* can be distinguished. One use of *We* can clearly be distinguished from *I* simply by saying the distinction depends on a notion of plurality. That is, when the children referred to themselves and others in joint reference they employed the form *We*, and when they referred to themselves alone they used the form *I*. But this account would need to be modified for two reasons. First, the uses of *We* involving joint reference tended to occur only when they were talking about depicted action; and second, I have noted that the children often used *We* in reference to independent action. The question becomes, then: How can the uses of *We* in reference to independent action be distinguished from uses of *I* in reference to independent action?

A more careful examination of the examples involving *I* and *We* in reference to independent action reveals two other points of contrast. First, the uses of *We* often co-occurred with time and manner adverbials. One finds that utterances with *We* also included *now*, *then*, and *first*, whereas the utterances with *I* rarely did. Another feature distinguishing the use of *I* and *We* is that *We* frequently co-occurred with particular modal forms referring to obligations (i.e., *should*, *hafta*) as motives for future actions. In contrast, the use of *I* with action verbs often did not involve modal forms.

At several different levels of analysis, the use of *I* and that of *We* can be distinguished. The co-occurrence patterns at each of these levels can be linked together at a higher level of analysis into broader activity frames. Just as was the case for the ego-anchored children's use of various self reference forms, the nonego-anchored children's use of *I* and *We* in reference to independent actions linked up with different clusters of notions organized around prototypes. *I* accompanied physical object play structured around action sequences in which talk referred to the child's desire to manipulate particular objects or to the child's actual manipulations, regardless of the degree of agentivity expressed. In contrast, *We* referred to independent action in sequences in which physical object play was organized around a plan. In such cases, an action was referred to that was part of a broader action sequence leading to an independent or jointly conceived goal. The motive for the action described transcended the individual's subjectivity. Although the child might carry out the action involved, it is as if the child distanced himself from taking full responsibility for the action. The action carried out was conducted in accordance with a plan for the achievement of a goal.

The following examples illustrate the contrastive use of *I* and *We* when referring to goal-directed actions.

(19) Keith (K) and mom (KM) are playing with toy people who can be placed on small bicycles.
    a. K: These are babies. They need to stay on that (be)cause they are resting in their beds. Their daddy is on his bicycle and he-/ I am gonna take their daddy off his bicycle.
    b. KM: Good idea.
    c. K: Umm (.) I cannot get him off!
    d.   (pulls man off bicycle)
    e.   There!

(20) Keith (K) and mom (KM) have been building structures with blocks. K lifts helicopter.

a. K: Look what I d& did.
b. KM: Opp. Did you close off the propellers?
c. K: Yeah.
d. KM: Did you put it away for the night?
e. K: No.
f. KM: No. (laugh) Don't be silly Mom.
g. K: We should. (pause) We should, um um, put the people
         out of it. Put one to bed. (holds plane looking at people
         inside, then places block flat on table)
h. KM: You gonna put them to bed?
i. K: Yeah (.) because they're crashed into a rock.

Note how, in example (19), the child's decision to take the daddy off his bicycle was not part of a broader activity frame. The decision seemed to be made as the child was manipulating the toys. Many of the uses of *I* were, in fact, in announcements of action sequences that were not conforming to the children's desires. For instance the statement *I cannot get him off* was uttered as the child actually tried to get the figure off the bike.

In contrast, *We* in example (20) was employed in the context of the child's descriptions of his plan of what needed to be done. Even his mother interpreted his action as part of an independent plan. In line (20h), Keith's mother did not respond by saying *We can do that* or the like but, rather, allowed the child to continue on his own. In this example, as in the others involving the use of *We* in reference to independent actions, the child's reference to a particular action can be contextualized as part of a broader sequence. This can account for several of the features noted to link up with the use of *We*. For instance, the use of time and manner adverbials in conjunction with *We* would follow if the child were referring to steps in a scripted sequence. It also would follow that *We* would occur more frequently in play with blocks, because block play often elicits talk about goal-directed action, and that *I* would occur in the manipulative activity task, because this task was noted to elicit more talk about immediate action descriptions. Note that it is, of course, possible for the forms to occur in other tasks. We see in example (20) that the child used both *I* and *We*. In line (20a), the child reported on an action he had just completed—an action that in fact was unplanned—and here we find that the child used the predicted form *I*. Thus, the use of *I* and *We* does seem to involve a contrast (see also Nelson, 1989). Although both are found in reference to independent actions being carried out by the speaker, *We* seems to have been used as a kind of marker of impersonal agency. The child indicated that although he was the instigator of the action referred to, the motive was not personal desire but, rather, broader goals.

The question remains: To what extent can one find a connection between the two different uses of *We*? I have noted that *We* was not found simply in references to independent actions but also when the child referred to self and other(s) in depicted action. At this point, we have no way of knowing whether the two uses of *We* existed side by side as independent form–function clusters, or whether the children saw some overarching connection between the two. It seems at least possible that the connection for the child was that the references to self and other in depicted action were also viewed as downplaying a notion of volition. The children might have been referring to self and other as actors rather than as agents, the distinction being that an actor is an animate participant, whereas reference to agency carries with it an implication of volition and responsibility. These data, though, are inconclusive. We can conclude simply that although the uses of *I* and *We* at times looked quite similar, there seems reason to believe that the children used these forms contrastively.

OTHER SELF REFERENCE FORMS: *MY, ME, OTHER,* AND *OWN NAME*

The Use of *My*

In considering each of the ego-anchored children I noted that *My* played a central role in the core contrast for each of the three children. One major difference between the ego-anchored and nonego-anchored children was that the nonego-anchored children rarely used *My*. One can nevertheless examine the core field of use of this form for the nonego-anchored children. My analysis shows that, by this point in development, the nonego-anchored children did not seem to link this form up with either high agentivity or a particular pragmatic force. The distinction between this form and the other self reference forms can be accounted for largely in terms of surface characteristics.

With regard to surface coding we find that *My* appeared in clauses with and without verbs. When appearing in utterances with verbs, it tended to be used in object position; and in such instances, *My* always modified a noun (e.g., *Now your bicycle crashes my bicycle*). When *My* was used in subject position it typically occurred in conjunction with a noun (e.g., *My tree trunk fell down*). Only once did Keith use *My* in subject position followed by a verb (*My don't know*). In contrast to the ego-anchored children, we find that the nonego-anchored children did not employ *My* in subject position in a way that deviated from adult input.

Turning to a consideration of the semantic level of coding, I examine whether the nonego-anchored children tended to use *My* with clauses expressing a particular degree of agentivity. In contrast to the ego-anchored children, there is no indication that the nonego-anchored children reserved the use of *My* for the expression of high agentivity. There was no preference among the nonego-anchored children for using *My* in utterances ranking either high or low with regard to semantic agentivity.

With regard to pragmatic function, there also does not appear to be a one-to-one mapping between use of the *My* form and pragmatic control. Recall that the ego-anchored children used *My* primarily in control acts. As is shown in Fig. 8.5, the nonego-anchored children used *My* primarily in assertions, though they also used it with control acts. More specifically, 34% of all uses of *My* were in control acts, whereas 51% of all uses of this form were in noncontrol acts. The finding that there was a slight preference for noncontrol acts relates to the general finding that the nonego-anchored children's language was more frequently coded as noncontrol acts.

The basic finding, with regard to the nonego-anchored children, is that their use of *My* was not linked with the semantic and pragmatic features, as was noted to be the case for the ego-anchored children. The nonego-anchored children did not use *My* in subject position in a way that deviated from English input. The use of *My* by the nonego-anchored children appears to be like that of adult speakers of English—the nonego-anchored children used it as a possessive pronoun.

The Use of *Me*

The use of *Me* was similar to the use of *My* by the nonego-anchored children in two ways. First, in contrast to some of the ego-anchored children, the nonego-anchored children did not use *Me* in subject position in a way that deviated from the adult English input they received. In addition, the use of *Me* did not link up with the specific semantic and pragmatic properties of agentivity and control that were coded. Nevertheless, the use of *Me* can be related to particular perspectives the children took on their role in action frames and to the way the children situated the self in stretches of discourse.

The following list includes all uses of *Me* by the three children in the first month of the study. Although the instances were not frequent, they nevertheless reveal some patterns:

(21) But I want that mine on me. (referring to microphone)

(22) Can you do some for me?

(23) You make a house with me.

(24) Mama, will you come outside with me?

(25) They don't look black to me.

(26) Me is a tray.

(27) This is what me and Lily did.

(28) Take me for a ride in the car. (singing)

(29) Yeah he gave me a piggyback ride.
(30) Can you help me put this um thing in his hand?

Most of these examples can be grouped together in terms of the case role of dative-"a conscious participant or recipient in events or states" (Givón, 1984a, p. 126). The uses of *Me* with prepositions expressed a relationship between the child and the action frame, and it was the role of the particular preposition to qualify this relationship. For instance, in example (22) the self acted as a kind of benefactor, whereas in examples (23) and (24) the self was viewed as a coparticipant (cf. Foley & Van Valin, 1984; Givón, 1984a, for further discussion of coagency and the use of *with*). A second use of *Me* is illustrated in examples (28)–(30). In these examples, *Me* was a dative/benefactive object that had been promoted to the direct object slot, thereby losing the prepositions indicating semantic case role. Whether the children's placement reflected a discourse-based strategy to promote second-ary topics or instead conformed to a general tendency in English to promote dative-benefactive objects remains a question for further empirical study.[1]

One can question whether the use of *Me* more generally reflected an underlying discourse-based strategy to take a particular perspective on the self. Considering example (27), we can question why the child did not select the *I* form (e.g., *This is what Lily and I did*). It could be that the choice of *Me* was related to the speaker's focus of interest. The switch in form could indicate that such information was nonfocused (see Zubin, 1979, for a more complete discussion of the relation between case marking and focus of interest). Looking at the context of example (27) helps clarify this distinction, as revealed in the more extended example (31):

(31) Researcher (R) brings over tray of blocks to table where Thomas (T) and Keith (K) stand.
   a. R: Look at this.
   b. K: (inaudible)
   c. R: You guys can build. (placing blocks on table)
   d. T: This is what me and Lily did.
   e. R: Yeah.

In line (31d), focus was placed on the building activity. Although this ap-proach remains speculative, it is interesting to relate (31) to reports of Bellugi (1971) and Brown (1973) concerning Adam, Eve, and Sarah's occasional use

---

[1]In a study of English texts, Givón (1984b) found that in two-object clauses, dative-bene-factive objects rarely appeared as indirect objects (only 16%) and, rather, tended to be promoted to direct object (84%), whereby they lose their semantically relevant case markers (e.g., *Tell her a story* vs. *Tell a story to her*).

of "pronouns designed to serve as surface objects, as 'nominative' pronouns or subjects" (Brown, 1973, p. 141). Bellugi (1971) noted that in such instances the the child transposed an adult utterance into a question. This is illustrated in the following sequences taken from Bellugi (1971, p. 100):

(32) Adult: I think you broke it.
      Child: Why me break it?
      Adult: You got some chocolate on it.
      Child: Why me get some chocolate on it?

According to Bellugi, at this phase, the child employs a strategy whereby reference to self in utterance-initial position is marked by *I*, whereas elsewhere within utterance boundary reference is marked with *Me*. Brown (1973) noted similar errors but offered no explanation for them. An alternative suggestion is that the selection of *I* versus *Me* is in part related to discourse factors having to do with focus. If self is not in focus then the child switches to *Me*. For the time being this must remain an empirical question. More examples need to be gathered, perhaps via elicitation techniques, to disentangle the alternative accounts.

In summary, I have noted that all three children used the form *Me* to refer to self as conscious participant. Like the ego-anchored children, the nonego-anchored children attempted to use this and the other self reference forms to situate the self differently in action frames. In addition, the nonego-anchored children used *Me* in utterances that de-emphasized the self's agentive characteristics. Focus was placed instead on the consciousness of the self in receiving and benefiting from action. In contrast, though, to the ego-anchored children's solutions, we find that the nonego-anchored children also attempted to coordinate the relationship between self and other in relation to action. For instance, issues of coagency now came up. In addition, we find that the use of *Me* may, perhaps, relate to broader discourse strategies involving focus of interest.

The Use of *Own Name*

As can be seen in Fig. 8.1, 8% of all uses of self reference forms involved the child's use of *Own Name*.[2] That the nonego-anchored children still employed such a form is rather surprising given that many studies of early grammatical development have noted that by this phase of language development, the use

---

[2]I do not provide a full discussion of other self reference forms used by the nonego-anchored children. Several groups of forms were used, including *mine(s)*, *let's*, first person plural forms (*us*, *our*), third person forms (*he*, *his*, *they*). I integrate into the present discussion the use of third person forms. The reader can find a more complete discussion of the other forms of self reference in Budwig (1986).

of *Own Name* has given way to the employment of pronominal forms (cf. Bellugi, 1971; Brown, 1973, among others). It may be that the use of this form is limited to a context not included in such previous studies.

In many ways the use of *Own Name* by the nonego-anchored children looked quite similar to that of the ego-anchored children. All 34 examples occurred in the context of photo labeling. Some examples from each of the children illustrate this:

(33) E: Eric.

(34) E: Here's Eric and Jeffrey.

(35) E: And that's Eric on a motorcycle without his hands.

(36) K: This is Keithy and this is Thomas.

(37) K: There's Keith under Thomas.

(38) K: I see Keithy talking.

(39) T: And Thomas.

(40) T: Thomas getting down.

(41) T: Thomas with a tennis ball.

Such instances often occurred in the context of question–answer routines, and frequently these utterances were accompanied by a pointing gesture. The use of *Own Name* rarely occurred with verbs; instead it occurred alone or in combination with deictic terms. At times, stative information was also given. Example (38) is particularly interesting, because we find double reference to the self. Keith referred first to himself as speaking subject with the pronominal form *I* and then to self depicted in the photo with the nominal form *Keithy*.

Although at first glance the nonego-anchored children's use of *Own Name* looks similar to that of the ego-anchored children, there are some important differences. Recall that one of the ego-anchored children, Jeffrey, at times employed the pronominal form *Me* in reference to photos. The nonego-anchored children also used pronominal forms at times in their references to the photos, but they never once employed first person singular forms, instead using *he*, *his*, *they*, *we*, and *our*. These pronominal forms appeared in a different discourse context from *Own Name*. All three nonego-anchored children relied on the various pronominal forms when they went beyond picture labeling and gave picture descriptions or short narrations about the photos. The following examples illustrate this usage:

(42) Keith (K) and mom (KM) are looking at the photo-book.

  a. K: I see Keithy talking. (pointing to photo)

  b. KM: And Keithy is talking?

  c. K: Yeah. They bumped heads. (pointing to same photo)

(43) Thomas (T) and Keith (K) are looking at photo-book with the researcher (R).
  a. T: Thomas getting down. (patting page)
  b. R: Thomas getting down, uhhuh.
  c. T: What's he gonna get?
  d. R: What do you think? I think it looks like he's doing something.
  e. K: He's gonna get a shovel. (looking at R)
  f. R: Umm that's a good guess.
  g. T: Maybe he's gonna get a tennis ball.
  h. R: Umhmm. Wanna turn the page?

In these examples, the children initiated reference to themselves with the use of *Own Name*, whereas they maintained reference to self with a first person plural or a third person form. For instance, in example (42), the form *Keithy* is found in line (42a), whereas the child referred to the actions of his peer and himself with *they* in line (42c). Likewise, in example (43), Thomas first labeled the photo with the nominal form (see line (43a)), and he sustained reference with the form *he* in lines (43c) and (43g).[3]

The question can be raised: Why did the children come up with this system? In particular, why did they exclude first person singular forms when talking about depicted self and why did they rely on either first person plural or third person pronominal forms? Although answers to these question deserve further examination, one can speculate that the nonego-anchored children reserved the use of the first person singular pronominal forms for the reporting of highly agentive or experiential events of the speaking subject. The use of first person singular forms seemed to be reserved for subjective accounts. It is intriguing that the first person plural form *We* could occur in reference to both ongoing and depicted experiences.

SUMMARY AND DISCUSSION

The discussion of the nonego-anchored children's use of various pronominal forms has pointed up ways in which the children's use of these forms more closely approximated use in the target system. Nevertheless, we have also seen that the children's use appeared different from that in adult English in certain respects. Likewise, the nonego-anchored children's use of self refer-

---

[3]The use of nominal and pronominal shifts in the proto-narrative descriptions of the nonego-anchored children presents an intriguing correspondence with the use of such forms as cohesive devices in later narratives about nonself protagonists (cf. Bamberg, 1987; Karmiloff-Smith, 1981).

ence forms shared both similarities and differences with that of the ego-anchored children. I now consider these similarities and differences.

The nonego-anchored children's use of self reference forms was similar to the ego-anchored children's in two respects. First, like the ego-anchored children, the nonego-anchored children linked the use of particular forms with a function cluster. The use of the forms was not arbitrary but, rather, motivated by various functional features. A second and related similarity between the two groups of children concerns the interrelationship between the uses of various forms. Not only did all six of the children link the use of forms with particular functional clusters; in addition, such form–function pairings were related to one another as part of a broader functional system. For example, I noted that all of the children made use of a core contrast of forms that linked up with a related set of functions. Thus all children constructed systems, rather than simple form–function pairings.

Despite these general similarities, the nonego-anchored children differed from the ego-anchored children in several important ways. First, I noted that none of the nonego-anchored children regularly used a variety of self reference forms in subject position in ways that deviated from adult input. That is, the nonego-anchored children never used *My* or *Me* as a subject pronoun. Thus, from the standpoint of the target language, the nonego-anchored children's use of forms was grammatically correct. Nevertheless, an analysis of functional aspects of self reference forms did reveal ways in which the target language and the nonego-anchored systems differed. The importance of this is that it shows that correct grammatical use need not be equated with a system that corresponds with adult usage. The difference between the ego-anchored systems and the nonego-anchored systems is more complex than a distinction between erroneous and error-free usage. Each group of children constructed systems of form–function contrasts, and what differed between the two groups was the specific nature of these contrasts.

The basic distinction between the ego-anchored and nonego-anchored systems of self reference is that the nonego-anchored children's systems were less tied to concrete action. I have noted that the ego-anchored children divided up the use of several self reference forms to mark various degrees of agentivity and control. In contrast, the nonego-anchored children used one and the same form when referring to various degrees of agentivity and control. For instance, I have noted that the use of *I* linked up with both agentive and nonagentive reference and was found both in control acts and in less dynamic descriptive language. Although the nonego-anchored children were less concerned with marking various perspectives on the self's role in concrete action frames, the notion of agentivity nevertheless played a role in the systems of self reference they developed. Rather than marking the concrete relation between act and self as participant, they were more likely to mark distinctions such as the underlying motives and intentions guiding action (i.e., in the contrastive use of *I* and *We*), and the relationship between concrete action and participant and the more general discourse context (i.e., switching focus of interest with the use of *Me*).

To close this section, I briefly consider whether, then, the nonego-anchored children used the self reference forms as markers of agentivity and control. Although I have pointed up some evidence that the use of particular forms (i.e., the contrast between *I* and *We*) was linked with notions of agentivity, albeit in a more complex relationship than in the case of the ego-anchored children, the analysis of other self reference forms (i.e., *My*) provides no evidence that agentivity and control played an organizing role. What seemed to be going on was a process of old forms integrating new functions, and new forms taking on old functions (see Slobin, 1973; Werner & Kaplan, 1984). That is, forms that previously were regularly employed to mark agentivity and control at this point are not, whereas newly introduced forms such as *We* function to mark distinctions related to agentivity and control.

What also is relevant is that simultaneous to aspects of development with regard to self reference forms, was the development of a variety of linguistic systems that have been noted to mark aspects of agentivity in the target language. For instance, the nonego-anchored children could now be said to be developing a system of case marking that cut across person; and they regularly employed prepositions, many of which qualified the relationship between participant and action. In addition, the nonego-anchored children made use of modal forms, which have been noted by Gerhardt (1990) to relate to an orthogonal dimension involving motives guiding agency. One more system coming into play at this point was that of voice. The children, through the use of voice contrasts, were able to take various perspectives on scenes that could, for instance, enhance or downplay agency (see Budwig, 1990). Although I am not concerned here with the specifics of the development of these systems, the important point is that such developments provided the children with a full range of devices for marking various aspects of agentivity and control. Thus, although the nonego-anchored children seemed, on the one hand, to be moving away from a one-to-one correspondence between self reference form and degree of agentivity and control, the issue of marking various aspects of agentivity and control still was central to the nonego-anchored children.

PART THREE

MECHANISMS OF DEVELOPMENT

The Organization of Linguistic Systems: Forms and Functions in Development

In Part II of this book, I have been concerned with the organization and reorganizations of the use of self reference forms by six children acquiring English as a first language. In this chapter I discuss the joint implications of the various case studies. In the first section, I pull together the separate findings from the various children. I consider two central questions. First, given that the discussion focused on two groups of children, I reconsider the evidence that these groups represent two phases in the organization of self reference systems rather than individual differences. Second, I consider the similarities and differences between the developmental paths traveled by the various children en route to an adultlike system. In the second section of this chapter, I am concerned with various ways to account for the original organizations of form and function by the ego-anchored children; and in the third section, I turn to the question of what leads children to give up their original systems.

In providing answers to these important questions, we see that at present, multiple factors can be noted to play a role in the original organization and reorganization of self reference forms and the functions that they serve. I suggest, in the final section of the next chapter, several avenues of future research that might help explain how various factors motivate the original construction and subsequent reorganization of self reference systems.

THE DEVELOPMENT OF A SYSTEM OF SELF REFERENCE

An Argument for a Developmental Path Between Ego-Anchored and Nonego-Anchored Self Reference Systems

In Part II of this book, I examined the self reference systems of six children, dividing the children into two groups. One group, referred to as ego-anchored, was studied longitudinally; and I argued that all three of these children made special use of self reference forms en route to an adultlike system. In contrast, another group of three children was said to use self reference forms in a way that looked more similar to adult usage. At this point I consider the evidence that these children's usage of self reference forms reflects a continuum of development, rather than the language of two distinct groups of children. That is, I discuss the evidence that by the end of the study the ego-anchored children looked like the nonego-anchored children. My discussion focuses on two issues: (a) the distribution of reference to self and other, and (b) the distribution of self reference forms.

The Distribution of Reference to Self and Other. One of the distinctions between the ego-anchored and nonego-anchored children concerned the proportion of time spent talking about self and others. In chapter 4 I noted that, as a group, the ego-anchored children spent the majority of time talking about themselves as main participants at the onset of the study. In contrast, the nonego-anchored children distributed their talk about self and other more equally. If the two groups of children represent two phases in development, one could expect that as the ego-anchored children became older they should begin to look more like the nonego-anchored children with regard to the distribution of self and other reference forms. In Part II of this book I noted evidence suggesting that this was the case. All three of the ego-anchored children looked more similar to the nonego-anchored children by the end of the study, though there were some individual differences. For instance, by the end of the study Jeffrey looked like the nonego-anchored children with respect to the distribution of self and other references, whereas Grice and Megan still referred primarily to themselves but showed a trend toward more talk about others than evidenced at the onset of the study.

Distribution of Self Reference Forms. At the onset of the study I noted two distinct patterns with regard to the six children's distribution of self reference forms. The ego-anchored group held together to the extent that they made use of multiple self reference forms, often in ways that deviated from the target language. In contrast, the nonego-anchored children relied primarily on one given form. The data reviewed in Part II of the book suggested that the ego-anchored children ended up looking like the nonego-anchored children to the extent that by the end of the study all six of the children relied primarily on one self reference form. In addition, the three ego-anchored children gave up the deviant uses of self reference forms noted at the onset of the study.

Summary. Taken together, the evidence from the longitudinal analyses of the distribution of self and other reference forms, as well as the analyses of the use of particular self reference forms, lend support for the claim that these were not two distinct groups of children—one that began with seemingly adultlike usage and one that built a temporary system. Rather, the separate analyses suggest a developmental route between the two groups of children such that by the end of the study the ego-anchored children looked more similar to the nonego-anchored ones. Whether this pattern holds for all English-speaking children is an empirical question (see later comments on future directions).

Similarities and Differences in the Ego-Anchored Children's Organization and Reorganization of Self Reference Systems

Much of Part II involved the detailed examination of the paths traveled by the three ego-anchored children en route to the more nonego-anchored systems of self reference. At this point I consider whether the children as a group showed any similarities in the sorts of developmental changes that took place en route to an adultlike system, or whether each child differed in the sorts of organizations and reorganizations that took place. I consider first the similarities and differences in the original organizations of the systems and then the subsequent reorganizations. Finally, I consider whether the individual pathways traveled share a common principle.

The Original Organizations. At the onset of the study I noted that all three ego-anchored children made use of multiple self reference forms to refer to themselves, and all three used these in ways that deviated from the adultlike system. Furthermore, in contrastively employing these forms, the children all drew upon a common core set of notions having to do with agency and control. Nevertheless, as was pointed out in Part II, there was a certain amount of variation between the ways in which the original systems were organized by the three children. Grice contrasted primarily between three forms of self reference. The majority of her utterances did not include verbs, and her self reference system involved primarily a fairly simple contrast between various pragmatic functions. *I* appeared primarily in assertions, *My* appeared in utterances about the self involving control, and *Me* appeared in both control acts and noncontrol acts tending to be aligned with a notion of self as receiver or benefactor.

Megan's original system also seemed to divide forms on the basis of pragmatic function, though she integrated a core set of semantic notions as well into this contrast. For instance, although *I* linked up with assertions, it also occurred in utterances in which self was experiencer, whereas *My* appeared in control acts, though often in utterances that expressed self as agent. Thus, Megan's system differed from Grice's to the extent that semantic agency played a central organizing role in the division between various forms.

Jeffrey's system was the most complicated of the three at the beginning. Like Megan, Jeffrey tied the use of particular forms to related semantic and pragmatic notions. In contrast to Megan's system, with its neat one-to-one mapping between clusters of semantic and pragmatic dimensions (i.e., assertion and experiencer), Jeffrey's system was somewhat more multifunctional. One form, *My*, linked up with both pragmatic control and pragmatic noncontrol, though its usage could be predicted based on semantic agency. *I* was typically found with noncontrol acts involving the expression of self as experiencer.

What was similar about all three children was their attempt to relate surface forms with semantic and pragmatic notions of agency and control. What differed were the specifics of these constellations. I now consider how the children moved from these form-function clusters to more adultlike usage.

The Reorganization of Self Reference Systems. Pulling together the findings presented in chapters 5, 6, and 7, we find three different routes into adultlike systems of self reference. I compare and contrast the two systems that differed most from one another, namely, those constructed by Megan and Jeffrey, and then I relate these two systems to that used by the third child, Grice.

Megan came up with a fairly straightforward way to move from a system of self reference organized around semantic and pragmatic notions to a less contextually driven system. As was noted earlier, and is represented in Fig. 9.1, Megan began with a contrast between three forms, each serving a distinct function. Megan's solution was simply to delete the extra forms and functions during Months II and III of the study. That is, Megan moved from the use of a variety of self reference forms to mark a variety of functions, to a phase in which she relied on one self reference form to talk about one function. During Months II and III Megan avoided using forms such as *My* and *Me*, and when referring to herself she neither used language to control nor made use of action verbs. By Month IV, she began using *I* multifunctionally and at the same time used *My* as a possessive pronoun (correctly) and *Me* as an object pronoun. Simultaneously, in Month IV, we find Megan making use

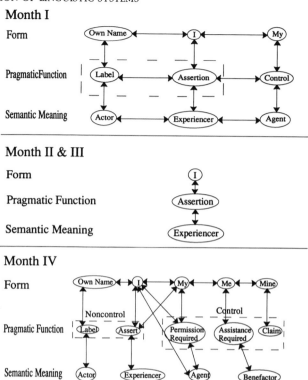

FIG. 9.1. Megan.

of a variety of control acts that linked up with different self reference forms. For instance, she used *I* in requests for permission: *Can I . . . ?*, *Me* occurred in requests for assistance: *Could help me?*, and *Mine* was now used in attempts to claim goods. Thus, Megan's solution to the problem of turning a unifunctional system into a plurifunctional system involved focusing on a particular form–function pair (and avoiding the others) and then suddenly making use of multiple resources.

A second solution was offered by Jeffrey. As is revealed in the analyses in chapter 5, Jeffrey began with a fairly neat unifunctional system. For Jeffrey, the process by which *I* became multifunctional was slow and protracted. Likewise, the deconstruction of the special use of *My* was very subtle and slow. Essentially what we see is Jeffrey trying to find a new functional contrast between *I* and *My*. As is shown in Fig. 9.2, by Month II Jeffrey began using *I* with action verbs but now contrastively employed *I* and *My*, depending on the motive for the action. That is, if the motive for the action was personal desire, Jeffrey employed *My*; and if the motive was an interpersonal or joint agreement, he switched to *I*. By Month III Jeffrey seemed to view *My* more similar to modal forms; here we find him uttering sequences

Month I

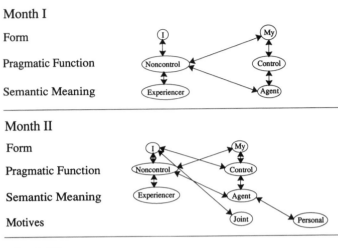

Month II

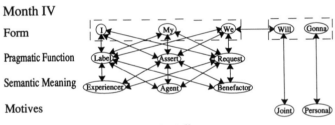

Month III
(Identical to Month II except WE replaces the
functions of MY and MY used as quasi-modal)

Month IV

Form

Pragmatic Function

Semantic Meaning

Motives

FIG. 9.2. Jeffrey.

such as *I m'ant to build a tower.* During Month III, Jeffrey also included new pronominal contrasts in the system, replacing the *I/My* distinction from Month II with an *I/We* distinction. By Month IV, the distinction between joint and personal motivations was marked with modal forms, and *I, My,* and *We* all became multifunctional. Thus Jeffrey went through an extremely protracted period of (a) adding new self reference forms, (b) reorganizing the functional clusters associated with given forms, and (c) adding new forms into the system.

I do not pursue a detailed analysis of the transformations of Grice's system of self reference. What is relevant here is that it integrated aspects of both of the solutions used by Jeffrey and Megan. Like the other children, Grice began with a fairly neat unifunctional system; and like the others, by Month IV *I* was employed multifunctionally. Along the way Grice also added a number of new resources to express previous functions. For instance, although early on Grice used *Me,* often in subject position, to mark the notion of self as recipient (i.e. *Me have airplane*), by the end of the study she said things like *I want the airplane for me*. As with Megan, the fading of *My* as a marker of control was sudden, and its disappearance was marked by the addition of a variety of request and control forms. But as with Jeffrey, *I* became multifunctional in a slow and protracted way. First Grice distinguished between *I* and *My* in terms of two broad pragmatic categories. During the subsequent months, Grice slowly changed this until *I* became multifunctional.

Given the variety of ways the three children moved from unifunctional systems to plurifunctional ones, the question remains whether one can generalize about the transformational process. The answer given here is affirmative. Regardless of the particulars, all three children started with relatively global, contextually restricted uses of forms and moved toward solutions involving hierarchical integration and differentiation. Not only did the children enter a wider range of communicative situations and need to express an increasingly varied set of communicative functions, but they also drew upon a larger array of linguistic resources. This sort of means–ends relationship was introduced into the psycholinguistic literature by Slobin (1973): "New forms first express old functions, and new functions are first expressed by old forms" (p. 184). It was more generally related to developmental changes across domains by Werner (1957) and Werner and Kaplan (1984) as the *orthogenetic principle*.

Before moving on in the next section of this chapter to ask why the children traveled the particular paths that they traveled en route to the adult system, I should emphasize how the approach to development offered here can be distinguished from other approaches. As was pointed out in chapter 1, many previous approaches to development in the child language literature have been concerned with ordering relations between given forms. The developmental-functionalist approach adopted here has been less concerned with the issue of which forms are acquired in which sequence and more concerned with the nature of the form–function pairings throughout ontogenesis.

To this extent, the approach adopted here comes closer to that put forth by Karmiloff-Smith (1979), who was also interested in the developmental transformations between individual forms and functions across development. The major distinction between Karmiloff-Smith's approach and this one is that I view development in light of the orthogenetic principle. Like Karmiloff-Smith, I have noted ways in which the developmental trajectory of an individual subsystem of forms moves from unifunctional to plurifunctional status. In addition, though, the construct of the orthogenetic principle has also allowed me to examine the unfolding of form–form and function–function relationships as well. As was pointed out in the first chapter of this book, the notion of development here is not equated with ontogenesis and is not viewed as a function of the data but, rather, as a construct that the researcher brings to the empirical examination of children's linguistic productions. Thus, although there were many changes in the monthly productions both within and between the children, I have found that the orthogenetic principle serves as a tool in the discovery of underlying similarities between the individual children.

ACCOUNTING FOR THE ORIGINAL ORGANIZATION OF SELF REFERENCE SYSTEMS

Thus far, I have outlined the course of development various children go through en route to adultlike usage of self reference forms. This discussion, though, has yet to grapple with the very important question of why the children organize the systems as they do and the related question of what factors might lead children to give up their original systems and push them to reorganize the systems as they do. Undoubtably, multiple factors influence both the organization and the reorganization of the self reference systems. In this section and the one that follows, I review various proposals that have been offered in the literature, considering such theories in light of the findings reviewed in Part II of this book. I begin the discussion in this section by asking what factors influence the children's original organizations of forms and functions, and I turn in the next section to a discussion of factors influencing subsequent reorganizations.

Maturational Accounts

As was noted in chapter 4, Radford (1990) suggested that children's early case errors can be attributed to their being at a lexical-thematic stage of development. The one significant discrepancy between Radford's account and the data of the three ego-anchored children concerns the use of nominative forms. As I noted, Radford predicted some sporadic use of nominative pronouns at this stage. The difference, though, is that he argued that such usage is nonproductive. There was little evidence that the ego-anchored children's frequent use of the nominative form *I*, was as part of a set phrase. Thus it is unclear how a maturational account such as Radford's would explain the original organization of the ego-anchored children's systems.

Cognitive Accounts

My discussion of cognitive factors that might play a role in the children's organization of self reference systems involves two perspectives. First, I consider the role of general cognitive strategies and second, I compare my findings to Slobin's observations of universal preferences for grammaticizing particular distinctions.

Cognitive Strategies. Undoubtably, the child brings to the task of constructing a grammar a number of general cognitive processing skills. Slobin (1971, 1973, 1982, 1985) referred to such processing strategies as Operating Principles—principles that guide the child's construction of grammar. I do not discuss the particular principles themselves but, rather, suggest that such principles are fundamental prerequisites for the construction of linguistic systems.

In considering the relationship between cognitive strategies and the ego-anchored children's construction of self reference systems, I draw upon related research by Tanz (1974). In attempting to account for the pattern of pronominal case errors found in data she reviewed of English-speaking children's early productions, Tanz appealed to two of Slobin's Operating Principles: (a) avoid exceptions, and (b) pay attention to the ends of units.[1] Tanz used the notion of cognitive strategies to explain patterns similar to the ones created by the ego-anchored children. The specifics of her argument fail to account for the actual patterns reported in Part II and highlight the need to go beyond a simple matching between an Operating Principle and what she referred to as case-marking errors. The basic pattern that Tanz attempted to account for involved the finding that English-speaking children tend to go through a phase of using the accusative pronouns in place of nominative ones, though the same children do not use the nominative forms where an accusative pronoun would be expected. This results in errors of the following sort: *Me a good boy* and *Me do it*.

According to Tanz, the child selects the accusative form as basic because it appears in a greater number of syntactic contexts than the nominative form; and abiding by the Operating Principle *avoid exceptions*, the child adopts the basic form even in subject position. Tanz also noted that because the accusative form tends to occur at the end of constituents, whereas the nominative form occurs at the beginning of constituents, the child could be drawing upon the strategy *Pay attention to the ends of units*, thereby selecting the accusative form as basic.

Tanz claimed that regularities in children's use of pronominal case markers can be accounted for by appealing to the notion of cognitive strategies. Although I am in general agreement with Tanz's proposal, there is an important incompatibility between Tanz's account and the data reported in Part II of this book. Tanz viewed the issue as one of children replacing

---

[1]Although Slobin has elaborated on the Operating Principles since Tanz developed her argument, I do not discuss such changes here because they are not directly relevant to the issues at hand (see Slobin, 1985, for a more recent discussion of his notion of Operating Principles).

nominative forms with accusative ones. The data presented here suggest that the children in this study used both nominative and accusative forms side by side. Because Tanz did not report distributional frequencies, I cannot assess whether this was the case for the children she examined. Given that the children in the present study made use of multiple forms in subject position, her arguments cannot be accepted. Likewise, paying attention to the ends of units cannot be drawn in to explain the frequent use of forms like *My* in subject position, because this form does not appear at the ends of units.

I do not propose general strategies that might better account for the findings but, rather, suggest that a satisfactory account for the original organization of pronominal systems will follow assessment of the ways children draw upon such principles for dealing with the interpretation, storage, and organization of linguistic material in combination with other motivating factors when constructing self reference systems. I now discuss some of the other potential motivating factors that could be working in combination with the Operating Principles discussed in this section.

Cognitive Predispositions. Another way of accounting for the sort of self reference systems constructed by the children would be to appeal to the notion of universal cognitive preferences. Based on evidence stemming from more than 15 languages, Slobin (1985) drew the conclusion that children across the world build similar early grammars. Before grammatical forms are employed in ways that conform with the language being acquired, such forms are first mapped onto a universal set of basic notions. Grammatical markers are first used in conjunction with particular Scenes (Fillmore, 1977) or activity-types. The claim is that the initial meaning categories receiving grammatical treatment by children across the world are minimally influenced by the structure of the specific input language and, rather, reflect universal ways of structuring conceptual material.

Slobin suggested that one of the first scenes to receive grammatical treatment by children acquiring structurally different languages is the manipulative activity scene. As was noted in chapter 1, this scene refers to a basic event in which a prototypical agent brings about a change of state in a patient. I have noted the extent to which children acquiring accusative and ergative languages at first similarly extend the use of accusative and ergative inflections to mark the manipulative activity scene. Striking parallels can be found between such usage and the three ego-anchored children's usage of personal pronouns. The children's use of *My* in subject position has been suggested to mark a notion of prototypical agency, just as the Kaluli and Russian children underextended the use of ergative and accusative inflections. The use of *My* is particularly interesting to the extent that the children have gone beyond the input to grammaticize a particular notion. It seems that children acquiring languages that are strikingly different have all drawn upon something like the manipulative activity scene when first using specific linguistic forms in the earliest phases of grammatical development. The various findings provide striking evidence for Slobin's claims that in the earliest phases of grammatical development children bring with them universal preferences to construct grammar in particular ways.

As striking as such evidence is, we nevertheless should keep in mind some important differences in the findings reported for the various language groups. Two main distinctions are noted here. One central difference between the data reported by Slobin for inflectional languages and that reviewed here is that the American children's marking of the manipulative activity scene has been noted to be limited to self reference. Although the Kaluli and Russian children were noted to mark the notion of prototypical agent, the American children simply marked self as prototypical agent. Another difference between the ego-anchored children and those studied by Slobin concerns the number of distinctions marked by the various children. The Kaluli and Russian children seemed to draw a contrast between prototypical agency and some general form of nonprototypical agency. Yet, in the case studies outlined in Part II, it was noted that the American children employed a range of forms to mark more particular kinds of deviations from the prototypical agency scene.

These differences are important because they point to the need for further research. Analyses would need to be carried out in order to determine the extent to which children acquiring other languages also limit their marking of the manipulative activity scene to self, and to determine the number of distinctions marked regarding prototypical and nonprototypical agency. This is to suggest that the differences noted at present may have more to do with the ways the researchers have approached their data than with differences in the children themselves.

In my discussion of universal cognitive predispositions, I have suggested that children bring to the task of constructing a language a collection of basic notions that they attempt to distinguish at the linguistic level. In formulating his position on Basic Child Grammar, Slobin (1985) suggested that it is the basic notions receiving early grammatical attention that are universal, claiming that the particular forms employed will vary depending upon the input language. With regard to the marking of agentivity and control, as I noted in chapter 2, other researchers have noticed a certain amount of overlap in the types of devices used by speakers of the languages of the world when marking prototypical agency and various deviations. This suggests that children may also be constrained by certain universal tendencies in the sort of forms they select to mark particular basic notions.

With regard to the present findings, we can speculate that the ego-anchored children's contrastive use of first person pronominal forms was influenced by the tendency in many languages to link the expression of degree of control with the use of case-marking contrasts. This suggests that cross-linguistically, one might find that when children create particular distinctions not found in the target language, there are some general patterns in the range of forms selected by children to do so. In the future it would be interesting to assess the extent to which universal preferences might play a role in recruiting particular sorts of formal devices in order to mark linguistically particular scenes or basic notions. Likely choices might include markers of enhanced transitivity, as well as linguistic devices that express the speaker's perspective on the utterance.

Language as a Problem-Solving Space. Karmiloff-Smith (1979, 1983, 1986) suggested that children treat language as a formal problem-solving space. Central to Karmiloff-Smith's position is the issue of what leads the children to go beyond successful input. Based on several empirical studies, Karmiloff-Smith outlined a three-phase sequence of development. Because the framework proposed by Karmiloff-Smith contributes to an understanding of both the ego-anchored children's organization and their subsequent reorganization of self reference forms, I review all three phases and then turn to a more complete discussion of Phase II, which provides a partial interpretation for the original organization of the ego-anchored children's self reference systems (see chapter 1 for further discussion).

Phase I is characterized as a time when the child's productions are guided by external stimuli. These utterances look like those produced by adult speakers of the language community, though Karmiloff-Smith suggested that the child lacks the ability to generalize across form–function pairs. The forms can be thought of as unifunctional homonyms. Thus the representations are stored separately. During Phase II the child works on gaining control of the linguistic representations, organizing them into a kind of subsystem. It is at this phase that the internal representations become the focus of the child's attention. Now the child goes beyond linguistic input, often creating distinct markers for forms that are plurifunctional. The claim is that "the externalization of such surface marking enables the child to keep distinct the functional relationships attached to a common phonological form" (Karmiloff-Smith, 1985, p. 35). At this second phase the child not only draws connections between the various uses of a single form but also begins forming systems of reference.

Finally at Phase III, the child begins to focus again on the sort of input received. Distinctions created by the child but not found in the target language fade out, and the child's speech at the behavioral level looks quite similar to that produced during Phase I, though during Phase III the forms are explicitly related and represented as a subsystem.

Relating Karmiloff-Smith's three-phase model to the data from the ego-anchored children, one can suggest that these three children were functioning at Phase II at the onset of the study. They had broken apart the range of meanings and functions associated with the self reference form *I* into several separate clusters, assigning one pronominal form to each of these clusters. We can interpret the ego-anchored children's nonadultlike usage of self reference forms as part of the children's attempts to render tangible the distinct functions common to the nominative form. This in turn not only allows the child to establish links between a form and its various functions but also represents a first step in the child's linking of various forms into a subsystem. The ego-anchored children's organization of a self reference system can be viewed as part of an ongoing process in which the child attempts to come to grips with language as a system of interconnected units.

Environmental Accounts

Two sorts of accounts that rely heavily on the environment in which the child is raised are now reviewed as potential accounts for why children might organize self reference forms as they do. I first discuss the impact of the input children receive. To what extent were the ego-anchored children's systems a by-product of the input they heard around them? Next I consider potential evidence that the children were sensitive to typological aspects of the language being acquired.

It is noncontroversial to suggest that the children's construction of pronominal systems was partially based on the input they received. I now consider how children's special use of self reference forms might be accounted for by regularities in linguistic input they receive. The specific issue of self reference becomes all the more complex to assess, because the child must grapple with the issue of shifting reference. Even if adult speech directed to these children were highly repetitive, grammatical, easy to process, and closely tied to the ongoing activity frame, it remains unclear how such input might have led the child to (a) untangle the issue of shifting reference, and (b) relate self reference forms with the meanings and functions noted in Part II of this book.

Input. To begin with, we should consider the sort of input concerning self reference that these children received. Did the caregivers similarly distribute their references between self and other? What forms (nominal and pronominal) did they use when talking with the children? Was there any evidence that the caregivers limited the use of particular forms with specific functions? Even if caregivers never produced utterances such as *My did it*, the possibility remains that they reserved the use of the possessive pronoun for emotionally charged acts of control, but used the nominal form *Mommy* referentially.

I begin my analysis of caregiver talk with a consideration of the distribution of caregivers' reference to themselves and their child. All three caregivers referred more to their child than to themselves. The importance of this is that unless the caregivers relied on nominal forms, the children were more likely to receive input involving second person reference forms than first person forms. Examining the forms used, it was found that when referring to their children, the caregivers tended to employ pronominal forms (primarily *you*). Use of the children's names was rare (see also Nelson, 1989). With regard to self reference, caregivers also relied heavily on pronominal forms. *I* was used most frequently, and *My* and *Mommy* were rarely used by any of the caregivers. Such findings reflect interesting differences between the caregivers' input and children's productions. For instance, although Jeffrey used *My* in almost half of his references to self in the first session, his mother never used this form in the same play session. Clearly the distributional patterns noted in Part II for the ego-anchored children did not match those found in their caregivers' data.

We can also consider the relationship between the forms that the caregivers used and the functions they served, examining the extent to which the children's patterning reflected patterning in the speech used by caregivers. An analysis examining form, meaning, and function clusters in the ego-anchored children's caregivers' speech to their children did not reveal any evidence that the caregivers' use of self reference forms was limited to the particular activity-types noted for their children. For instance, all the mothers used *I* in clauses ranking high and low in agentivity, although their children were noted to restrict the use of *I* to clauses ranking low. The functional analysis reveals that the caregivers rarely used any of the self reference forms in conjunction with control acts. When a self reference form appeared in conjunction with a control act, then this tended to be *I* in requests, such as *Can I have a piece of cake?* or *Can I have some tea please?* in the context of pretend play. In addition, the caregivers rarely used *My* in ownership claims or other acts of control. Rather, the use of *My* often functioned to specify information so the child could locate or identify a particular referent in conversations where control was not at issue.

The various analyses concerning caregivers' input reveal that the children were not merely copying the forms they heard in the input around them. Nevertheless, much remains unclear about the specific role that the caregivers' input played in the children's formulations. It is interesting that although none of the caregivers restricted the use of particular self reference forms to a specific semantic and pragmatic cluster, it has been noted that all of the caregivers tended to use *I* in a functional cluster similar to that used by their children (see Budwig, in press). It also can be noted that the caregivers tended to make use of expansions and partial repetitions in dialogues in which the children referred to themselves, and it could be that caregiver input played a role in the children's attempts to deal with shifting reference. It would be important in the future to examine more closely the extent to which adult input provides the child with structural information about the system being acquired (see chapter 10 for further discussion).

By attending to input, the children might not only receive information concerning relationships between various pronominal forms but also obtain information about the positioning of elements. Ervin (1961), in a study of the verbal determinants of word association, noted some factors about English usage that can be related to the present discussion. She reported that words that do not tend to occur in sentence-final position (e.g., nominative pronouns, copulas, and function words) do not tend to occur alone. In contrast, words that occur in final position (e.g., nouns, accusative pronouns, intransitive verbs) also appear alone in answers to questions. This implies that the child is not likely to hear words like *I* or *My* alone as responses to questions, or in sentence-final position, though the child might hear instances of *Me* or *Mommy* in such contexts. Such regularities in the input could lead the children to relate the self reference forms in specific ways.

In the future it seems essential to look more carefully at the sort of contrasts the child actually is confronted with when listening to spoken input. In the present study, when the caregivers asked their children questions, it was noted that the form *you* was actually pronounced *ya*, as in, for instance, *What ya gonna do?* The children then were actually presented with a contrast between *you* and *ya*. Keeping in mind that the ego-anchored children's pronunciation of *My* often sounded like *Ma*, the question can be raised: Did the children create the *Ma* form in an attempt to build a formal correspondence with the second person form *ya*?

Another way the children might have arrived at a possessive construction in subject position in a way that deviated from the target language, based on input they received, is as follows. The caregivers often repeated what the child had just stated that he or she was going to do; for instance, we find *You're gonna build a house.* In such instances, it could be the case that the children interpreted the forms *you are* in their contracted version as the possessive pronoun *your*, which could help to explain why the ego-anchored children came to use *My* in subject position alone without a noun. Although at present these points are mere speculations, they nevertheless remind us of the need to consider the actual speech units that the child is confronted with when attempting to construct a self reference system.

As one final suggestion regarding the role that input may play, one should keep in mind the range of input that particular children might receive in their daily interactions and the role that different kinds of input play on the children's constructions. For instance, the children in the present study spent a good proportion of their days interacting with similar-aged peers in a day-care setting. At present we know very little about the extent to which peer input influences children's constructions of self reference systems. It could be that as children enter into the peer culture, and conflicts over control and dominance become important issues, particular linguistic forms become salient at this age. Along similar lines, it seems important also to consider the input such children receive in nondyadic interactions, which are common in the day-care setting. Given that children receive input from multiple sources, it seems that we must begin to think about how such varied input might be used selectively by the child in constructing a self reference system.

Typological Factors. A second way in which the environment may impact on the sort of grammatical systems children construct is related to particular structural properties of the language being acquired. At the level of input, we considered the extent to which the ego-anchored children's patterning of forms and functions related to regularities in the actual input they received. At a slightly different level, we can also consider the extent to which specific ways a particular language categorizes meaning play a role in the child's original categorization. Bowerman (1985) suggested that children are sensitive to and make use of clues from the target language when constructing grammar. In contrast to Slobin, who argued for a language-neutral starting point, Bowerman contended that the children's earliest meaning categories associated with grammatical forms are biased by the semantic structure of the target language. I now consider whether the ego-anchored children's linkages of form and meaning are related to structural properties of English.

The comparison with Slobin's discussion of Kaluli and Russian children's early use of inflections pointed up both some similarities and some differences between the children. One might speculate that because the Russian and Kaluli children made use of inflectional devices, their use of such forms was not restricted to self. In contrast, the English-speaking children were drawing on first person forms and therefore restricted the notion of agency to self. Similarly, recall that the Kaluli and Russian children marked a binary distinction between prototypical and nonprototypical agency, whereas the distinctions the English-speaking children made were multiple (i.e., prototypical agent, experiencer, affected agent, etc.). One suggestion is that although all children may attempt to mark some general distinction involving the manipulative activity scene, the actual number of distinctions made may depend on language-particular factors. These comments are necessarily speculative. In order to tease apart the relative influence of structural properties of particular languages, future research must carefully select languages that contrast in ways that would allow one to address this question.

Discussion

Much of my discussion above has argued for the active role of the child in constructing grammar. I have suggested that children bring with them to the task of constructing a self reference system a set of cognitive strategies that assists the children in interpreting input and subsequently organizing forms into grammatical systems. The evidence reviewed here suggests that agentivity and control are notions that will play a central organizing role in children's construction of grammar across the world. Children acquiring English, as well as children acquiring structurally different languages, will attempt to mark distinctions between what I have referred to as the prototypical agentivity scene and particular deviations. The question remains whether all English-speaking children will select self reference forms as a means of marking such a distinction. It could be that children mark similar notions with other forms. I have argued that given a range of forms offered by a particular language, some subsystems will be more likely candidates for the marking of agentivity and control than others. I have suggested that given that the English-speaking children in this study were not regularly referring to others, they borrowed first person forms for the purposes of marking agentivity and control. Whether other English-speaking children might adopt other forms is a topic for future investigation.

It is important to stress that according to the present account the child is guided by preferences to mark quite generally the notions of agentivity and control. The actual number of distinctions drawn by children and the particular devices employed are dependent on the child's interpretation of structural properties of the input received. The specific number of distinctions marked will vary according to typological and interactional factors. Thus environmental factors and cognitive factors all play a role, suggesting that a certain amount of interlanguage and intralanguage variation is to be expected.[2]

The framework outlined thus far could be interpreted to imply that the children were attempting to construct grammatical systems without regard to the various functions language serves in the child's interactions with others. It seems necessary to consider also the role such factors might play in motivating the sorts of contrasts constructed by the children. Previous research reviewed in Part I of this book has highlighted the extent to which children contrastively employ sound patterns and intonation to mark various language functions in their speech before they combine words (see Carter, 1975; Halliday, 1975; Painter, 1984). The children may attempt to mark function similarly when contrastively employing multiword utterances.

This leaves the question why the children choose the self reference system to mark such a distinction. Silverstein (1985) claimed that there are networks of functional regularities across languages that are located in equivalent forms. The child may not acquire the semantic values until a later point, after first using the forms only pragmatically. Such a suggestion fits the developmental trends reported to the extent that two of the ego-anchored children first organized the use of the self reference forms primarily around a pragmatic

---

[2]For alternative ways to employ self reference forms in English see Gerhardt, 1988, and Nelson, 1989.

contrast. Future research should collect data from children who have yet to produce word combinations in order to draw conclusions of this sort.

A second factor that has not received much treatment in the literature concerning organizational processes concerns the extent to which the child's growing notions of agentivity and control interact with other factors in leading to various organizations of the self reference forms. Children begin working on self reference systems with different conceptions of agentivity and control; and such distinctions may lead to variations in the ways form, meaning, and pragmatic function are related. It would be fruitful as well to collect data from children who have had qualitatively different experiences with agency and control, because such experiences might lead them to very different beliefs about such notions. As just one example, one could examine language data from children who have had little experience manipulating objects or moving as independent agents due to lack of full use of limbs.

In sum, I have presented only some very general ideas about what led the ego-anchored children in this study to organize self reference forms as they did. Any adequate account is going to need to consider mutual influences of multiple factors. The tentative framework put forth here has been developed in light of findings from the examination of a few children's organization of a specific linguistic subsystem. In the future, it is essential that more children be studied and that the developmental unfolding of other linguistic systems be carefully investigated. I discuss this further in the final chapter.

ACCOUNTING FOR THE REORGANIZATION
OF SELF REFERENCE SYSTEMS

Given the highly systematic nature of the ego-anchored children's use of self reference forms at the start of the study, the question arises: What led the children to give up these systems in favor of a system that conformed more to that found in the target language? I have claimed that the children moved developmentally from a phase of using multiple self reference forms, each linked with a distinct meaning and functional cluster, to one of using the forms multifunctionally as adults do. I turn now to various accounts that could shed light on possible motivations for such changes. I begin my discussion with a consideration of Radford's (1990) maturational hypothesis. Next I discuss cognitive factors, and finally I consider accounts that emphasize environmental influences. I focus exclusively on approaches that attempt to offer a specific solution to the problem at hand.

Maturational Accounts

Radford (1990) claimed that the transition from lack of productive use of nominative case marking to adultlike usage can be accounted for by the *maturational hypothesis*. According to his account, children begin at a lexical-thematic stage and subsequently progress to a functional-nonthematic stage. Although there is a certain amount of overlap in the examples of child speech offered here and by Radford, there are some important differences between the two data sets. Most significantly, it is unclear how the ego-anchored children's protracted development can be explained as a two-stage biologically determined process. It should also be noted that the ego-anchored children's use of accusative forms in nominative position was first restricted to first person and later appeared with third person forms at a time when first person nominative forms were frequent.

Cognitive Accounts

In this section I examine Karmiloff-Smith's approach, also reviewed earlier, because it is the most specific attempt within cognitive approaches to account for the kind of protracted development and reorganization of self reference forms described in Part II of this book. I have noted that the ego-anchored children's organization of self reference forms at the onset of the study could be related to Phase II of Karmiloff-Smith's three-phase account of children's language development. One interpretation of the children's use of the various self reference forms early on in the study is that the children were attempting to gain control over the system by rendering each of the functions of a given form tangible. One can now suggest that when the ego-anchored children began to reorganize their self reference systems to conform with the target language, they had successfully consolidated the relationship between form–function pairs. The children no longer needed to externalize the overall organization via the use of distinct linguistic markers. According to Karmiloff-Smith's model, during Phase III, the additional markers fade away and the children start to devote more attention to the input they receive in evaluating previous hypotheses and formulating new ones. Slowly the use of the nominative form *I* becomes more frequent, and the cluster of semantic and pragmatic factors associated with its use expands to include new functions and meanings previously covered by the other self reference forms. At the same time children are working on self reference forms as a linguistic sub-system, they are working on other systems as well. Connections between the various subsystems may contribute to the consolidation process. For instance, I have noted that the children were acquiring a variety of devices that began to take over functions related to those served by the self reference system. Although Karmiloff-Smith's three-phase account focuses primarily on one particular linguistic system, other models, such as the Competition Model (see MacWhinney & Bates, 1989), more directly handle the relationship between various linguistic systems.

It is central to Karmiloff-Smith's account that input is used in a new way by children during Phase III. During Phase II, children were said to be focusing on the dominant form–function pattern in the input. During Phase III, at a point at which the children have rendered tangible the links between form and function, the children begin making use of input that previously was ignored. What is central in my analysis is the claim that monitoring of input per se did not motivate the reorganization of the ego-anchored children's system. Rather, I suggest that children used the input in a new way. With regard to the transition from ego-anchored to nonego-anchored functioning, I have noted that only after an extended phase of employing self reference forms unifunctionally, did the children begin employing them plurifunctionally. An examination of the individual differences in the children's decisions with regard to how the other self reference forms were to be employed highlights the fact that input cannot be taken as the motivating factor. Some children simply avoided the use of the other self reference forms, allowing them to resurface a few months later after reevaluating how they were used in the target system, whereas other children seemed more ready to work simultaneously on the various self reference forms. That some forms were avoided suggests that the children were not yet clear how they fit into the system. This implies that input monitoring had not instructed the children on how to make use of such forms.

I also have noted that some forms, such as *My*, were tried out as part of another subsystem—in this instance, as a modal form. This suggests that children were not always reorganizing forms in a direction that corresponded with input but might test out other alternatives along the way. This finding supports Karmiloff-Smith's claim that the children, at Phase III, are not merely remodeling their systems in terms of input. It also highlights the need to consider the specifics of how children build systems not only of form–function patterns but also of relationships between form–form and function–function relationships (see also Bates & MacWhinney, 1989).

Environmental Accounts

One might want to hypothesize that the children all began changing their use of self reference forms because something in their linguistic environment changed. Two possible accounts for why the children might reorganize their system are pursued here. First I consider evidence as to whether the children's changes related to potential changes in caregiver input. I also consider whether children reorganized their self reference systems for reasons related to communicative pressure.

Changes in Caregiver Input. One particular hypothesis might be that the caregivers of the nonego-anchored children provided their children with distinct input patterns regarding form and function of self reference forms. Analyses of caregiver input for the nonego-anchored children (Quick, 1991), as well as comparisons of the ego-anchored children's caregivers across the various months of study revealed no significant changes (Budwig, in press). These findings, which, interestingly enough, showed that all of the caregivers tended to restrict the usage of *I* to a cluster of low agentivity and assertions, contained no evidence that the children's patterns changed over time due to corresponding changes in the input (see Budwig, in press, for a review of this argument).

Communicative Pressure. One might hypothesize that the children reorganized their self reference systems to conform better to the target language because they wanted to be more effective communicators. In fact, communicative pressure fares poorly as a motivating factor. It is generally assumed to play, at best, a minor role in the reorganizational process (see Bamberg, 1987; Bowerman, 1982; Karmiloff-Smith, 1979, 1983). Although the ego-anchored children's systems were organized differently from those of the target language, much of the output was grammatical, and communicative partners did not have difficulty making sense of the children's utterances. Even when the children produced utterances that were not grammatical, for instance substituting *My* or *Me* for *I* in subject position, such usage rarely led to communicative breakdowns. As has been previously noted, many caregivers were unaware of such usage in their children's speech.

Although communicative pressure per se cannot be viewed as a sufficient motivating factor, it is possible that children are led to reorganize their systems in part by other factors related to the communicative context. As children's communicative contexts change, it seems likely that the kinds of grammatical systems may also become reorganized. One sort of change seems relevant to the present discussion. As the children begin to become more independent and verbal, they gradually move into a wider range of social situations. They begin interacting with a number of others, rather than primarily with caregivers who are familiar with their needs. Givón (1979, 1985) has suggested that as communicators move beyond communicating with intimates to communicating with strangers they create a more elaborate grammatical system. This holds across the lifespan. With regard to the children in the present investigation one might want to claim that as the children began to communicate with a wider array of others, their repertoire of self reference forms was integrated into a broader paradigm of referential devices, including second and third person forms. In addition, as the functions of children's discourse developed, the children might have needed to draw on pronominal and nominal devices to serve other functions concerning text coherence. This might have led the children to find alternative means to mark degree of agentivity and control. And it seems likely that with time, the children might have recognized that a clear contrast at the linguistic level between various language functions may become disadvantageous for a communicator needing to rely on a system with more subtle boundaries between such acts as requests and assertions.

Ervin-Tripp (1977) convincingly argued for the need to consider the extent to which the growth of conversation stimulates linguistic change. Although in recent years researchers have directed more attention to the various functions language serves in early childhood, and though we know a great deal more about pragmatic aspects of child language development, the actual relationship between language structure, language function, and developmental change has continued to be virtually ignored. It seems, though, that a complete understanding of the factors motivating children to reorganize early systematizations of forms, meanings, and functions will ultimately come from a closer examination of the role communicative factors play in such a process.

Discussion

This discussion of potential factors influencing the children's reorganization of the self reference systems has emphasized a process-oriented view. After an extended phase of linguistically marking various functions with distinct forms, the child is said to gain control over the organization of the relation between form and function to the extent that the externalization process is no longer necessary. The child then gradually begins to encode in a single form a cluster of related meanings and functions that were previously encoded in several separate forms. The process described here whereby the children began using self reference forms plurifunctionally is more complicated than that described by Karmiloff-Smith with regard to her examination of determiners. Although the children did begin to use *I* multifunctionally, they did not seem to use the other forms immediately in an adultlike way.

The process of reorganization does seem motivated by a web of interrelated factors. In Part II, I highlighted some of the complexity involved when discussing the use of devices other than self reference forms to mark notions related to agentivity and control. I suggested that around the time the children no longer employed self reference forms to mark the notion of prototypical agency, they began marking a set of related notions including degree of control and motivations for action with a range of forms. The children began breaking down the notions of agentivity and control into several related notions that were marked in different parts of the grammar. Although particular cognitive notions contribute to subsequent development, experience with novel linguistic forms also may lead the child to new categorizations. The direction of mapping cannot be viewed as merely unidirectional (see also Kuczaj, 1982; Schlesinger, 1977). Finally, in considering multiple factors influencing the child's reorganization of the self reference system, one must also consider the extent to which changing communicative demands and the child's changing notions of agentivity and control play a contributing role in this process.

In summary, it has been suggested that the children studied began with some core notions of what deserves grammatical treatment. Based on an assessment of structural information about the language being acquired and various communicative factors, they began using particular linguistic forms to mark various distinctions concerning agentivity and control. At some later point, as a consequence of the mutual influences of changing notions of human action, communication, and language as a system, the children gradually reorganized the relationship between form–function pairs. The specific mechanisms guiding the reorganization process are at this point quite vague. It seems clear, however, that future research could examine this issue more carefully. Details of some possibilities are discussed in the next chapter.

Conclusions

In this chapter, I discuss the implications of the present study for functional approaches to child language. I reconsider the notion of language function, as well as the notion of development. In addition, I consider the relationship of the perspective adopted in this book to central issues in the study of child grammar. In the concluding section, I discuss directions for future research.

IMPLICATIONS OF THE PRESENT STUDY FOR FUNCTIONAL APPROACHES TO CHILD LANGUAGE

The Notion of Function

This study illustrates the extent to which children organize linguistic forms around a broad cluster of notions having to do with meaning and pragmatic function. Where does this leave us with regard to current theorizing about language function? In this section I return to three topics that came up in the review of the literature on language function in chapter 1, and I relate the current findings to these topics. The three issues to be pursued here include: (a) the nature of linguistic categories, (b) the role of semantics and pragmatic notions in functionalist accounts, and (c) the notion of activity-types.

The Nature of Linguistic Categories. As was noted in chapter 1, it has become increasingly common for researchers studying children's early grammatical development to suggest that semantic–cognitive correspondences play important roles in the early phases of language development. Although the theories differ, one central assumption has been that categories such as *agent* represent discrete categories for the child. Many child language researchers whose work was reviewed in chapter 1 were noted to posit a category such as *agent-action* that included examples like *My open that* and *Eve read.* Recent discussions in the linguistics literature have challenged such a claim, suggesting that the notion of agentivity is actually composed of several interrelated components such as control, volition, and animacy (see DeLancey, 1984; Lakoff, 1977, 1986).

The findings of the present investigation suggest that the children studied were not treating agentivity as a discrete category. They did not always treat subjects of verbs like *open* and *read* alike. Utterances including references to the self with *open* were usually encoded as involving the prototypical agentivity scene, whereas utterances involving *read* only occasionally were encoded in a similar way. Furthermore, the children's categorization of verb types did not accord with any theory of verb semantics outlined thus far. The children were said to be working with slippery categories that involved a combination of notions of agency and control, using fairly subtle distinctions that cut across semantic and pragmatic levels of analysis. These findings call into question the usefulness of any attempts to work with discrete categories, especially those based on current linguistic theory, in helping us understand children's construction of early grammar.

Semantics Versus Pragmatics. Previous literature has often separated these levels of analysis. In the literature on early child grammar, there has been a tendency to emphasize the extent to which children are concerned with mapping the relation between linguistic forms and some set of underlying conceptual meanings. The emphasis on the relationship between form and meaning can be related to the prevalent assumption in the child language literature that language encodes reality. Although such a view is clearly not false, it underestimates the extent to which language is a tool that helps the child constitute reality. Just as children draw linguistic distinctions between various meanings, it also makes sense that they would attempt to organize the use of particular linguistic forms around their budding notions of language function. It should be noted that researchers have found that children are capable of working on language at a purely formal level without relating form and meaning. In addition, it seems that function will not play an organizing role for the acquisition of all linguistic forms. The question remains, nevertheless: To what extent do children draw upon their budding notions of function in constructing a language system?

Form, Meaning, and Function in Early Child Language. One of the central questions regarding early grammatical development has involved the nature of children's early linguistic categories. I have suggested here that one way to approach this issue is by starting with the level of form. By examining the children's contrastive use of self reference forms and considering the kinds of categories they used, I have found that the child relies on rather broad clusters of properties. With regard to the marking of agentivity and control in early child grammar, I have found it fruitful to rely on the notion of activity-types-clusters of properties that cut across both the semantic and pragmatic levels in ways that pattern into linguistic gestalts (see Lakoff & Johnson, 1980). Such clusters are made up of experiential properties and are characterizable in terms of the ways children interact with their environment. The categories have prototype effects; no one property is essential, but the category is centered instead around a prototype defined in both semantic and pragmatic terms. At various points in development some of the properties of the activity-type may be more central than others. Although changes can be noted across development in the configuration of these patternings, at all times the children's categorizations consist of a bundle of properties that cluster together in regular ways.

Thus the present work suggests not only that researchers should attend to both semantic and pragmatic factors when studying early grammatical development but also that the sorts of relationships between form and function will not necessarily pattern in adultlike ways. We need to find ways of arriving at the child's construction of such clusters. I have suggested that in the future, rather than starting with broad categories of semantic meaning or pragmatic function, it would be advantageous to begin one's functional analysis with form contrasts.

The Notion of Development

In the preceding chapters, I have outlined a specific notion of development that has been used in this research. In Part I it was noted that much of the functionalist work that has been carried out has focused primarily on some ways in which children's patterning of linguistic forms differs from adultlike usage. Very little explicit discussion can be found in much of the functionalist work on how development is defined. I have attempted to illustrate explicitly a particular stance taken toward development that involves the examination of form–function relations over time. This view of development has become increasingly popular over the last 15 years in much of the functionalist work, though there is little explicit mention of this change (see Budwig, 1993, for further illustration).

This particular construct focuses on changes in form–function pairings and can be contrasted with a view held by both functionalists and others, under which development in child language is perceived in terms of ordering sequences in the development of form. Thus development, here, is studied by examining the ways in which forms not only relate to one another over time, but also cluster with various semantic meanings and pragmatic functions. This sort of approach acknowledges that the first use of the form may be qualitatively, as well as quantitatively, different from subsequent uses. It switches focus away from what Brown (1973) referred to as *obligatory contexts*, toward an analysis of how forms are used at any given stage of development. This view of protracted development is quite different from other approaches, mainly but not exclusively nonfunctionalist, that view development as an all-or-none process.

In addition to illustrating explicitly an alternative view of development in terms of the protracted nature of the construction of linguistic systems, I have attempted, in the research described here, to find a common way to characterize the developmental patterns discussed in Part II. Although it is far from clear what factors motivate children to organize and reorganize their linguistic systems as they do, what does become apparent is that there is a common pattern to the processes of the various children's development outlined here. Regardless of the particulars, all of the ego-anchored children began with relatively global, contextually restricted uses of forms and slowly moved toward solutions involving hierarchical integration and differentiation. As the children entered into a wider range of communicative situations and needed to express an increasingly varied set of communicative functions, they drew upon an increasing array of linguistic resources. Although we are beginning to be more explicit about the notion of development within functionalist approaches, future research will also need to address explicitly the relationship between such a view and several central issues in the study of early child grammar. After considering the impact of a functionalist approach on various methodological issues, I return to a brief discussion of some of these themes.

Methodological Issues

Appealing to the notion of language function and development outlined here affects one's stance toward methodological issues in important ways. In this section, I briefly discuss various methodological issues, with particular focus on both the collection and the analysis of data. Although none of the particular methodological points are new, they often have been overlooked in studies of early grammatical development and therefore are made explicit here.

Data Gathering Procedures. Clearly technological advances in recent years have greatly assisted in arriving at the findings reported here. First, the importance of working with video when studying early child grammar from a functionalist standpoint cannot be stressed enough. No matter how rich one's contextual notes might be, they would not allow one the array of information necessary to code the various semantic and pragmatic parameters used in this study. Only with the aid of video data can one begin to arrive at the broad range of properties that co-occur with the use of particular forms. In the present study, working with high-quality wireless microphones also assisted in picking up subtle contrasts in the child's selection of form. Without such equipment it would have been quite difficult to note subtle differences between utterances such as *My do it* and *I do it* in the children's speech.

In addition, the present study has highlighted the advantages of examining grammatical development within the context of a variety of communicative partners. As Ervin-Tripp (1977) argued, the range of forms used by speakers is greatly influenced by the sorts of interaction settings sampled. With regard to the present study, it has been noted that particular forms were more likely to occur in interactions taking place with specific partners. Struggles over control of goods and participation in activities were likely to occur in interactions with peers. It is of interest that very few of the data sets drawn by researchers from computerized data banks such as CHILDES (under the direction of Snow and MacWhinney; see MacWhinney, 1991) included samples involving agemates. Peer data are important not only because they highlight ways children relate form, meaning, and function that might not be found when examining data stemming from adult-child interactions, but also because one can begin to make use of findings concerning different distributional patterns of particular forms in the distinct settings as a clue to how the children actually organize such forms. To this extent, more attention ought to be given in the future to aspects such as interactive partner and setting when collecting data.

One last point concerning data collection concerns the use of naturalistic data. In contrast to many previous naturalistic studies, this study was carefully designed in ways that allowed for the collection of particular kinds of talk. Hypotheses developed on the basis of pilot data, permitted the formulation of some expectations concerning the elicitation of the range of devices of interest in a relatively natural and quick manner. In the present study, given the focus on the linguistic marking of agentivity and control, it seemed important to set up the situation in such a way that children were bound to run into struggles over control of objects. Likewise, children could be given objects that could be manipulated only by adults, thus eliciting talk about mediated agency. The general point is that a certain amount of structuring of the environment can enhance the nature of the data base. Although none of the mothers interviewed at the end of the project had tuned into the specific focus on agentivity and control, the structuring nevertheless provided a rich data base with hundreds of examples of form contrasts that were of interest. Future research within a functionalist approach should continue to find ways to collect naturalistic data, and to arrange the environment so as to enhance the data set.

Data Analysis. One central point relevant to data analysis concerns the importance of distributional analyses. By beginning a functional analysis with a series of distributional analyses, one is in a better position to assess the relationship between form, meaning, and function. Such a procedure allows us to examine a range of contrasts with which the child is working.

I have also noted that distributional analyses based on forms alone represent only a first step in approaching the data. The task becomes one of working out a way to relate distributional patterns of forms with analyses that take into account a broad range of semantic and pragmatic parameters. Two directions of analysis have been proposed here. First, one must begin with some preconceived notions concerning general distinctions the child might be attempting to mark. To this end one can draw upon basic notions noted to play a role in the acquisition of related forms in other languages (see Slobin, 1985). In addition, one can make use of findings concerning ways particular categories are marked in other languages.

At the same time that one works with certain expectations, one must also keep an eye open for patterns that may be unique to the data at hand. Thus original categories are refined in light of preliminary analyses. In this study much of the refinement of the coding scheme took place during the pilot stages when working with data stemming from other children. Nevertheless, it was necessary in some instances to break apart particular levels of the coding scheme or to collapse across categories in order to account for the regularities at hand.

Finally, the importance of coding across several linguistic, as well as nonlinguistic, layers of analysis must also be stressed. Only by considering an array of verbal and nonverbal characteristics can one arrive at the sorts of categories that children might be using. And I have shown the importance of analyzing individual children's data before collapsing across children, because many interesting patterns and differences are washed out in grouped analyses. Recent technological advancements in computer-aided analysis such as CLAN have made such an endeavor more possible in recent years (see MacWhinney, 1991).

RELATIONSHIP TO ISSUES CENTRAL TO THE STUDY OF CHILD GRAMMAR

Three issues have been central to most previous discussions of the acquisition of early grammar, and it seems important to consider such issues in light of the framework presented here. I begin by considering whether there is evidence for underlying syntactic relations in early child language. Next I discuss the issue of continuity and discontinuity in early language development. A third theme concerns the issue of the psychological reality of children's early grammatical categories.

Syntactic Relations in Early Child Language

The extent to which children should be credited with knowledge of underlying syntactic relationships has been an issue receiving much attention in the literature concerning children's first word combinations (see Bloom et al., 1975; Bowerman, 1975; Braine, 1976; Gleitman & Wanner, 1982; Radford, 1990). With regard to the present study, can we say that the ego-anchored children had the notion of a sentence subject in mind, or were they working at a different level of abstraction? Bloom et al. (1975) argued that the children in their study used the same words in a particular sentence position to convey a variety of semantic roles (e.g., agent, possessor). Based on such findings, Bloom et al. credited the children with more abstract knowledge about superordinate categories such as subject. Such a claim has not gone unchallenged (see Bowerman, 1975; Braine, 1976). Bowerman, for example, suggested that identity of word order patterns is not necessarily sufficient evidence for the presence of syntactic functions.

Even if word order were to be taken as adequate evidence, the findings from the present study lead us to question whether the children examined by Bloom et al. actually were using similar words to encode a variety of semantic relationships. Although utterances such as *My open that* were argued to express the relation Agent–Action and *My teapot* would have been categorized as Possessor–Possessed, the findings of the present study indicate that these children may have been expressing a single notion related to control in both instances. This points up the methodological problem of knowing whether the children were in fact using similar words to express different semantic relations. The findings of the present study lend support to the conclusion put forward by Braine (1976), who found no evidence for such abstract categories. Braine suggested that children are working with more limited notions. Evidence that this is the case can also be found in the children's marking of agentivity and control in this study. I have noted that the children linguistically categorized self as agent differently from other as agent in the early phases of development. Thus in utterances like *I like vanilla*, *My open that*, *Adam read*, and *Mommy eat* it is not clear that the ego-anchored children were expressing the same underlying relation. The present study offers no evidence that the children were working with fairly abstract syntactic relations in the early phases of grammatical development. This position is also consistent with formal approaches to early child grammar (see, for instance, Radford, 1990).

Continuity and Discontinuity in Early Child Language

Given that there is no firm evidence that the ego-anchored children were working with syntactic categories, we are led to the issue central to much of the current literature in early child grammar, concerning continuity and discontinuity. If we start with the assumption that the categories in early child speech are organized differently from those that figure in adult grammars, we must account for how the child breaks into the adult system (see Atkinson, 1982, for further discussion). The position outlined earlier with regard to development has been viewed in light of the orthogenetic principle, outlined in Werner and Kaplan (1984). Accordingly, the position adopted here is similar to Werner and Kaplan's concerning developmental transformations, namely, that both continuity and discontinuity are necessarily entailed. Although the introduction of novel forms and functions into the system obviously implies discontinuity, the manner in which these additions enter the system is protracted. I have noted the gradual way in which old is replaced by new, and this fits well with a continuity position (see also Lock, 1978, 1980).

Furthermore, I have noted that at times neither forms nor functions are added in some novel way; instead, the relationship between forms and functions is reorganized in terms of hierarchical organization and increasing differentiation. This sort of developmental sequence can be compared to that proposed in recent discussions of semantic bootstrapping (see, for instance, Pinker, 1989), where it is argued that the syntactic representations themselves are not developing out of semantic representations; instead, children gradually make use of correlations between semantic and syntactic representations.

The Psychological Reality of Children's Early Grammatical Categories

A third issue that has received much attention in the literature on early child grammar concerns the psychological reality of the categories. In other words, do the sorts of categories outlined with regard to the children's marking of agentivity and control actually correspond to concepts that the child is working with in constructing language? Several different proposals have been made in the literature concerning the nature of children's early word combinations. What evidence is there that those outlined for the children who participated in the present study correspond to notions that the child may be using? The position adopted here is based on the assumption that variations in form are not random but, rather, systematic. By placing linguistic contrasts at the center of one's analysis, one has a rich source to draw upon. One can move from the level of form and attempt to account for the range of contrasts employed.

In an attempt to arrive at the sort of categories that are functioning within early child speech, one must do more than account for a statistically significant proportion of the data. I have noted, for instance, that most of Megan's use of *my* could be related to a set of pragmatic features. Nevertheless, the study of exceptions pointed up further linkages the child could be drawing. In drawing conclusions concerning the scope of children's categories, examination of the contrastive use of forms can be instructive in pointing out distinctions that also might otherwise have gone unnoticed. For instance, I have noted that many examples of the use of *Me* by Grice resembled instances involving *My* in that both were associated with high agentivity and control. In digging deeper for a potential contrast, I noted that all the utterances with *Me* expressed the more specific category of affected agent.

It should be obvious that an analysis that begins at the level of contrasts of forms in no way ensures that one can arrive at psychologically real categories. Clearly the children in the present study may have been making even more distinctions or may have incorporated notions into the distinctions reviewed here that have gone unnoticed. Nevertheless, the suggestion here is that contrasts in the children's use of forms provide an excellent point of departure in identifying categorization schemes that correspond to ones children may be employing.

IMPLICATIONS FOR OTHER AREAS OF STUDY

The present study has implications for many other areas of research, two of which are discussed here. First, it seems that researchers interested in the development of social cognition could make use of the present findings in attempting to arrive at young children's budding notions of self and other. Researchers have noted the difficulties in making such assessments at phases of development at which children will not yet participate in extensive interviews. The sorts of patterns in the children's speech presented in this study could be used in structuring a preliminary framework for researching young children's social conceptions. Although clearly, children may not attempt to distinguish at the linguistic level all social cognitive notions they work with, the distinctions marked by the children in the present study, such as the subtle distinctions in agency, are far more refined than those described in the literature (see discussion in chapter 2, and Budwig & Wiley, in press).

The present study also has implications for researchers interested in both language and communicative disorders. If the methodology of the present study were to be extended to the examination of children targeted as having language or communicative difficulties, we could examine whether these children's language productions differ from those of normally developing children. The methodology also allows the researcher to gather information about the sorts of linguistic distinctions with which such children are working. This methodology is especially advantageous for young children who have difficulty with less naturalistic testing settings. Such research not only provides potential diagnostic measures but also could show alternative paths to particular domains of language.

CONCLUDING COMMENTS

This study can be contextualized within the tradition of a growing number of studies that illustrate that the early uses of a variety of linguistic forms are tied closely to a related set of semantic and pragmatic factors. Although this may be the case for many areas of grammatical development, we still know relatively little about why some areas of language are more likely than others to be dealt with in this way by young children. In the future, studies ought to examine more closely this patterning in a cross-linguistic perspective. It seems equally important to find out which forms do not link up with functional clusters in early development. I suggest that children are most likely to draw upon semantic and pragmatic notions when beginning to use linguistic markers that encourage the speaker to adopt a perspective or point of view. Thus deixis, modality, and voice would be likely areas for form–function pairings.

It seems important, also, to begin looking at the developmental relationship between linguistic systems at various points in time. In the present study, it has been suggested that as the children gave up their special patterning of self reference forms, other changes appeared in the system. For instance, children began regularly using an array of pronominal forms to refer to others. In addition, modal forms became quite frequent. The relationship between these developments and the children's special pronominal usage is clearly worth future study. Elsewhere I have noted that 2-year-old children began to use *get* and *be* passives contrastively to mark nonprototypical kinds of agency. Again, we know little about the connections between the *get/be* usage and children's use of pronominal forms. We therefore need longitudinal studies designed to look at the interrelationship between various subsystems (see Gerhardt, 1988; Nelson, 1989). Much of the research within functionalist approaches has focused on particular pockets with little attention to the interconnections between these areas at various points in time.

In the present study, I have also attempted to show how little we know about developmental changes in linguistic subsystems. Although some functionalist work within child language has aimed to document the nonadultlike ways children link forms to various semantic or pragmatic functions, I have sought to understand better the series of transformations that take place en route to an adultlike system. This study can be seen as reflecting a gradual change within functionalist approaches, in its revised view of development. It has been a rather common procedure in studies of early child language to work with the notion of obligatory context (see Brown, 1973). Until children use a given form 90% of the time in contexts where it would be expected, their use of that form often has been thought to reflect little more than incomplete mastery. In the present study, an attempt has been made to illustrate the wealth of information that can be gathered about early language development at a time when children often use forms in ways that deviate from the language they are acquiring. Rather than questioning whether a given form is being used appropriately, I have noted how various forms are used at any developmental point in time.

This approach, then, radically changes the view toward development and suggests a shift toward the assumption that development takes place in small increments over time. There is a growing amount of evidence that such a view is consistent with the cross-linguistic patterns of language acquisition (see, for instance, Berman & Slobin, 1994; Bloom, 1991; Tomasello, 1992). It seems likely that in the future, as researchers move away from fairly static notions of development, the kinds of questions raised with regard to development will continue to change as well. Within functionalist perspectives this has meant a decrease in focus on the order of acquisition of one form in relation to other (a popular focus at a time when researchers sought cognitive explanations for acquisition sequences) and an influx in studies that have attempted to describe the phases children go through from their first use of a given form to adultlike usage.

Although there have been recent changes in the view of child language development within functionalist perspectives, one area that we still know surprisingly little about concerns the mechanisms that move the child from one phase of development to the next. One of the biggest challenges for future research within this area is the achievement of a better understanding of the variety of factors involved in this process. I now briefly outline some steps that need to be taken in order to understand better the nature of the process in the particular domain that has been investigated here.

As was noted in chapter 9, until recently many functionalist accounts have appealed either to universal cognitive explanations or to language-typological explanations in describing how the child links form and meaning in early child language. More recently there has been a growing consensus that these factors combine in complex ways. For instance, although Slobin (1985) developed the notion of a universal Basic Child Grammar, his recent work highlighted the extent to which young children can and do adopt patternings that look quite like the language they are acquiring (see Slobin, 1990). Conversely, though Bowerman (1985) originally was a strong proponent for the view that children are quite flexible in adopting the meaning distinctions marked in the target language, her most recent work also suggested that children do not mark particular spatial notions even if their language requires them to do so (Bowerman & Choi, 1994). Although there is growing consensus for a position that supports the rich interplay between cognitive predispositions and the input children receive regarding language-specific solutions, it is clear that much more research is needed to understand this relationship better. I now discuss one avenue of research I am currently pursuing in an attempt to contribute to such an understanding.

One major problem that becomes apparent as functionalists acknowledge the complexity of factors that influence children's form–function patternings is the difficulty in making clear predictions. Most recently (see Budwig, 1993b, 1993c, in press) I suggested that what would greatly contribute to our understanding of factors influencing the organization and reorganization of forms and functions are studies in which language input is varied, though typology is held the same. More specifically, I suggested that much previous cross-linguistic research has been based on assumptions about language typology, rather than careful attention to input children receive.

As one example, my own recent reanalysis of the caregivers' input for the children studied in the present research revealed some unexpected pattern-ings of form and function that could not be predicted from what we know about the English language (see Budwig, in press). As was noted in chapter 9, the caregivers relied primarily on one self reference form in referring to themselves in subject position, namely, *I*; and although they used this form in a variety of semantic and pragmatic contexts, they did show a tendency to reserve the use of *I* for contexts involving a cluster of mental state verbs in noncontrol acts. Elsewhere (Budwig, in press), I suggested that one partial explanation for this may lie in the parents' interactive goals, in particular, their attempts to accentuate their children's agency and play down their own. Recent work in the area of language socialization has highlighted the extent to which caregiver beliefs link up with the linguistic forms they use (see Miller & Hoogstra, 1992; Schieffelin & Ochs, 1986), and Lin (1993) illustrated that American caregivers who express distinct beliefs about their children in an interview situation also organize conversation in distinct ways. What is not yet known is whether these two groups of caregivers also provide children with distinct linguistic input regarding self and other reference forms.

Previous research in the area of language socialization and individual differences does suggest that caregivers who speak the same language provide children with different input patterns. If we can identify pockets of language in which children learning the same language receive varied input, this would provide us with an important variable to help tease apart the relative contributions of cognitive predispositions and language-specific factors in the children's construction of grammar. Combining the study of within-language variation with the study of cross-linguistic variation also will allow us to draw distinctions between input factors and typological factors in the children's construction of linguistic systems. Such a program can help us understand better the linguistic, social, and conceptual factors influencing children's construction of linguistic systems.

References

Ames, L. (1952). The sense of self of nursery school children as manifested by their verbal behavior. *The Journal of Genetic Psychology, 81,* 193–232.

Atkinson, M. (1982). *Explanations in the study of child language development.* Cambridge, England: Cambridge University Press.

Austin, J. (1962). *How to do things with words.* Oxford, England: Oxford University Press.

Bamberg, M. (1987). *The acquisition of narratives.* Berlin: Mouton de Gruyter.

Bamberg, M. (1991). Narrative activity as perspective taking: The role of emotionals, negations, and voice in the construction of the story realm. *Journal of Cognitive Psychotherapy, 5,* 275–290.

Bamberg, M., Budwig, N., & Kaplan, B. (1991). A developmental approach to language acquisition: Two case studies. *First Language, 11,* 121–141.

Barber, E. (1975). Voice—beyond the passive. *Proceedings of the Berkeley Linguistic Society, 1,* 16–24.

Bates, E., Bretherton, I., & Snyder, L. (1988). *From first words to grammar: Individual differences and dissociable mechanisms.* Cambridge, England: Cambridge University Press.

Bates, E., & MacWhinney, B. (1987). Competition, variation and language learning. In B. MacWhinney (Ed.), *Mechanisms of language acquisition* (pp. 157–193). Hillsdale, NJ: Lawrence Erlbaum Associates.

Bates, E., & MacWhinney, B. (1989). Functionalism and the competition model. In B. MacWhinney & E. Bates (Eds.), *The crosslinguistic study of sentence processing* (pp. 3–73). Cambridge, England: Cambridge University Press.

Bellugi, U. (1971). Simplification in children's language. In R. Huxley & E. Ingram (Eds.), *Language acquisition: Models and methods* (pp. 95–117). London: Academic Press.

Benveniste, E. (1971). *Problems in general linguistics.* Coral Gables, FL: University of Miami Press.

Berman, R. (1979). Form and function: Passives, middles, and impersonals in modern Hebrew. *Proceedings of the Berkeley Linguistics Society, 5,* 1–27.

Berman, R., & Slobin, D. (1994). *Different ways of relating events in narrative: A crosslinguistic developmental study.* Hillsdale, NJ: Lawrence Erlbaum Associates.

210

Bloom, L. (1991). *Language development from two to three.* Cambridge, England: Cambridge University Press.

Bloom, L., Lightbown, P., & Hood, L. (1975). Structure and variation in child language. *Monographs of the Society for Research in Child Development, 40*(2, Serial No. 160).

Bowerman, M. (1975). Commentary on structure and variation in child language. *Monographs of the Society for Research in Child Development, 40*(2, Serial No. 160).

Bowerman, M. (1982). Reorganizational processes in lexical and syntactic development. In E. Wanner & L. Gleitman (Eds.), *Language acquisition: The state of the art* (pp. 319–346). Cambridge, England: Cambridge University Press.

Bowerman, M. (1985). What shapes children's grammars? In D. Slobin (Ed.), *The crosslinguistic study of language acquisition* (Vol. 2, pp. 1257–1319). Hillsdale, NJ: Lawrence Erlbaum Associates.

Bowerman, M., & Choi, S. (1994, January). *Linguistics and nonlinguistic determinants of spatial semantic development: A cross-linguistic study of English, Korean, and Dutch.* Paper presented at the 18th Annual Boston University Conference on Language Development, Boston, MA.

Braine, M. (1976). Children's first word combinations. *Monographs of the Society for Research in Child Development, 41*(Serial No. 164).

Brown, R. (1973). *A first language: The early stages.* Cambridge, MA: Harvard University Press.

Budwig, N. (1981). *The role of language in two-year-old peers' play.* Unpublished manuscript, University of California, Berkeley.

Budwig, N. (1986). *Agentivity and control in early child language.* Unpublished doctoral dissertation, University of California, Berkeley.

Budwig, N. (1989). The linguistic marking of agentivity and control in child language. *Journal of Child Language, 16,* 263–284.

Budwig, N. (1990). The linguistic marking of non-prototypical agency: An exploration into children's use of passives. *Linguistics, 28,* 1221–1252.

Budwig, N. (1993a). Perspectives on the form-function relationship across 25 years of the SCLRF meetings. In E. Clark (Ed.), *Proceedings of the Twenty-Fifth Annual Child Language Research Forum* (pp. 297–306). Stanford, CA: Center for the Study of Language and Information.

Budwig, N. (1993b, April). *Two year olds' talk about self and other: A cross-linguistic comparison.* Paper presented to the New York Child Language Group, New York, NY.

Budwig, N. (1993c, May). *Indexing self and other in parent-child interactions.* Paper presented at The National Academy of Education Spencer Fellows Forum, Stanford, CA.

Budwig, N. (in press). What influences children's patterning of forms and functions in early child language? In D. Slobin, J. Gerhardt, A. Kyratzis, & J. Guo (Eds.), *Social interaction, social context, and language: Essays in honor of Susan Ervin-Tripp.* Hillsdale, NJ: Lawrence Erlbaum Associates.

Budwig, N., & Bamberg, M. (in press). Functional approaches to language development. In N. Budwig & M. Bamberg (Eds.), *Theoretical approaches to language development.* San Francisco: Jossey-Bass.

Budwig, N., Strage, A., & Bamberg, M. (1986). The construction of joint activities with an agemate: The transition from caregiver-child to peer interaction. In J. Cook-Gumperz, W. Corsaro, & J. Streeck (Eds.), *Children's worlds and children's language* (pp. 83–108). The Hague: Mouton.

Budwig, N., & Wiley, A. (in press). What language reveals about children's categories of personhood. In L. Sperry & P. Smiley (Eds.), *Learning about self and other through conversation. New directions for child development series.* San Francisco: Jossey-Bass.

Bullock, M. (1979). *Aspects of the young child's theory of causation.* Unpublished doctoral dissertation, University of Pennsylvania, Philadelphia.

Burke, K. (1969). *A grammar of motives.* Berkeley: University of California Press.

Carter, A. (1975). The transformation of sensori-motor morphemes into words: A case study of the development of *more* and *mine. Journal of Child Language, 2,* 233–255.

Carter, A. (1978a). The development of systematic vocalizations prior to words: A case study. In N. Waterson & C. Snow (Eds.), *The development of communication* (pp. 127–138). Chichester: Wiley.

Carter, A. (1978b). From sensori-motor vocalizations to words: A case study of the evolution of attention-directing communication in the second year. In A. Lock (Ed.), *Action, gesture, and symbol* (pp. 309–349). London: Academic Press.

Chafe, W. (Ed.). (1980). *The Pear stories: Cognitive, cultural, and linguistic aspects of narrative production.* Norwood, NJ: Ablex.

Charney, R. (1980). Speech roles and the development of personal pronouns. *Journal of Child Language, 7,* 509–528.

Chomsky, N. (1957). *Syntactic structures.* The Hague: Mouton.

Chomsky, N. (1975). *Reflections on language.* New York: Pantheon.

Clark, E. (1978). Awareness of language: Some evidence from what children say and do. In A. Sinclair, R. Jarvella, & W. Levelt (Eds.), *The child's conception of language* (pp. 17–43). Berlin: Springer-Verlag.

Clark, E. (1985). The acquisition of Romance, with special reference to French. In D. I. Slobin (Ed.), *The crosslinguistic study of language acquisition* (Vol. 1, pp. 687–782). Hillsdale, NJ: Lawrence Erlbaum Associates.

Comrie, B. (1976). *Aspect.* Cambridge, England: Cambridge University Press.

Comrie, B. (1981). *Language universals and linguistic typology.* Chicago: University of Chicago Press.

Cook-Gumperz, J., Corsaro, W., & Streeck, J. (Eds.). (1986). *Children's worlds and children's language.* The Hague: Mouton.

Cooley, C. (1908). A study of the early use of self-words by a child. *Psychological Review, 15,* 339–357.

Corsaro, W. (1985). *Friendship and peer culture in the early years.* Norwood, NJ: Ablex.

Croft, W. (1987). *Categories and relations in syntax: The clause-level organization of information.* Unpublished doctoral dissertation, Stanford University, Stanford, CA.

Croft, W. (1990). *Typology and universals.* Cambridge, England: Cambridge University Press.

DeLancey, S. (1984). Notes on agentivity and causation. *Studies in Language, 8,* 181–213.

DeLancey, S. (1987). Transitivity in grammar and cognition. In R. Tomlin (Ed.), *Coherence and grounding in discourse* (pp. 53–68). Amsterdam: John Benjamins.

DeLancey, S. (1990). Crosslinguistic evidence for the structure of the agent prototype. *Papers and Reports on Child Language Development, 29,* 141–147.

Demuth, K. (1984). *Aspects of Sesotho language acquisition.* Bloomington: Indiana University Linguistics Club.

Deutsch, W., & Budwig, N. (1983). Form and function in the development of possessives. *Papers and Reports on Child Language Development, 22,* 36–42.

de Villiers, P., & de Villiers, J. (1974). On this, that and the other: Nonegocentrism in very young children. *Journal of Experimental Child Psychology, 18,* 438–447.

Duranti, A. (1985). Sociocultural dimensions of discourse. In T. A. Van Dijk (Ed.), *Handbook of discourse analysis: Disciplines of discourse* (Vol. 1, pp. 193–230). London: Academic Press.

Eilfort, W., Kroeber, P., & Peterson, K. (Eds.). (1985). *Papers from the Parasession on Causatives and Agentivity.* Chicago: Chicago Linguistic Society.

Ervin, S. (1961). Changes with age in the verbal determinants of word-association. *The American Journal of Psychology, 74,* 361–372.

Ervin, S., & Miller, W. (1964). The development of grammar in child language. *Monographs of the Society of Research in Child Development, 29,* 9–34.

Ervin-Tripp, S. (1972). On sociolinguistic rules: Alternation and co-occurrence. In J. Gumperz & D. Hymes (Eds.), *Directions in sociolinguistics: The ethnography of communication* (pp. 213–250). New York: Holt, Rinehart & Winston.

Ervin-Tripp, S. (1977). From conversation to syntax. *Papers and Reports on Child Language Development, 13*, 1–21.

Ervin-Tripp, S. (1981). How to make and understand a request. In H. Parret, M. Sbisa, & J. Verschueren (Eds.), *Possibilities and limitations of pragmatics* (pp. 195–210). Amsterdam: John Benjamins.

Ervin-Tripp, S. (1989). Speech acts and syntactic development: Linked or independent? *Berkeley Science Report, 61,* Institute of Cognitive Studies, University of California, Berkeley.

Ervin-Tripp, S. (1993). Constructing syntax from discourse. In E. Clark (Ed.), *Proceedings of the Twenty-Fifth Annual Child Language Research Forum* (pp. 333–341). Stanford, CA: Center for the Study of Language and Information.

Ervin-Tripp, S., & Gordon, D. (1986). The development of requests. In R. Schiefelbusch (Ed.), *Communicative competence: Assessment and intervention* (pp. 61–95). Baltimore, MD: University Park Press.

Ervin-Tripp, S., & Mitchell-Kernan, C. (Eds.). (1977). *Child discourse.* New York: Academic Press.

Fillmore, C. (1968). The case for case. In E. Bach & R. T. Harms (Eds.), *Universals in linguistic theory* (pp. 1–88). New York: Holt, Rinehart & Winston.

Fillmore, C. (1977). Topics in lexical semantics. In R. Cole (Ed.), *Current issues in linguistic theory* (pp. 76–138). Bloomington: Indiana University Press.

Firbas, J. (1964). On defining the theme in functional sentence analysis. *Travaux Linguistique de Prague, 1,* 267–280.

Firth, J. (1951). *Modes of meaning.* London: The English Association.

Foley, W., & Van Valin, R. (1984). *Functional syntax and universal grammar.* Cambridge, England: Cambridge University Press.

Gee, J. (1985). An interpretive approach to the study of modality: What child language can tell the linguist. *Studies in Language, 9,* 197–229.

Gee, J., & Savasir, I. (1985). On the use of "will" and "gonna": Towards a description of activity-types for child language. *Discourse Processes, 8,* 143–175.

Gerhardt, J. (1983). *Tout se tient: Towards an analysis of activity-types to explicate the interrelation between modality and future reference in child discourse.* Unpublished doctoral dissertation, University of California, Berkeley.

Gerhardt, J. (1988). From discourse to semantics: The development of verb morphology and forms of self-reference in the speech of a two-year-old. *Journal of Child Language, 15,* 337–393.

Gerhardt, J. (1990). The relation of language to context in children's speech: The role of HAFTA statements in structuring 3-year-olds' discourse. *Papers in Pragmatics, 4,* 1–57.

Gerhardt, J., & Savasir, I. (1986). The use of the simple present in the speech of two 3-year-olds: Normativity not subjectivity. *Language in Society, 15,* 501–536.

Givón, T. (1979). *On understanding grammar.* New York: Academic Press.

Givón, T. (1984a). *Syntax: A functional-typological approach* (Vol. 1). Amsterdam: John Benjamins.

Givón, T. (1984b). Direct object and dative shifting: Semantic and pragmatic case. In F. Plank (Ed.), *Objects: Towards a theory of grammatical relations.* New York: Academic Press.

Givón, T. (1985). Function, structure, and language acquisition. In D. Slobin (Ed.), *The crosslinguistic study of language acquisition* (Vol. 2, pp. 1005–1028). Hillsdale, NJ: Lawrence Erlbaum Associates.

Givón, T. (1990). *Syntax: A functional-typological introduction* (Vol. 2). Amsterdam: John Benjamins.

Gleitman, L., & Wanner, E. (1982). Language acquisition: The state of the state of the art. In E. Wanner & L. Gleitman (Eds.), *Language acquisition: The state of the art* (pp. 3–48). Cambridge: Cambridge University Press.

Golinkoff, R., Harding, C., Carlson, V., & Sexton, M. (1984). The infant's perception of causal events: The distinction between animate and inanimate objects. In L. Lipsitt & C. Rovee-Collier (Eds.), *Advances in infancy research* (Vol. 3, pp. 145–151). Norwood, NJ: Ablex.

Goodenough, F. (1938). The use of pronouns by young children: A note on the development of self-awareness. *The Journal of Genetic Psychology, 52*, 333–346.

Gopnik, A. (1980). *The development of non-nominal expressions in one to two year old children.* Unpublished doctoral dissertation, Oxford University.

Gordon, D., Budwig, N., Strage, A., & Carrell, P. (1980, October). *Children's requests to unfamiliar adults: Form, social function, age variation.* Paper presented at the Fifth Annual Boston University Conference on Language Development, Boston, MA.

Gordon, D., & Ervin-Tripp, S. (1984). The structure of children's requests. In R. Schiefelbusch & J. Pickar (Eds.), *The acquisition of communicative competence* (pp. 295–321). Baltimore: University Park Press.

Grice, H. (1975). Logic and conversation. In P. Cole & J. L. Morgan (Eds.), *Syntax and semantics: Vol. 3. Speech acts* (pp. 41–58). New York: Academic Press.

Gruber, J. (1965). *Studies in lexical relations.* Unpublished doctoral dissertation, Massachusetts Institute of Technology, Cambridge, MA.

Gumperz, J. (1976). Language, communication and public negotiation. In P. Sanday (Ed.), *Anthropology and the public interest: Field work and theory* (pp. 273–292). New York: Academic Press.

Gumperz, J. (1982). *Discourse strategies.* Cambridge, England: Cambridge University Press.

Guo, J. (1993). Discourse motivations for the development of modal auxiliaries. In E. Clark (Ed.), *Proceedings of the Twenty-Fifth Annual Child Language Research Forum* (pp. 315–323). Stanford, CA: The Center for the Study of Language and Information.

Gvozdev, A. N. (1949). *Formirovanie u rebenka grammaticeskogo stroja russkogo jazyka.* Moscow: Izd-vo Akademii Pedagogiceskix Nauk RSFSR.

Halliday, M. (1973). *Explorations in the functions of language.* London: Arnold.

Halliday, M. (1975). *Learning how to mean: Explorations in the development of language.* London: Arnold.

Harris, Z. (1951). *Methods in structural linguistics.* Chicago: Chicago University Press.

Hickmann, M. (1987). *Social and functional approaches to language and thought.* London: Academic Press.

Holisky, D. (1987). The case of the intransitive subject in Tsova-Tush (Batsbi). *Lingua, 71*, 103–132.

Hopper, P., & Thompson, S. (1980). Transitivity in grammar and discourse. *Language, 56*, 251–299.

Huttenlocher, J., Smiley, P., & Charney, R. (1983). Emergence of action categories in the child: Evidence from verb meaning. *Psychological Review, 90*, 72–93.

Huxley, R. (1970). The development of the correct use of subject personal pronouns in two children. In G. B. Flores d'Arcais & W. Levelt (Eds.), *Advances in psycholinguistics* (pp. 141–165). Amsterdam: North Holland.

Hymes, D. (1974). *Foundations in sociolinguistics: An ethnographic approach.* Philadelphia: University of Pennsylvania Press.

Jackendoff, R. S. (1990). *Semantic structures.* Cambridge, MA: MIT Press.

Kaplan, B. (1983a). Genetic-dramatism: Old wine in new bottles. In S. Wapner & B. Kaplan (Eds.), *Toward a holistic developmental psychology* (pp. 53–74). Hillsdale, NJ: Lawrence Erlbaum Associates.

Kaplan, B. (1983b). A trio of trials. In R. Lerner (Ed.), *Developmental psychology: Historical and philosophical perspectives* (pp. 185–228). Hillsdale, NJ: Lawrence Erlbaum Associates.

Karmiloff-Smith, A. (1979). *A functional approach to child language*. Cambridge, England: Cambridge University Press.

Karmiloff-Smith, A. (1981). Getting developmental differences or studying child development. *Cognition, 10*, 151–158.

Karmiloff-Smith, A. (1983). Language development as a problem-solving process. *Papers and Reports on Child Language Development, 22*, 1–22.

Karmiloff-Smith, A. (1986). From meta-processes to conscious access: Evidence from children's metalinguistic and repair data. *Cognition, 23*, 95–147.

Kolodziej, P., Deutsch, W., & Bittner, C. (1991). Das Selbst im Spiegel der Kindersprache [The self in the mirror of child language]. *Zeitschrift für Entwicklungspsychologie and Paedagogische Psychologie, 23*(1) 23–47.

Kuczaj, S. II. (1982). On the nature of syntactic development. In S. Kuczaj II (Ed.), *Language development: Syntax and semantics* (Vol. 1, pp. 37–81). Hillsdale, NJ: Lawrence Erlbaum Associates.

Kuroda, S. Y. (1973). Where epistemology, grammar, and style meet—a case study from Japanese. In S. Anderson & P. Kiparsky (Eds.), *A Festschrift for Morris Halle* (pp. 377–391). New York: Holt, Rinehart & Winston.

Kyratzis, A. (1993). Pragmatic and discursive influences on the acquisition of subordination-co-ordination. In E. Clark (Ed.), *Proceedings of the Twenty-Fifth Annual Child Language Research Forum* (pp. 324–332). Stanford: The Center for the Study of Language and Information.

Lakoff, G. (1977). Linguistic gestalts. In W. Beach, S. Fox, & S. Philosoph (Eds.), *Papers from the 13th Regional Meeting of the Chicago Linguistic Society* (pp. 236–287). Chicago: Chicago Linguistic Society.

Lakoff, G. (1986). *Women, fire, and dangerous things: What categories reveal about the mind*. Chicago: University of Chicago Press.

Lakoff, G., & Johnson, M. (1980). *Metaphors we live by*. Chicago: University of Chicago Press.

Leopold, W. (1939). *Speech development of a bilingual child: A linguist's record: Vol. 1. Vocabulary growth in the first two years*. Evanston, IL: Northwestern University Press.

Levinson, S. (1979). Activity types and language. *Linguistics, 17*, 356–399.

Levinson, S. (1983). *Pragmatics*. Cambridge, England: Cambridge University Press.

Lewis, M., & Brooks-Gunn, J. (1979). *Social cognition and the acquisition of self*. New York: Plenum Press.

Lin, A. (1993). *The child as conversational partner: The creation of participation roles as cultural activity*. Unpublished doctoral dissertation, Clark University, Worcester, MA.

Lock, A. (Ed.). (1978). *Action, gesture and symbol: The emergence of language*. London: Academic Press.

Lock, A. (1980). *The guided reinvention of language*. London: Academic Press.

Loveland, K. (1984). Learning about points of view: Spacial perspective and the acquisition of "I/You." *Journal of Child Language, 11*, 535–556.

Lyons, J. (1982). Deixis and subjectivity: Loquor ergo sum? In R. J. Jarvella & W. Klein (Eds.), *Speech, place, and action* (pp. 101–124). London: Wiley.

MacWhinney, B. (1991). *The CHILDES project: Tools for analyzing talk*. Hillsdale, NJ: Lawrence Erlbaum Associates.

MacWhinney, B., & Bates, E. (Eds.). (1989). *The crosslinguistic study of sentence processing*. Cambridge, England: Cambridge University Press.

Maratsos, M. (1979). Learning how and when to use pronouns and determiners. In P. Fletcher & M. Garman (Eds.), *Language acquisition: Studies in first language development* (pp. 225–239). Cambridge, England: Cambridge University Press.

McNeill, D. (1963, August). *The psychology of "you" and "I": A case history of a small language system*. Paper presented at American Psychological Association Symposium on Child Language: Structural Aspects, Philadelphia, PA.

Mead, G. (1934). *Mind, self, and society*. Chicago: University of Chicago Press.

Mead, G. (1938). *Philosophy of the act.* Chicago: Open Court.

Miller, P., & Hoogstra, L. (1992). Language as a tool in the socialization and apprehension of cultural meanings. In T. Schwartz, G. White, & C. Lutz (Eds.), *New directions in psychological anthropology* (pp. 83–101). New York: Cambridge University Press.

Nelson, K. (1989). Monologue as the linguistic construction of self in time. In K. Nelson (Ed.), *Narratives from the crib* (pp. 284–308). Cambridge, MA: Harvard University Press

Ochs, E. (1979). Transcript as theory. In E. Ochs & B. Schieffelin (Eds.), *Developmental pragmatics* (pp. 43–72). New York: Academic Press.

Ochs, E. (1988). *Culture and language development.* Cambridge, England: Cambridge University Press.

Ochs, E., & Schieffelin, B. (Eds.). (1979). *Developmental pragmatics.* New York: Academic Press.

Painter, C. (1984). *Into the mother tongue: A case study in early language development.* London: Frances Pinter.

Paprotté, W., & Sinha, C. (1987). A functional perspective on early language development. In M. Hickmann (Ed.), *Social and functional approaches to language and thought* (pp. 203–222). London: Academic Press.

Park, T. (1971). *The acquisition of German morphology.* Unpublished manuscript, Psychological Institute, Bern.

Piaget, J. (1926). *The language and thought of the child.* New York: Harcourt.

Piaget, J. (1930). *The child's conception of physical causality.* Totowa, NJ: Littlefield, Adams.

Piaget, J. (1954). *The construction of reality in the child.* New York: Basic Books.

Pike, K. (1982). *Linguistic concepts: An introduction to tagmemics.* Lincoln: University of Nebraska Press.

Pinker, S. (1984). *Language learnability and language development.* Cambridge, MA: MIT Press.

Pinker, S. (1988). Learnability theory and acquisition of a first language. In F. Kessel (Ed.), *The development of language and language researchers: Essays in honor of Roger Brown* (pp. 97–119). Hillsdale, NJ: Lawrence Erlbaum Associates.

Pinker, S. (1989). *Learnability and cognition: The acquisition of argument structure.* Cambridge, MA: MIT Press.

Poulin-Dubois, D., & Schultz, T. (1988). The development of the understanding of human behavior: From agency to intentionality. In J. Astington, P. Harris, & D. Olson (Eds.), *Developing theories of mind* (pp. 109–125). Cambridge, England: Cambridge University Press.

Quick, H. (1991). *Maternal input and children's use of self reference forms: A functional approach.* Unpublished manuscript, Clark University, Worcester, MA.

Radford, A. (1990). *Syntactic theory and the acquisition of English syntax.* Cambridge, England: Basil Blackwell.

Rosch, E. (1978). Principles of categorization. In E. Rosch & B. Lloyd (Eds.), *Cognition and categorization* (pp. 27–48). Hillsdale, NJ: Lawrence Erlbaum Associates.

Sacks, H., Schegloff, E., & Jefferson, G. (1974). A simplest systematics for the organization of turn-taking in conversation. *Language, 50,* 696–735.

Saksena, A. (1980). The affected agent. *Language, 56,* 812–826.

Savasir, I. (1984). *How many futures?* Unpublished master's thesis, University of California, Berkeley.

Schieffelin, B. (1985). Acquisition of Kaluli. In D. I. Slobin (Ed.), *The crosslinguistic study of language acquisition* (pp. 525–593). Hillsdale, NJ: Lawrence Erlbaum Associates.

Schieffelin, B. (1990). *The give and take of everyday life: Language socialization of Kaluli children.* Cambridge, England: Cambridge University Press.

Schieffelin, B., & Ochs, E. (Eds.). (1986). *Language socialization across cultures.* Cambridge, England: Cambridge University Press.

Schlesinger, I. (1977). The role of cognitive development and linguistic input in language acquisition. *Journal of Child Language, 4,* 153–169.

Schlesinger, I. (1988). The origin of relational categories. In Y. Levy, I. Schlesinger, & M. Braine (Eds.), *Categories and processes in language acquisition* (pp. 121–178). Hillsdale, NJ: Lawrence Erlbaum Associates.

Searle, J. (1969). *Speech acts*. Cambridge, England: Cambridge University Press.

Searle, J. (1979). *Expression and meaning*. Cambridge, England: Cambridge University Press.

Shepherd, S. (1980). *Creoles and language acquisition: Parallels in the expression of modality.* Paper presented at the Third Biennial Conference, Society for Caribbean Linguistics, Aruba.

Shipley, E., & Shipley, T. (1969). Quaker children's use of "thee": A relational analysis. *Journal of Verbal Learning and Verbal Behavior, 8*, 112–117.

Shultz, T. (1980). Development of the concept of intention. In W. Collins (Ed.), *The Minnesota Symposium on Child Psychology, 13* (pp. 131–164). Hillsdale, NJ: Lawrence Erlbaum Associates.

Silverstein, M. (1985). The functional stratification of language and ontogenesis. In J. Wertsch (Ed.), *Culture, communication, and cognition: Vygotskian perspectives* (pp. 205–235). Cambridge, England: Cambridge University Press.

Silverstein, M. (1987). The three faces of "function": Preliminaries to a psychology of language. In M. Hickmann (Ed.), *Social and functional approaches to language and thought* (pp. 125–164). London: Academic Press.

Silverstein, M. (1991). A funny thing happened on the way to the form: A functionalist critique of functionalist developmentalism. *First Language, 11*, 143–179.

Skinner, B. F. (1957). *Verbal behavior.* New York: Appleton-Century-Croft.

Slobin, D. (Ed.). (1971). *The ontogenesis of grammar: A theoretical symposium.* New York: Academic Press.

Slobin, D. (1973). Cognitive prerequisites for the development of grammar. In C. A. Ferguson & D. I. Slobin (Eds.), *Studies of child language development* (pp. 175–208). New York: Holt, Rinehart & Winston.

Slobin, D. (1981). The origins of grammatical encoding of events. In W. Deutsch (Ed.), *The child's construction of language* (pp. 185–199). London: Academic Press.

Slobin, D. (1982). Universal and particular in the acquisition of language. In E. Wanner & L. Gleitman (Eds.), *Language acquisition: The state of the art* (pp. 128–170). Cambridge, England: Cambridge University Press.

Slobin, D. (1985). Crosslinguistic evidence for the Language-Making Capacity. In D. Slobin (Ed.), *The crosslinguistic study of language acquisition* (Vol. 2, pp. 1157–1256). Hillsdale, NJ: Lawrence Erlbaum Associates.

Slobin, D. (1988). From the Garden of Eden to the Tower of Babel. In F. Kessel (Ed.), *The development of language and language researchers: Essays in honor of Roger Brown* (pp. 9–22). Hillsdale NJ: Lawrence Erlbaum Associates.

Slobin, D. (1990). The development from child speaker to native speaker. In J. Stigler, R. Shweder, & G. Herdt (Eds.), *Cultural psychology: Essays on comparative human development* (pp. 233–256). Cambridge, England: Cambridge University Press.

Tanz, C. (1974). Cognitive principles underlying children's errors in pronominal case-marking. *Journal of Child Language, 1*, 271–276.

Tomasello, M. (1992). *First verbs: A case study of early grammatical development.* Cambridge, England: Cambridge University Press.

Tomlin, R. (Ed.). (1987). *Coherence and grounding in discourse.* Amsterdam: John Benjamins.

van Oosten, J. (1986). *The nature of subjects, topics and agents: A cognitive explanation.* Bloomington: Indiana University Linguistics Club.

Van Valin, R. (1991). Functionalist linguistic theory and language acquisition. *First Language, 11*, 7–40.

Van Valin, R. (1993). A synopsis of role and reference grammar. In R. Van Valin (Ed.), *Advances in role and reference grammar.* Amsterdam: John Benjamins.

Vendler, Z. (1967). *Philosophy in linguistics.* Ithaca: Cornell University Press.

Vila, I. (1987). *Emergence and use of the Castillian pronominal system in early language.* Unpublished manuscript, Universitat de Barcelona, Department de Psicologia Evolutiva i de l'Educacio.

Werner, H. (1957). The concept of development from a comparative and organismic point of view. In D. B. Harris (Ed.), *The concept of development: An issue in the study of human behavior* (pp. 125–148). Minneapolis: University of Minnesota Press.

Werner, H., & Kaplan, B. (1984). *Symbol formation.* Hillsdale, NJ: Lawrence Erlbaum Associates.

Wolf, D. (1982). Understanding others: A longitudinal case study of the concept of independent agency. In G. Forman (Ed.), *Action and thought: From sensorimotor schemes to symbolic operations* (pp. 297–327). New York: Academic Press.

Wolf, D., Rygh, J., & Altshuler, J. (1984). Agency and experience: Actions and states in play narratives. In I. Bretherton (Ed.), *Symbolic play* (pp. 195–217). New York: Academic Press.

Zubin, D. (1979). Discourse function of morphology: The focus system in German. In T. Givón (Ed.), *Syntax and semantics: Vol. 12. Discourse and syntax* (pp. 469–504). New York: Academic Press.

Author Index

Subject Index

223